# REVISE EDEXCEL GCSE (9–1)
# Religious Studies B
## CATHOLIC CHRISTIANITY AND ISLAM

REVISION GUIDE

Series Consultant: Harry Smith

Author: Tanya Hill

## A note from the publisher

In order to ensure that this resource offers high-quality support for the associated Pearson qualification, it has been through a review process by the awarding body. This process confirms that this resource fully covers the teaching and learning content of the specification or part of a specification at which it is aimed. It also confirms that it demonstrates an appropriate balance between the development of subject skills, knowledge and understanding, in addition to preparation for assessment.

Endorsement does not cover any guidance on assessment activities or processes (e.g. practice questions or advice on how to answer assessment questions), included in the resource nor does it prescribe any particular approach to the teaching or delivery of a related course.

While the publishers have made every attempt to ensure that advice on the qualification and its assessment is accurate, the official specification and associated assessment guidance materials are the only authoritative source of information and should always be referred to for definitive guidance.

Pearson examiners have not contributed to any sections in this resource relevant to examination papers for which they have responsibility.

Examiners will not use endorsed resources as a source of material for any assessment set by Pearson.

Endorsement of a resource does not mean that the resource is required to achieve this Pearson qualification, nor does it mean that it is the only suitable material available to support the qualification, and any resource lists produced by the awarding body shall include this and other appropriate resources.

**For the full range of Pearson revision titles across KS2, KS3, GCSE, Functional Skills, AS/A Level and BTEC visit:**
www.pearsonschools.co.uk/revise

 Pearson

Published by Pearson Education Limited, 80 Strand, London, WC2R 0RL.

www.pearsonschoolsandfecolleges.co.uk

Copies of official specifications for all Pearson qualifications may be found on the website: qualifications.pearson.com.

Text and illustrations © Pearson Education Ltd 2017
Typeset and illustrated by Kamae Design
Produced by Out of House Publishing
Cover illustration by Miriam Sturdee
Picture research by Alison Prior

The right of Tanya Hill to be identified as author of this work has been asserted by her in accordance with the
Copyright, Designs and Patents Act 1988.

First published 2017

20 19 18 17

10 9 8 7 6 5 4 3 2 1

**British Library Cataloguing in Publication Data**
A catalogue record for this book is available from the British Library.

ISBN 978 1 292 13386 7

Printed in Italy by Lego

**Acknowledgements**
*We are grateful to the following for permission to reproduce copyright material:*

**Figures**
Figures on pages 75, 78, 121, 122 from *Revise Edexcel: Edexcel GCSE Religious Studies* by Tanya Hill, Pearson Edexcel, 2012, pp.5, 8, 14, 31. Reproduced by permission of Pearson Edexcel.

The publisher would like to thank the following for their kind permission to reproduce their photographs:

(Key: b-bottom; c-centre; l-left; r-right; t-top)

**123RF.com:** 38r, 41; **Alamy Stock Photo:** Aurelian Images 49, Stuart Aylmer 22br, Rafael Ben-Ari 22t, Clark Brennan 63, Chronicle 50t, 52l, Chronicle 50t, 52l, Digital Image Library 6, Everett Collection Historical 44, 59, Everett Collection Historical 44, 59, Paul Fearn 15, GL Archive 47, 50b, Tim Graham 24, David Grossman 17, Lanmas 55, Andy Medina 20, RealyEasyStar / Fotografia Felici 27b, jozef sedmak 30, Trinity Mirror / Mirrorpix 58, Rod Williams 33; **Bridgeman Art Library Ltd:** Christ on the Cross with the Virgin, Saint John and Saint Dominic (oil on canvas), Titian (Tiziano Vecellio) (c.1488-1576) / San Domenico, Ancona, Italy / Alinari 5, The Fall, after 1479 (oil on panel) (detail of 13000), Goes, Hugo van der (c.1440-82) / Kunsthistorisches Museum, Vienna, Austria 7, The Woman Taken in Adultery, 1653 (oil on canvas), Poussin, Nicolas (1594-1665) / Louvre, Paris, France 34, Window w25 depicting the Trinity (stained glass), English School, (15th century) / York Minster, Yorkshire, UK 2; **The Catholic Agency for Overseas Development:** CAFOD 23b; **Getty Images:** Bettman 48, Alex Bowie 48r, DEA / A. DAGLI ORTI 23, Vincenzo Fontana 29, Julian Kumar / GODONG 19, Philippe Lissac 18, Alberto Pizzoli 16, Print Collector 35, 50c; **Aidan McRae Thomson:** 3; **Pax Christi:** 42; **Prison Fellowship:** 34b; **Shutterstock.com:** 22r, 52r, 62, Africa Studio 38, Art Man 9, Andi Berger 11tr, Alena Brozova 4, DGLimages 11bl, Goodluz. 11c, Monkey Business Images 10, 11br, pbombaert 14, Rawpixel.com 12, Sakhorn 36, Ventura 26, Kiev Victor 22cl, wong sze yuen 11tl

All other images © Pearson Education

**Text**
Surah extracts on pages 69, 70, 72, 73, 75, 78, 82, 84–86, 88, 90–106, 108–112, 116–120, 122–124, 126, 127, 129–131, Sahih International, The Qur'an: English Meanings and Notes, Riyadh: Al-Muntada Al-Islami Trust, 2001–2011; Jeddah: Dar Abul-Qasim 1997-2001; and Surah extracts on pages 81, 87, 113, translated by Mohsin Khan, Dar-us-Salam Publications, March 1999, https://dar-us-salam.com, 713.722.0419. Reproduced with permission.

# Contents

# The Trinity

The **Trinity** is the way Catholic Christians believe God is revealed to the world – their belief in **One God** who has made himself known in three different ways – **Father**, **Son** and **Holy Spirit**.

## The nature of the Trinity

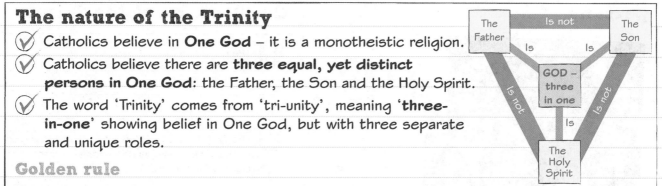

- ✓ Catholics believe in **One God** – it is a monotheistic religion.
- ✓ Catholics believe there are **three equal, yet distinct persons in One God**: the Father, the Son and the Holy Spirit.
- ✓ The word 'Trinity' comes from 'tri-unity', meaning '**three-in-one**' showing belief in One God, but with three separate and unique roles.

### Golden rule

Remember: the Trinity is not the idea that Catholic Christians believe in three gods.

## The Trinity in worship and belief

- Catholics **bless themselves** by making the sign of the cross and offer prayers 'in the name of the Father, Son and Holy Spirit'.
- The Trinity is used in **special services**, e.g. in baptism and confirmation ceremonies when oil is used to make the sign of the cross.
- **Prayers** such as the Lord's Prayer and statements of belief such as the Nicene Creed and Apostles' Creed refer to the Trinity.
- Some **hymns** sung during **Mass** refer to the Father, Son and Holy Spirit.
- The beliefs of the Trinity are at the centre of each Catholic's relationship with God.

## The importance of the Trinity

For Catholic Christians, God's nature and acts are a 'mystery'; they believe they cannot 'know' everything about him.

The Trinity helps them understand the three ways God has tried to reveal himself – through the Father, the Son and the Holy Spirit. They can understand God better by relating differently to these three aspects.

Catholic Christians believe that each part of the Trinity is equally important, as each reveals a different aspect.

## The Trinity and the Nicene Creed

The Nicene Creed is an important statement of belief about the roles of the Trinity:

- The **Father** is the powerful creator of everything – 'maker of heaven and earth, and of all that is, seen and unseen'.
- The **Son** is Jesus Christ, who came to Earth as God in human form (incarnation) and was crucified to redeem humanity's sins – 'For us men and for our salvation, he came down from heaven.'
- The **Holy Spirit** is the invisible power of God that works within the world today to guide and inspire human beings – 'the giver of life, who proceeds from the Father and the Son'.

## Using evidence to develop your answer

Use quotations as evidence to help explain your answer. For example, you could use quotations from the Nicene Creed on the left and the Bible, e.g. 'Therefore go and make disciples of all nations, baptising them in the name of the Father and the Son and the Holy Spirit.' (Matthew 28:19)

**Now try this**

Outline **three** beliefs about the Trinity. **(3 marks)**

Aim to write three separate sentences – one for each belief.

# God as a Trinity of persons

The origin and development of the Catholic Christian idea of the Trinity is found in the Bible.

## Nature of God as a Trinity of persons

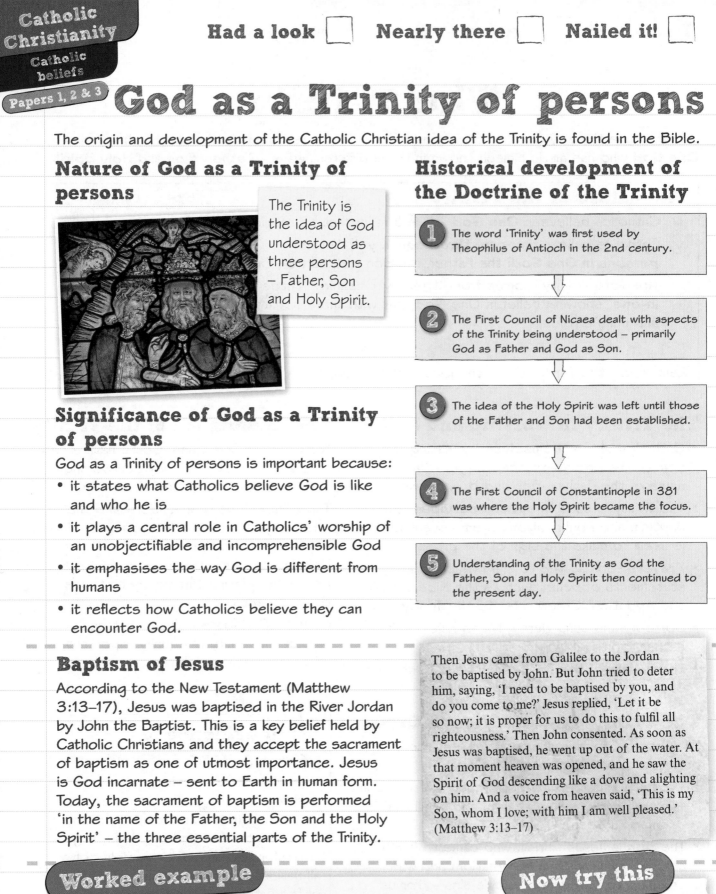

The Trinity is the idea of God understood as three persons – Father, Son and Holy Spirit.

## Significance of God as a Trinity of persons

God as a Trinity of persons is important because:

- it states what Catholics believe God is like and who he is
- it plays a central role in Catholics' worship of an unobjectifiable and incomprehensible God
- it emphasises the way God is different from humans
- it reflects how Catholics believe they can encounter God.

## Historical development of the Doctrine of the Trinity

**1** The word 'Trinity' was first used by Theophilus of Antioch in the 2nd century.

**2** The First Council of Nicaea dealt with aspects of the Trinity being understood – primarily God as Father and God as Son.

**3** The idea of the Holy Spirit was left until those of the Father and Son had been established.

**4** The First Council of Constantinople in 381 was where the Holy Spirit became the focus.

**5** Understanding of the Trinity as God the Father, Son and Holy Spirit then continued to the present day.

## Baptism of Jesus

According to the New Testament (Matthew 3:13–17), Jesus was baptised in the River Jordan by John the Baptist. This is a key belief held by Catholic Christians and they accept the sacrament of baptism as one of utmost importance. Jesus is God incarnate – sent to Earth in human form. Today, the sacrament of baptism is performed 'in the name of the Father, the Son and the Holy Spirit' – the three essential parts of the Trinity.

> Then Jesus came from Galilee to the Jordan to be baptised by John. But John tried to deter him, saying, 'I need to be baptised by you, and do you come to me?' Jesus replied, 'Let it be so now; it is proper for us to do this to fulfil all righteousness.' Then John consented. As soon as Jesus was baptised, he went up out of the water. At that moment heaven was opened, and he saw the Spirit of God descending like a dove and alighting on him. And a voice from heaven said, 'This is my Son, whom I love; with him I am well pleased.' (Matthew 3:13–17)

## Worked example

Explain **two** reasons why the Trinity is important for Catholics. **(4 marks)**

One reason why the Trinity is important for Catholics is for their understanding of God. They believe in One God who is understood in three different ways – Father, Son and Holy Spirit. Another reason is that Catholics believe God is a mystery and they cannot 'know' everything about him. The Trinity helps them to understand three aspects of him and relate to him better.

## Now try this

Outline **three** features in the history of the teaching of the Trinity. **(3 marks)**

In this answer, the student has given two different reasons to explain the importance of the Trinity for Catholics. Each reason has been stated and then developed with further information.

# Creation

Catholic Christians believe that the Bible Creation story in the first book of Genesis contains theological truths about God's nature, but they also accept the scientific creation theories.

Catholics believe God created the world in six days with a seventh day of rest.

In the beginning God created the heavens and the earth. Now the earth was formless and empty, darkness was over the surface of the deep, and the Spirit of God was hovering over the waters. (Genesis 1:1–2)

Genesis 1–3 tells the story of how God created the world. It is an important story as it reveals aspects of God to help Catholics know what he is like.

## Literal and metaphorical interpretations of the story

Different Christians may interpret the story of Creation in different ways.

**Literalists** (also known as Creationists) believe that:

- the Creation story told in the Bible is **literally true** because the Bible is the literal 'word of God'
- God created the world in six, 24-hour days
- scientific explanations about the world, such as the Big Bang Theory of evolution, are wrong.

**Non-literalists** believe that:

- God created the world, but **not exactly** how the Bible story tells it
- the Genesis story of Creation is more myth than fact, e.g. the word 'day' used in the Creation story is a **metaphor** for a much longer period of time
- science and religion together explain how the world came to exist and there is no conflict between the two; the Bible explains **why** the Creation happened and science explains **how**.

This is a **metaphorical** interpretation of the Creation story believed by most Catholics and supported by Pope Francis as a scientist and the leader of the Catholic Church.

## Nature and characteristics of God in the Creation story

Catholics use the Creation story to understand what God is like.

**1** **Omnipotent** – all-powerful, as demonstrated through the way he used his power to create the world and everything in it.

**2** **Eternal** – he had no start and will have no end.

**3** **Compassionate, benevolent and caring** – by creating the world, God shows his loving nature. The final and most important part of his Creation was making it fit for his greatest achievement, human beings.

## Use of supporting quotes

Try to use relevant quotes to support any points you make in exam answers. For this topic, you could use:

Then God blessed the seventh day and made it holy, because on it he rested from all the work of creating that he had done. (Genesis 2:3)

Then God said, 'Let us make mankind in our image, in our likeness...' (Genesis 1:26)

## Now try this

Explain **two** ways in which the Christian Creation story can be interpreted. In your answer you must refer to a source of wisdom or authority.     **(5 marks)**

This style of question asks you to explain **two different** reasons; to achieve the fifth mark available you must refer to a source of wisdom or authority for Catholics.

Catholic
Christianity
Catholic
beliefs
Papers 1, 2 & 3

Had a look ☐   Nearly there ☐   Nailed it! ☐

# The significance of the Creation account

The Creation account contained in the Bible is very important for Catholic Christians. It helps them to understand their special nature, place and purpose within the world.

## The Creation story and its importance

> So God created mankind in his own image, in the image of God he created them; male and female he created them. God blessed them and said to them, 'Be fruitful and increase in number; fill the earth and subdue it. Rule over the fish in the sea and the birds in the sky and over every living creature that moves on the ground.' (Genesis 1:27–28)

By making humans in his image, Catholics believe that God shows they are different – they are the final and highest part of his Creation. As such, they are given the responsibility of caring for his Creation.

## Humanity's relationship with Creation

Catholics accept the ideas of dominion and stewardship, which others believe are in conflict with each other. Catholics, however, believe these ideas can work together: God has given humans dominion over the world, and the responsibility of that power is to care for the world through stewardship. Catholics believe they have a special relationship with the world as God's Creation.

Catholics accept the idea of **dominion** – the idea that God gave them power or control over the world.

Catholics also accept the idea of **stewardship** – a God-given responsibility to care for the world.

This answer successfully states three different ways, and so clearly answers the question.

## Implications for these beliefs

Catholics believe:

- they were given a purpose on Earth from God – to worship God, care for his Creation and other people, have children and be good stewards

- through caring for the world, they are showing love and gratitude towards God and his Creation

- they will be accountable to God after death for how they treated the world as his Creation.

### Worked example

Outline **three** ways in which the Creation story shows humans are special. **(3 marks)**

One way is that Catholics believe they were 'made in the image of God'. Another way is that they believe God set humans above other animals in terms of importance. A third way is that Catholics believe they were given the responsibility of stewardship for God's Creation.

Remember, you must show knowledge and understanding of the issue as well as the skills of analysis and evaluation.

### Now try this

'The world is here for humans to use as they please.'
Evaluate this statement considering arguments for and against.
In your response you should:
- refer to Catholic teachings
- reach a justified conclusion. **(15 marks)**

# The Incarnation

The word 'incarnation' means 'becoming flesh' and is used by Catholic Christians to explain how God **became human** through Jesus and lived and died in the world.

## The importance of Jesus

Catholic Christians believe Jesus is the incarnate **Son of God**.

- His birth fulfilled the Old Testament prophecy of **Christ** coming to Earth as a **Saviour** promised by God – so God took human form to be present within the world.

- Jesus is the 'Son' part of the three ideas (the **Trinity**) that make up the Christian understanding of God.

- 'In the beginning was the Word...' (John 1:1). Catholics believe Jesus is God – the eternal Word who was, is and always will be.

## Jesus in the Bible

- Information about the life and death of Jesus is found in the Bible in the first four books of the **New Testament**: Matthew, Mark, Luke and John – books known as the 'Gospels'.

- Accounts in the New Testament describe Jesus' birth, life and death. Jesus experienced life as any other human. The pain he suffered when he died on the cross was not reduced because he is God.

The Word became flesh and made his dwelling among us. We have seen his glory, the glory of the one and only Son, who came from the Father, full of grace and truth. (John 1:14)

Christ on the cross

## Jesus as the 'Divine Word'

Though Jesus was human, he was **Divine**, which means he was God. Catholics believe the Bible gives us examples of how Jesus is Divine.

- ☑ Jesus is **omnipotent** (Matthew 28:18) and **omniscient** (John 21:17).
- ☑ Jesus **forgave sins** (Mark 2:5–7).
- ☑ Jesus **performed miracles** (e.g. John 21:25).
- ☑ People **worshipped** and **prayed** to Jesus (Matthew 2:11).
- ☑ Jesus was **resurrected** after death (Mark 16:1–20).

## Jesus as incarnate Son

It is easier for Catholics to understand and relate to Jesus, as he was human and experienced the same problems we do.

- ☑ He was **born to a human** mother – Mary – as a 'normal' baby (Luke 2:7).
- ☑ He had a **human body** (Luke 24:39).
- ☑ He demonstrated **human characteristics** such as tiredness, thirst and hunger.
- ☑ He showed **human emotions** such as amazement (Matthew 8:10), anger (John 2:15–17) and sorrow (John 11:35).
- ☑ He **prayed** to God (John 17).
- ☑ He **died** on the cross (Romans 5:8).

## Worked example

Explain **two** reasons why the Incarnation is important for Catholic Christians today.                    **(4 marks)**

The Incarnation gives Catholic Christians today hope as Jesus is viewed as the Saviour of the world who allows our sins to be forgiven. His resurrection shows Catholics there is an afterlife and provides hope that they will be able to go to heaven.

The Incarnation also helps Catholic Christians to understand what God is like. Jesus is believed to be part of God and was sent to Earth to help humans, so Catholics believe this shows that God cares about them enough to send Jesus in human form.

## Now try this

Outline **three** ways in which Jesus is shown as Divine in the Bible.          **(3 marks)**

Make sure you write **three** sentences, each with a different idea.

# Events of the Paschal Mystery

The Paschal Mystery is one of the central ideas of the Catholic faith linked to redemption and salvation. It refers to the events of the passion, death and resurrection of Jesus.

**Life** – He is the Son of God who came to Earth in human form (Incarnation). He was born to the Virgin Mary and lived his life as the Bible says.

**Resurrection** – He was brought back to life three days after his crucifixion: 'He is not here; he has risen!' (Luke 24:6)

**What Catholics believe about Jesus**

**Death** – He was crucified on the cross to save – or redeem – the sins of the whole world: 'Carrying his own cross, he went out to the place of the Skull (which in Aramaic is called Golgotha). There they crucified him, and with him two others – one on each side and Jesus in the middle.' (John 19:17–18)

**Ascension** – '...he left them and was taken up into heaven.' (Luke 24:51)

## Redemptive efficacy

Three days after his crucifixion, Jesus rose from the dead and spoke to his disciples.

The term 'redemptive efficacy' refers to Catholic Christians' belief that the Paschal Mystery – Christ's suffering (passion) on the cross, resurrection after death and ascension into heaven – redeems all mankind and provides the chance of an afterlife: 'dying he destroyed our death, rising he restored our life' (CCC 1067). Catholics commemorate these events through the celebration of sacraments, during the season of Lent and the festival of Easter.

## The Paschal Mystery and Luke 24

In the descriptive biblical account of the resurrection of Jesus in Luke 24, even the disciples find it difficult to accept he had risen from the dead as it is such a miraculous event.

The women ... found the stone rolled away from the tomb, but when they entered, they did not find the body of the Lord Jesus. (Luke 24:1–3)

They were startled and frightened, thinking they saw a ghost. He said to them, 'Why are you troubled, and why do doubts rise in your minds? Look at my hands and my feet. It is I myself! Touch me and see; a ghost does not have flesh and bones, as you see I have.' (Luke 24:36–39)

This answer asks for **two** reasons, so consider what these could be. Then explain each one fully, developing your point and using an example, if appropriate, to show you understand the question.

## Worked example

Explain **two** reasons why the events in the Paschal Mystery are important to Catholics today. In your answer you must refer to a source of wisdom or authority. **(5 marks)**

The events of the Paschal Mystery underpin Catholics' daily lives through following Jesus and his example.

Jesus' death and resurrection provide evidence of an afterlife and the hope that there is new life after death with God and Jesus in heaven. The Catholic Catechism states: 'The Paschal Mystery of Jesus, which comprises his passion, death, resurrection, and glorification, stands at the centre of the Christian faith because God's saving plan was accomplished once and for all by the redemptive death of his Son Jesus Christ.'

## Now try this

Outline **three** Catholic beliefs about the Paschal Mystery. **(3 marks)**

Remember, this style of question asks for **three** different beliefs. Write three sentences, each including a different fact, to answer this question successfully.

# Jesus' life, death and resurrection

**Salvation** for Christians refers to being saved from sin through belief in Jesus and God's **grace**, while **redemption** is how Christians believe this can be achieved through Jesus' sacrifice. The events of Jesus' life, death, resurrection and ascension into heaven are important to Catholics.

## Salvation

Salvation – or the saving from sin through God's grace – is understood by Christians to bring about the mending of the relationship between God and humanity, which was broken when Adam and Eve disobeyed God in the Garden of Eden.

You will need to know all of John 3:10–21.

You will need to know all of Acts 4:8–12.

## The role of Christ in salvation

Christians believe that through God sending Jesus to Earth, the sins of humanity are forgiven. Jesus, who was perfect and without sin, offered redemption for humans through sacrificing his life, as shown in the Bible:

For God so loved the world that he gave his one and only Son, that whoever believes in him shall not perish but have eternal life. (John 3:16)

Jesus is 'the stone you builders rejected, which has become the cornerstone'. Salvation is found in no one else, for there is no other name under heaven given to mankind by which we must be saved. (Acts 4:11–12)

## The grace of God

- The grace of God is understood by Catholics to refer to all the good things in life, including life itself, which are given by God.
- This is also taken to include the gift of resurrection – Catholics believe it is through God's grace that they will be saved.
- They believe God is merciful and will forgive them and cleanse their souls of sin if they repent and try to redeem themselves.
- Catholicism focuses on God's grace through the life, death and resurrection of Jesus, whose example Catholics believe they should follow to attain eternal life in heaven with God.

## The significance of salvation and grace

Restore the relationship between God and humanity.

Confirm belief in an all-powerful and loving God.

Allow humans to understand the importance of being reconciled with others.

Give humans hope that they can be rewarded in the eternal afterlife.

**Salvation and grace**

Remind us of the importance of the events in Jesus' life in the sacrament of Mass and in the reciting of creeds.

## Now try this

'The events of the life, death and resurrection of Jesus are the most important Catholic beliefs today.'
Evaluate this statement considering arguments for and against.
In your response you should:
- refer to Catholic teachings
- refer to different Christian points of view
- reach a justified conclusion.

You must include teachings in your response (which may involve including a quote), differing Christian views on this topic, as well as a conclusion once you have considered all the arguments and evidence.

**(15 marks)**

# Eschatology

**Eschatology** means 'end times' – the end of a human life or the end of the world.

## Catholic beliefs...

**1** ...about resurrection
Catholics believe death is not the end and Jesus' resurrection proves there is life after death.

> I am the resurrection and the life. The one who believes in me will live, even though they die. (John 11:25)

**2** ...about life after death
- The soul is the spiritual and immortal part of a human.
- Death is only the end of the body – a 'physical' death.
- Souls that have been saved either go to heaven or to purgatory.
- Souls that have not achieved salvation go to hell.

**3** ...about judgement
Catholics accept and that those who have lived as God intended will be rewarded with heaven, while those who remain with some sin may experience temporary punishment in purgatory. Others will face eternal separation from God in hell.

> For we must all appear before the judgment seat of Christ, so that each of us may receive what is due us for the things done while in the body, whether good or bad. (2 Corinthians 5:10)

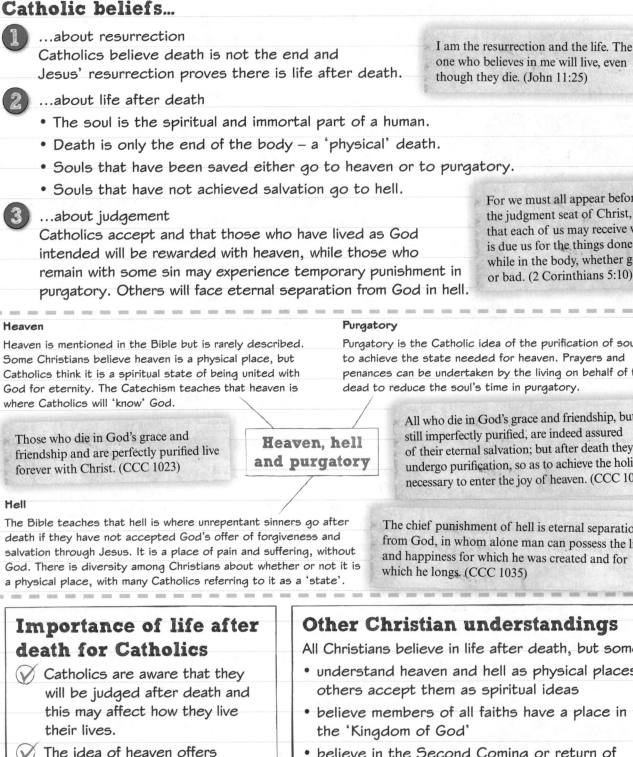

### Heaven

Heaven is mentioned in the Bible but is rarely described. Some Christians believe heaven is a physical place, but Catholics think it is a spiritual state of being united with God for eternity. The Catechism teaches that heaven is where Catholics will 'know' God.

> Those who die in God's grace and friendship and are perfectly purified live forever with Christ. (CCC 1023)

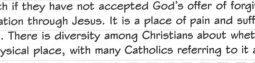
**Heaven, hell and purgatory**

### Purgatory

Purgatory is the Catholic idea of the purification of souls to achieve the state needed for heaven. Prayers and penances can be undertaken by the living on behalf of the dead to reduce the soul's time in purgatory.

> All who die in God's grace and friendship, but still imperfectly purified, are indeed assured of their eternal salvation; but after death they undergo purification, so as to achieve the holiness necessary to enter the joy of heaven. (CCC 1030)

### Hell

The Bible teaches that hell is where unrepentant sinners go after death if they have not accepted God's offer of forgiveness and salvation through Jesus. It is a place of pain and suffering, without God. There is diversity among Christians about whether or not it is a physical place, with many Catholics referring to it as a 'state'.

> The chief punishment of hell is eternal separation from God, in whom alone man can possess the life and happiness for which he was created and for which he longs. (CCC 1035)

## Importance of life after death for Catholics

- ✓ Catholics are aware that they will be judged after death and this may affect how they live their lives.
- ✓ The idea of heaven offers comfort when a loved one dies.
- ✓ The idea of death is easier to cope with.

## Other Christian understandings

All Christians believe in life after death, but some:
- understand heaven and hell as physical places; others accept them as spiritual ideas
- believe members of all faiths have a place in the 'Kingdom of God'
- believe in the Second Coming or return of Jesus from heaven to Earth
- see life as a test for the final judgement; others see belief in God as more important.

**Now try this**

Outline **three** Catholic beliefs about eschatology.  **(3 marks)**

# Marriage

Marriage is an important rite of passage in Christianity. Catholic Christians teach that it is a sacrament, believing it to be a lifelong union between a man and a woman made before God and society. It is also seen as the correct context to have a sexual relationship and children.

## Catholic teachings on marriage

Catholics believe marriage is a sacred bond designed by God.

 God created male and female so they could become 'one flesh' through the **sacrament** of marriage.

…what God has joined together, let no one separate. (Mark 10:9)

The intimate community of life and love which constitutes the married state has been established by the Creator and endowed by him with its own proper laws … God himself is the author of marriage. (CCC 1603)

 Pope Francis taught that marriage was 'not just good, but beautiful' at an interreligious conference in Rome where he and 400 religious leaders and scholars met to discuss faith teachings on marriage.

 Marriage is a **secure environment** to have children and raise them within the Catholic faith.

④ Marriage establishes a permanent, faithful and stable relationship between husband and wife, thereby also providing stability.

Catholics would respond by arguing that marriage is intended to be sacred and holy because it is blessed by God and he is part of it. They would not accept cohabitation even in today's modern society.

## Importance of marriage within society

☑ Marriage is seen to provide stability within society.

☑ It joins a couple who love each other and want to make a commitment and demonstrate their love.

☑ Marriage is also seen to provide the stable basis for children, as a married couple are expected to build their family around the marriage structure.

☑ Children raised within the family unit can help to strengthen society.

## Other Christian attitudes

- Although marriage should be for life, some Christians now accept divorce – recognising that marriages sometimes fail – and accept the idea of second marriages.

- Not all Christians wish to marry, so there may be alternative views on the importance of marriage.

## Non-religious attitudes

- Humanists do not accept marriage as a religious institution blessed by God, but they do accept marriage in a secular sense as a couple making a **commitment** to each other.

- It is possible to have a Humanist wedding, although this is not accepted legally and a civil ceremony would also be required.

- Those with other non-religious attitudes may have widely differing personal views; some may not see the need for marriage, instead preferring to **cohabit**; others believe weddings are expensive and unnecessary.

## Now try this

Outline **three** beliefs about marriage for Catholics.                    (3 marks)

# Sexual relationships

Catholic Christians strongly believe that a sexual relationship should only take place between a man and woman who are married to each other.

**Marital** – the only correct context for a sexual relationship is within marriage, as this is what God intended.

**Key Catholic beliefs on sexual relationships**

**Unitive** – marriage creates a sacred union or bond between husband and wife.

**Procreative** – the purpose of sex is to have children and every sexual act should be open to the possibility of a child.

## Bible and Catechism teachings

> Marriage should be honoured by all, and the marriage bed kept pure, for God will judge the adulterer and all the sexually immoral. (Hebrews 13:4)
>
> God blessed them and said to them, 'Be fruitful and increase in number; fill the earth and subdue it.' (Genesis 1:28)
>
> You shall not commit adultery. (Exodus 20:14)
>
> In marriage the physical intimacy of the spouses becomes a sign and pledge of spiritual communion. (CCC 2360)
>
> The Sacrament of Matrimony enables man and woman to enter into Christ's fidelity for his Church. Through conjugal chastity, they bear witness to this mystery before the world. (CCC 2365)

## Sexual relationships outside marriage

Catholics believe:

- casual relationships are wrong – marriage is intended for sexual relationships
- adultery is forbidden in the Ten Commandments, which are rules from God
- married couples should be faithful to each other, as promised in the marriage vows
- being sexually pure before entering into marriage is important.

## Homosexuality

Catholics believe sexual activity between homosexual couples is wrong because:

- the Catholic Church does not recognise marriage between homosexuals and any sexual activity outside marriage is not permitted
- the purpose of sex is for **procreation** (Genesis 2:24) and this cannot happen within a homosexual relationship.

## Other Christian attitudes

Although many **other Christians** believe sex is special and should take place within marriage, they also believe that sex can deepen a relationship and can be for pleasure as well as for procreation. Although they still view infidelity as wrong, they may be more accepting of a sexual relationship before marriage if the future intention is to get married.

## Catholic response

Catholic Christians maintain that sex is part of the sacrament of marriage and should only take place within marriage between husband and wife for the procreation of children. They do not condone either pre-marital or extra-marital sex.

## Non-religious attitudes

**Humanists** generally believe that consenting adults should be allowed to have a sexual relationship provided it does not harm anyone else. **Atheists** may hold a variety of personal views, but are generally unlikely to regard sex before marriage or homosexuality as a problem.

### Now try this

Explain **two** reasons why Catholics believe sex should only take place within marriage. In your answer you must refer to a source of wisdom or authority.    **(5 marks)**

Had a look ☐    Nearly there ☐    Nailed it! ☐

Catholic
Christianity
Marriage and
the family
Paper 1

# Families

Family life is very important to Catholics. They believe that it has set purposes regarding the education of children, procreation and stability for society as a whole.

## Types of families

There are many different types of family within society today.

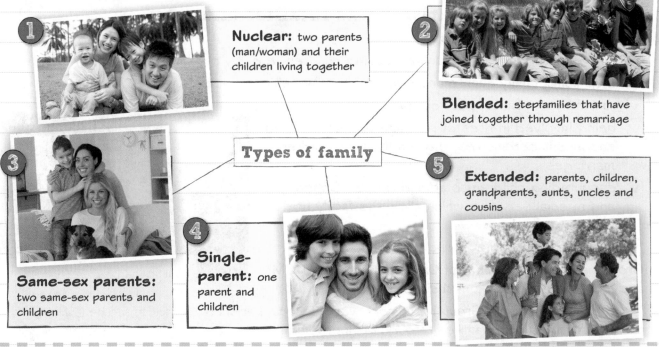

**1** Nuclear: two parents (man/woman) and their children living together

**2** Blended: stepfamilies that have joined together through remarriage

Types of family

**3** Same-sex parents: two same-sex parents and children

**4** Single-parent: one parent and children

**5** Extended: parents, children, grandparents, aunts, uncles and cousins

Provides the right place for a married couple to have children.

Provides stability and security for society as children can be raised in the correct social and moral setting.

**Catholic teachings on the purpose and importance of family**

Educates and teaches children the difference between right and wrong.

Raises children as Catholic Christians and introduce them to the Catholic faith.

## Bible teachings on family

Children are a heritage from the Lord, offspring a reward from him. (Psalms 127:3)

Children, obey your parents in the Lord, for this is right. 'Honour your father and mother'....' Fathers, do not exasperate your children; instead, bring them up in the training and instruction of the Lord. (Ephesians 6:1–4)

Parents do not embitter your children, or they will become discouraged. (Colossians 3:21)

## Catholic response to different family types

Catholics believe family is important for raising children correctly. They prefer the traditional nuclear family unit with a mother and father as first role models and teachers, as they feel this reflects the idea of family first shown in the Bible with Adam and Eve. However, today, many other Christians would accept that other kinds of families also provide a stable upbringing for children.

## Familiaris Consortio: 'The Fellowship of the Family'

This was written by Pope John Paul II in 1981 to describe the position of the Catholic Church on the meaning and role of marriage and the family. Verses 36–85 detail the importance of the family and the support it provides:

...parents must be acknowledged as the first and foremost educators of their children. (36)

parents must trustingly and courageously train their children in the essential values of human life. (37)

## Now try this

Outline **three** Catholic beliefs about the family.                    **(3 marks)**

# Support for the family in the Catholic parish

Catholics believe it is their duty to do all they can to support both their own and other families. They can offer pastoral care to families who need help in the local parish.

## How the Catholic parish helps families and why

The parish can help families by:

- ☑ supporting couples who are expecting children, e.g. by organising classes
- ☑ organising family events and special family worship services
- ☑ running parental support classes
- ☑ being involved in rites of passage and conducting sacrament ceremonies, e.g. baptism of children, marriages
- ☑ encouraging children to attend Sunday School and special services, which allow the family unit to worship together
- ☑ providing counselling support.

Groups such as the Union of Catholic Mothers (UCM) actively support families in their local parish.

The organisation Family Group Movement works in local parishes to celebrate and unite families through projects and events.

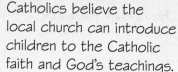

Catholics believe the local church can introduce children to the Catholic faith and God's teachings.

## The sacraments

The Catholic parish can guide and support families as they take part in the sacraments. This could involve the christening or confirmation of a child, preparation for a couple getting married, Holy Communion or the anointing of the sick. The Catholic community comes together to mark and celebrate baptisms and weddings, for example, to recognise their importance and the commitment they demonstrate.

## Counselling

Many Catholic communities offer counselling services such as Care Service. Ministers or priests may also counsel couples if they are experiencing conflict or struggles within the family. Many Catholic parishes have Family Groups, which are friendship groups drawn from the parish who spend time together each month for a variety of activities. They aim to support and provide fellowship as well as a community feel and a source of outreach.

> The parish is the Eucharistic community and the heart of the liturgical life of Christian families; it is a privileged place for the catechesis of children and parents. (CCC 2226)

State each way clearly and then develop it by adding another sentence to show specifically what you mean. You could also include an example or case to explain.

## Now try this

1 Explain **two** ways in which the local Catholic parish can help families. **(4 marks)**

2 'The Catholic parish should be responsible for helping the family.'
   Evaluate this statement considering arguments for and against. In your response you should:
   - refer to Catholic teachings
   - reach a justified conclusion. **(12 marks)**

# Family planning

Catholics believe the purpose of a sexual relationship is procreation and they hold differing views about family planning and the regulation of births from other Christian denominations.

## Types of contraception

Contraception is the intentional prevention of pregnancy. There are two types of contraception – natural and artificial. Natural methods include the rhythm method, where a couple only have sex at times of the month when the woman is likely to be less fertile. Artificial methods include the condom and pill, which are man-made objects designed to prevent pregnancy.

## Catholic beliefs

Catholics believe:

* the purpose of sex is to have children, so each sexual act should be open to the possibility of a child
* contraception could encourage immoral behaviour and promiscuity, and lead to STIs
* natural forms of contraception are acceptable, but artificial forms which put a barrier between husband and wife are not
* the **Humanae Vitae** of Pope Paul VI affirms the Catholic belief that artificial contraception is not acceptable, but Pope Francis amended this position by saying contraception to prevent the spread of diseases, e.g. the Zika virus, is the 'lesser of two evils' and is acceptable.

As for you, be fruitful and increase in number; multiply on the earth and increase upon it. (Genesis 9:7)

Catholics believe this instruction to Adam and Eve in the first book of the Bible proves God's wish for humans to procreate, which makes contraception a sin against God.

## Non-religious attitudes

People may choose to use contraception for many reasons unconnected with religion. For example:

* they want to plan when to have a family and control its size
* they are not ready to have children
* pregnancy could harm the mother
* as the woman is the one who bears the child, she may want to decide what happens to her body
* they want to be safe from STIs
* the couple carry genetic disorders.

Humanists do not generally object to the use of contraception. They may argue that each person's individual situation should be considered rather than applying a general rule. This view is based on an ethical theory called **situation ethics**.

## Other Christian attitudes

Other Christians, including Anglicans and other types of Protestants, may hold contrasting views to Catholics as they generally believe:

* using artificial methods of contraception does not go against God's teaching
* contraception is a sensible method of planning families to give smaller families an improved quality of life
* sex can be for pleasure as well as procreation.

## Catholic response

Catholics would respond to any alternative views by maintaining that they should not use contraception as they should follow God's wishes and have a family.

### Now try this

Explain **two** reasons why Catholics do not accept the use of artificial contraception.  **(4 marks)**

Make sure you state each reason in one sentence and then explain it further in a second sentence.

13

# Divorce

Divorce is the legal termination of a marriage. Catholic Christians believe in the sanctity of marriage and, for this reason, do not accept divorce.

## Marriage is for life

Catholics believe marriage is a gift from God and is for life, symbolised by the marriage vows and the ring representing an unbroken circle.

## Teachings on divorce

He answered, 'Anyone who divorces his wife and marries another woman commits adultery against her. And if she divorces her husband and marries another man, she commits adultery.' (Mark 10:11–12)

Between the baptized, 'a ratified and consummated marriage cannot be dissolved by any human power or for any reason other than death'. (CCC 2382)

Divorce is a grave offence against the natural law. (CCC 2384)

Divorce is immoral also because it introduces disorder into the family and into society. (CCC 2385)

Therefore what God has joined together, let no one separate. (Mark 10:9)

These quotes demonstrate Catholic ideas. Use them in support of your reasons in exam questions.

## Catholic teachings

1. Marriage is for life, so divorce is not recognised by the Catholic Church.

2. Marriage is a sacrament and divorce would break the promises made before God.

3. Jesus spoke against divorce and reminded that marriage unites a man and woman as 'one flesh'.

4. As Catholics believe marriage is for life, remarriage after divorce is not accepted and is seen as a form of adultery. A divorced person wishing to remarry would not be able to have a Catholic Church ceremony.

## Annulment

In special cases, Catholics accept an annulment – making invalid – of the marriage (a Decree of Nullity). There are strict guidelines for this. Reasons can include:

- one partner hiding information such as a previous marriage
- the inability to have children
- the inability to understand the commitment of marriage.

## Other Christian attitudes

Other Christian churches, including Protestant churches, agree that marriage is a lifelong relationship. However, some accept that marriages sometimes break down, and that divorce may be the only option to avoid the continued suffering (including that of children) of those involved in an unhappy marriage.

## Non-religious attitudes

**Non-religious** people may also believe that marriage breakdown can cause problems within the family and understand that divorce is sometimes necessary. They do not associate marriage with religion, so do not feel that promises to any sort of god have been broken. They also have no issue with remarriage.

Catholics would respond by maintaining that marriage is the best environment for raising children in a stable society. In cases of abuse, Catholics may suggest a separation but would not recognise divorce.

### Now try this

Outline **three** Catholic beliefs about divorce.   **(3 marks)**

Had a look ☐    Nearly there ☐    Nailed it! ☐

Catholic
Christianity
Marriage and
the family
Paper 1

# Men and women in the family

Catholics recognise the equal value of both men and women, especially within the family. In today's society, equality between men and women is an important idea.

## Bible sources on the roles of men and women

### Created equal but different

Catholics accept the Genesis (1:27) account that men and women were created in God's image, and that they have different but equal and complementary roles: man was created physically different to work the land, while woman was designed to assist him. Catholics stress the dignity of work in the home because of its importance for the family.

### The patriarchal view

A more openly patriarchal view is found in Ephesians, with women instructed to obey their husbands, although in return men are also told to love, respect and protect their wives.

Submit to one another out of reverence for Christ. Wives, submit yourselves to your own husbands as you do to the Lord. (Ephesians 5:21–22)

### Traditional family roles

It is not good for the man to be alone; I will make a helper suitable for him... Then the Lord God made a woman from the rib he had taken out of the man, and he brought her to the man. (Genesis 2:18, 2:22)

A literal interpretation is that men are the head of the household with women looking after the home. Another interpretation is that men and women are intended to work together alongside each other equally. The Catholic Church values traditional family models.

### Alternative family roles

Many Christians today may feel that the traditional idea of men as providers and women as carers is outdated. They may argue that either can equally provide or take care of the home and children.

There is neither Jew nor Gentile, neither slave nor free, nor is there male and female, for you are all one in Christ Jesus. (Galatians 3:28)

## Catholic teaching

The family is the original cell of social life... Authority, stability, and a life of relationships within the family constitute the foundations for freedom, security and fraternity within society... Family life is an initiation into life in society. (CCC 2207)

This teaching shows how men and women form the essential building blocks of both the family unit and wider society.

## Non-religious and other Christian attitudes

Humanists and atheists are likely to accept more modern interpretations of the roles of men and women within the family. They believe in the equality of men and women and support their roles, as long as they are happy in them.

Many Christians of other denominations might also agree with this view, although others may still hold on to the traditional views suggested in the Bible.

Catholics would respond to these views by emphasising the importance of the family, and maintaining that the Bible's teachings are still valid. They believe that men and women have different but equally valuable roles within the family.

## Now try this

Outline **three** Catholic beliefs about the roles of men and women in the family.    **(3 marks)**

Make sure each belief you give is different.

# Gender prejudice and discrimination

Many people, including Catholics, believe men and women should be treated equally, although this is not always practised. If a person is treated unfairly, this is known as **discrimination**.

## Gender prejudice and discrimination

**1** **Gender prejudice or sexism** is when a person is judged to be superior or inferior depending on their gender.

**2** **Gender discrimination** is when a person is treated differently as a direct result of their gender.

## Role of women

Women play a very important part in the life of the Catholic Church – as Ministers of the Eucharist, Altar servers and Readers.

However, Catholicism does not permit women to be ordained as priests or bishops. Catholics believe that as a priest represents Jesus who was male, a woman cannot fulfil this role.

There has been some opposition both within and outside the Catholic Church to the debate on the ordination of women, but no change has as yet come about.

## Theology of the body

Most Catholics follow John Paul II's teaching on the 'Theology of the Body', a doctrine on the human body. It maintains that, although there is apparent equality between men and women, the ordination of women is not an area where this should apply. It firmly holds on to the belief that women cannot be ordained as priests.

## Catholic opposition to gender inequality

Some Catholic charity organisations work for gender equality, including CAFOD (Catholic Agency for Overseas Development). They believe gender inequality is against human rights. They use Catholic teachings such as the responsibility of stewardship to care for all people to support their views as well as traditional Bible teachings about all humans being equal. The Catechism also appears to oppose gender inequality:

> There exist also *sinful inequalities* that affect millions of men and women. These are in open contradiction of the Gospel... (CCC 1938)

## Non-religious and other Christian attitudes

Many Humanists and atheists are likely to hold the same views as Christians that men and women are equal, albeit for different reasons. Humanists would argue that everyone should be given the same opportunities, including those of different genders.

Other Christian denominations also work for gender equality, e.g. allowing women to become vicars and bishops in the Church of England.

## Catholic response

> For as woman came from man, so also man is born of woman. But everything comes from God. (1 Corinthians 11:12)

Catholics would maintain that men and women are made equal but different. They believe that their roles and positions are also different, equal and complementary.

## Now try this

'Men and women should be treated the same in all areas of life.'
Evaluate this statement considering arguments for and against. In your response you should:
• refer to Catholic teachings  • refer to different Christian points of view  • reach a justified conclusion.

**(12 marks)**

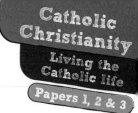

# Sacramental nature of reality

Catholic Christians and some other denominations believe that sacraments are outward visible signs, established by Jesus, of an inward spiritual blessing or grace. Christians can receive this grace and experience God's power during special ceremonies, rites or rituals.

> The seven sacraments touch all the stages and all the important moments of Christian life: they give birth and increase, healing and mission to the Christian's life of faith. (CCC 1210)

Catholics believe all creation is an expression of God's presence, and that he is close and active within the world, even though he does not have a physical presence.

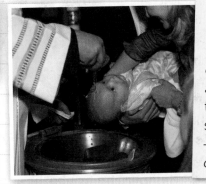

Catholics recognise seven sacraments, which are at the centre of their faith and accompany them throughout all stages of their lives – infant baptism is often the first.

---

### 1 Baptism

Infant baptism is a sacrament marking the entry of a new believer into the Church. Light represents Jesus as the 'Light of the world' and water as essential to life as a method of cleansing. Parents and godparents make promises on the child's behalf.

### 2 Confirmation

Children make the promises made for them in infant baptism for themselves. Anointing with oil and laying on of hands symbolise the gift of the Holy Spirit.

### 3 Marriage

A man and a woman are joined together through vows – 'till death do us part'. The symbol of the ring represents marriage's lifelong commitment.

### 4 Ordination/holy orders

A person enters holy orders to become a priest. During ordination, he is presented to the assembly and asked to commit to performing the duties of the priesthood. A bishop lays his hands on him and offers a prayer to invoke the power of the Holy Spirit, giving him the authority to represent Christ on Earth.

**The seven sacraments**

### 7 Reconciliation (penance)

Catholics believe priests have the power to forgive sins on God's behalf. Many Catholics attend reconciliation or confession weekly, telling the priest through a grille or curtain of sins committed since their last confession. The priest then absolves them of their sins and may ask them to perform a penance such as saying a particular prayer.

### 6 The Eucharist

The service to bless and share bread and wine, representing the body and blood of Jesus, in remembrance of the Last Supper Jesus shared with his disciples. Catholics believe in **transubstantiation** – that the bread and wine actually become the body and blood of Jesus when blessed by the priest using Jesus' words, even though they outwardly look the same. Catholics believe they actually receive Jesus into their bodies.

### 5 Anointing of the sick

Someone seriously ill or dying is blessed by the priest and is anointed by oil that has been blessed on the eyes, ears, nose, lips and hands, bringing spiritual strength. This is often the last sacrament a person receives before death.

---

## Diversity of interpretation

**Orthodox Christians** recognise seven sacraments (the seven sacred mysteries): baptism, Chrismation, marriage, ordination, anointing of the sick, the divine liturgy and reconciliation.

Most **Protestant Christians**, such as those in the Church of England, recognise only two sacraments – baptism and the Eucharist – because they are the only two specifically mentioned in the New Testament. However, some Protestant Christians, do recognise all seven as Catholics do.

**Now try this**

Outline **three** features of the sacrament of baptism.

**(3 marks)**

# Liturgical worship

Liturgical worship is a form of worship carried out in public by a group of people which follows a set pattern. The sacrament of the Eucharist – or Mass as Catholics call it – is particularly important as it symbolically re-enacts the Last Supper that Jesus shared with his disciples.

## Nature and significance

The Eucharist is the central act of divine worship in the Catholic Church because:

✓ many of the other sacraments are celebrated through its framework

✓ it reminds Catholics of Jesus' sacrifice

✓ it follows God's commandment to 'honour the Sabbath' and Jesus' instructions to remember the Last Supper

✓ it allows Catholics to feel God's presence.

Priest performing the Eucharist

Catholics believe the Eucharist or Mass is at the centre and linked to all the other sacraments, which affirm belief in God and Jesus. They believe that through it God's presence, power and love are shown, which fulfils their spiritual needs.

## Structure of the Mass

Priest processes towards the sanctuary of the church.

⮟

Greeting song and welcome.

⮟

Penitential rite – reflection time and prayer.

⮟

Liturgy of the Word – scripture readings.

⮟

The priest speaks to the congregation.

⮟

Liturgy of the Eucharist – presentation of the bread and wine, prayers, breaking of the bread and sharing of the wine, followed by distribution of the Eucharist.

⮟

Final prayers, blessing and dismissal.

## 'Source and summit of Christian life'

The Eucharist is 'the source and summit of the Christian life'. 'The other sacraments, and indeed all ecclesiastical ministries and works of the apostolate, are bound up with the Eucharist and are oriented towards it…' (CCC 1324)

## Lumen Gentium

The *Lumen Gentium* is one of the principal documents of the Second Vatican Council, which gives guidance on key Catholic Church teachings. Section 7 describes the unifying importance of the sacrament of the Eucharist:

Really partaking of the body of the Lord in the breaking of the Eucharistic bread, we are taken up into communion with Him and with one another. (*Lumen Gentium* 7)

## Significance of Catholic liturgical worship

- Catholics believe liturgical worship strengthens people's relationship with God through a set service of rituals and actions, including set prayers, hymns and time for reflection.

- It involves locations in a church, such as the altar, which create focal points to remind Catholics of Jesus' sacrifice.

- Many Catholics feel it is an appropriate way of showing respect to God.

## Diversity

In some evangelical denominations, such as **Pentecostal churches**, services may be less formal. Although there is a minister to guide the service, everyone is free to contribute. Services of this type may include hand clapping, singing and even dancing. **Baptist church** services may also be less formal in their structure, while **Quaker services** include sitting quietly and only speaking when a follower has something to say.

## Now try this

Outline **three** features of liturgical worship for Catholics.                    **(3 marks)**

# Liturgy of the funeral rite

Catholics have set funeral rites that are performed when a person dies.

## The funeral rite in the home

When a Catholic Christian dies there may be a vigil – a prayer service – the night before the funeral, which can be held either in the home of the deceased or in the church. A priest will lead the family in prayers to remember the person who has died.

## Aims of funeral rites

**1** To say goodbye to the deceased, celebrate their life and provide support and closure for friends and family.

**2** To express the hope of resurrection and eternal life with God shown through the death of Jesus.

**3** The committal (burial of the body) shows the communion between the Church on Earth and in heaven – the person's body returns to the Earth.

**4** A time for the Catholic community to unite in prayer.

| | | | | | |
|---|---|---|---|---|---|
| The corpse is carried to the church in a procession of clergy and mourners. | During the procession the Office of the Dead is recited or sung. | The coffin is placed in the church and covered with a pall. | The Paschal candle is put by the head of the coffin as a symbol of baptism. | Requiem Mass is said or sung as an offering. | The coffin is solemnly perfumed with incense and sprinkled with holy water. |

## The funeral rite at the cemetery

The Catholic Church prefers burial over cremation as some Catholics believe in the resurrection of the actual body after death. The coffin is carried to consecrated ground (holy ground) and buried while the priest recites prayers. A gravestone marks the location of the person after most burials.

The funeral rite in the church

A farewell to the deceased is his final 'commendation to God' by the Church. It is 'the last farewell by which the Christian community greets one of its members before his body is brought to its tomb'. (CCC 1690)

## Preparing for a funeral

Vincent Nichols, Archbishop of Westminster, produced two resources to help guide mourning families in preparing for a funeral:

**1** 'Guide for preparing a Catholic funeral' – a leaflet indicating the purpose and nature of a Catholic funeral that offers simple guidance for friends and family.

The purpose of the Catholic Funeral Liturgy is to offer worship and thanksgiving to God… to pray for the deceased, and to offer support to the bereaved. (Catholic Parish of Bishop Stortford)

**2** 'Preparing for my funeral' – a simple A4 sheet of questions designed to help people indicate their preferences for their own funeral to ensure it reflects their Catholic faith.

## Now try this

1 Outline **three** features of Catholic funeral rites. **(3 marks)**

2 'Catholic funeral rites have no purpose in modern life today.' Evaluate this statement considering arguments for and against. In your response you should:
   - refer to Catholic teachings
   - reach a justified conclusion.
   **(12 marks)**

Consider why Catholics have funeral rites and what they aim to achieve. Consider also why some non-religious people may still appreciate a funeral even if they hold no religious beliefs.

# Prayer

Christian Catholics believe prayer is a way of communicating with God. They believe they can speak and listen to God through prayer, which is a sign of faith and brings them closer to God.

## Different types of prayer and worship

Catholics use different types of prayer for different occasions. They follow Jesus' teaching by reciting the Lord's Prayer, have set structures for formal services such as the Mass and use personal informal prayer when they wish to speak to God privately.

## Importance of prayer

- Communication with God through prayer helps Catholics develop a personal relationship with him, deepening their faith.

- Catholics can worship God through prayer or ask for help in times of trouble. It provides comfort and assurance as well as hope that God will answer.

- Bible teachings and the Catechism both remind Catholics of the importance of prayer for **petition** and **intercession** – 'Prayer is the raising of one's mind and heart to God or the requesting of good things from God' (CCC 2590) – or for thanksgiving and praise – 'pray continually, give thanks in all circumstances; for this is God's will for you in Christ Jesus' (1 Thessalonians 5:17–18).

### Set formulaic prayers

Catholics often use such prayers in services such as the Eucharist or Mass, together with rosary beads to help them focus. Many prayers reflect key Catholic beliefs and may praise or thank God for what he has done and provided. The Sign of the Cross prayer recognises the symbol of the cross Catholics make, while the Hail Mary prayer recognises the importance of the Virgin Mary.

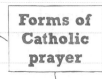

### Forms of Catholic prayer

### The Lord's Prayer

The Bible provides guidance on how Catholics should pray. The Lord's Prayer (Matthew 6:9–14, CCC 2759) is the most famous set prayer, which it is believed Jesus taught to his followers. It has key Catholic beliefs about God, e.g. his power, forgiving nature and directions on how to live life well. It is spoken during Mass, as part of the Rosary, and many Catholics also recite it daily.

**Sign of the Cross prayer**
In the name of the Father, and of the Son, and of the Holy Spirit. Amen.

**Hail Mary prayer**
Hail Mary, full of grace. Our Lord is with thee. Blessed art thou among women and blessed is the fruit of thy womb, Jesus. Holy Mary, Mother of God, pray for us sinners now and at the hour of our death. Amen.

Our Father, Who art in heaven, Hallowed by Thy name; Thy kingdom come; Thy will be done on earth as it is in heaven. Give us this day our daily bread; and forgive us our trespasses as we forgive those who trespass against us; and lead us not into temptation, but deliver us from evil. (The Lord's Prayer)

### Informal extempore prayer

Informal prayer is not set and may be said without any prior preparation. It might include meditation, contemplation and silent personal reflection. Such prayers can be performed alone or in a group outside a formal service.

## Now try this

Explain **two** reasons why prayer is important to Catholics. In your answer you must refer to a source of wisdom or authority.    **(5 marks)**

You must give **two different** reasons in your answer and develop each one by giving an example or new information. Remember to also include a quote from a source of wisdom or authority.

Had a look ☐   Nearly there ☐   Nailed it! ☐

Catholic
Christianity
Living the
Catholic life
Papers 1, 2 & 3

# Popular piety

Popular piety includes the various forms of worship or prayer that Catholic Christians practise – either alone or in a community group.

## The Rosary

A form of Catholic prayer including the recitation of sets of the Apostles' Creed, Hail Mary, the Lord's Prayer and Glory Be. The Rosary reminds Catholics of key beliefs such as Mary's importance, the nature of God and Jesus' significance. It may be said on special occasions, with others in a formal church setting or individually. It demonstrates devotion to the Catholic faith, helps Catholics to understand its key elements, provides time for reflection and allows a closer relationship with God.

## Eucharistic adoration

The Catholic practice of exalting God's greatness through honouring the Eucharistic presence of Christ. During the Mass, Catholics believe the bread and wine become the body and blood of Jesus (transubstantiation), and that by sharing in them, they are sharing in the person of Jesus. Eucharistic adoration is where the bread and wine are given devotion in the same way as Jesus himself. The ceremony may include Bible readings, hymns, prayers and time for silent reflection on the Eucharist's importance; Catholics feel it brings them closer to Jesus and God. They also reflect on the importance of Jesus' sacrifice and the significance of the bread and wine.

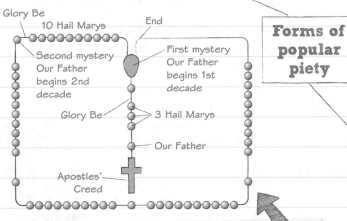

Glory Be
10 Hail Marys
End
Second mystery
Our Father
begins 2nd
decade
First mystery
Our Father
begins 1st
decade
Glory Be
3 Hail Marys
Our Father
Apostles'
Creed

Forms of popular piety

## Stations of the Cross

A series of images showing Jesus on the day of his crucifixion and an accompanying set of prayers. They enable Catholics to make a spiritual pilgrimage through reflection on the events of the Passion (Jesus' suffering and death). Usually, a series of fourteen (numbered) images are arranged in sequence and Catholics travel from image to image, stopping at each 'station' to say selected prayers and reflect. This can be done individually or in a procession and often happens during the festival of Lent and on Good Friday.

The rosary (without a capital 'R') is also the name given to the prayer beads Catholics use to count the prayers being spoken.

## Importance of popular piety

The religious sense of the Christian people has always found expression in various forms of piety surrounding the Church's sacramental life, such as the veneration of relics, visits to sanctuaries, pilgrimages, processions, the stations of the cross, religious dances, the rosary, medals. (CCC 1674)

The Catechism emphasises the importance of different forms of worship and recognises that variety helps to inspire devotion among Catholic followers.

## Other Christian attitudes

Although the forms of piety on this page are primarily Catholic practices, they are also regarded as important by some other Christian denominations. **Protestants** recognise the importance of remembering the Stations of the Cross and may take part in the ritual. They do not, however, recognise the Rosary or have the same understanding of the Eucharist, so may celebrate this differently.

## Now try this

Explain **two** reasons why popular piety is important for Catholics.        **(4 marks)**

Include **two different** reasons and state each one clearly. Then develop your answer by giving an example or supporting your reason with new information.

# Pilgrimage

A **pilgrimage** is a journey religious believers make to holy places of spiritual, biblical and historical significance. Pilgrimage also represents an inner spiritual journey and journey of faith.

## The history of Catholic pilgrimage

- The first recorded Christian pilgrim is thought to have been St Helena (248–328CE), who travelled to the Holy Land.
- Pilgrims also went to sites such as Rome or places where visions of saints or the Virgin Mary are believed to have been seen.
- During the Middle Ages, pilgrimages became a lot more common.
- The Crusades prevented some pilgrims travelling to the Holy Land in the 12th century.

## Purpose of Catholic pilgrimage

1. To visit places of importance associated with particular religious events or people.

2. To strengthen a pilgrim's faith and help them feel closer to God.

3. To visit places associated with saints or visions of Mary to ask for help or healing powers, or to give thanks.

4. To join with others who hold the same beliefs to trace the roots of their religion.

### Jerusalem, Israel

A holy city for all Christians and where Jesus celebrated the Last Supper and was crucified. Catholics trace Jesus' footsteps and visit places such as the Garden of Gethsemane where he was betrayed and arrested.

Places of Catholic pilgrimage

### Lourdes, France

An important pilgrimage site for Catholics. An apparition of the Virgin Mary was seen here in 1858 by a 14-year-old girl, Bernadette Soubirous. She followed the instructions given to her in the vision and a sacred healing spring appeared. Many Catholics go there hoping to be healed, although the Church has only verified 69 cases.

### Walsingham, Norfolk

In 1061, a woman received a vision of the Virgin Mary who showed her Jesus' home in Nazareth. A replica of the home was built in Walsingham as many could not make the journey to Israel. It is a popular place of pilgrimage where Catholics reflect on Jesus' human form and pray for themselves and the world.

### Rome, Italy

A place of historical importance for Catholics, as Vatican City is the home of the pope and the Curia, and is the centre of the Christian Church in the West. It has seven great basilicas and many sites and relics associated with apostles, saints and martyrs. Catholics visit Rome to receive blessings and sacraments, as well as to pray and reflect.

> Pilgrimages evoke our earthly journey toward heaven and are traditionally very special occasions for renewal in prayer. For pilgrims seeking living water, shrines are special places for living the forms of Christian prayer 'in Church'. (CCC 2691)

> Catholic Church sources of authority recognise the importance of pilgrimage as an opportunity to renew and confirm their faith.

## Other Christian views

Other Christian denominations may not place the same level of significance on pilgrimage as Catholicism. Some may feel it is more important to be close to God in a church rather than to travel to other places. Many may also feel that the money and time used for pilgrimage could be used to help others instead.

## Now try this

Explain **two** reasons why pilgrimage is important for Catholics today. In your answer you must refer to a source of wisdom or authority. **(5 marks)**

# Catholic social teaching

Social teaching is about Catholic action in society to improve it and be part of it. Helping others individually and in the worldwide community is an important Catholic teaching.

## Love of neighbour

'Love your neighbour as yourself.' There is no commandment greater than these. (Mark 12:31)

The Bible contains Jesus' teaching about helping others. The Church Catechism also promotes this idea and Catholics are taught to look after those around them.

## Justice, peace and reconciliation

Catholics believe it is important to:

☑ be fair towards others (e.g. treat people the same)

☑ achieve peace with others (e.g. not be in conflict)

☑ make up after conflict (say sorry and reconcile).

Ideas of justice, peace and reconciliation, along with working together and bringing about change, are key Catholic teachings.

## Evangelii Gaudium

The earth is our common home and all of us are brothers and sisters. If indeed 'the just ordering of society and of the state is a central responsibility of politics', the Church 'cannot and must not remain on the sidelines in the fight for justice'. (*Evangelii Gaudium* 183)

Each individual Christian and every community is called to be an instrument of God for the liberation and promotion of the poor, and for enabling them to be fully a part of society. (*Evangelii Gaudium* 187)

The *Evangelii Gaudium* is an address by Pope Francis on the Catholic Church's mission in the modern world that promotes the following:

**1** The Catholic Church and all Catholics have a responsibility to build a better world.

**2** Christian teachings, such as loving your neighbour and the Catholic view on justice, are key to help bring change to the world.

**3** Helping those who are poor is specifically mentioned, with every Christian having a role in bringing about justice and equality.

## Parable of the Sheep and the Goats

The Parable of the Sheep and the Goats (Matthew 25:31–46) contains a teaching about helping others. People who are charitable and caring are rewarded by God. Individual Catholics, such as Mother Teresa or Oscar Romero, are role models and examples of how Catholics believe they should act and behave, so that they will be rewarded by eternal life with God.

## Catholic agency worldwide

Agencies such as CAFOD:

* work to fight poverty and injustice
* help people to help themselves
* tackle challenges such as climate change, inequality, HIV and AIDS
* help out in times of crisis – providing clean water, food and shelter for those in need
* speak out against unjust governments.

**Why?**

* They believe every human deserves dignity.
* They are guided by Catholic values of compassion, solidarity and hope.
* They put Catholic teachings into action.
* They believe all humans are God's children.

## Now try this

Explain two Catholic teachings on social justice. In your answer you must refer to a source of wisdom or authority.

**(5 marks)**

# Mission and evangelism

**Evangelism** is the Christian practice of sharing and spreading the belief in salvation through Christ with others. **Missionary work** is a type of evangelical work where an individual or group is sent to a particular area to provide aid, for example through educational or medical work.

## Missionary and evangelical work

- Christianity has a long history of evangelism. Examples of early missionaries include the first disciples and St Paul in the Mediterranean area during the 1st century CE.

- Today, Catholic missionaries and evangelicals work within the current Church structure to grow and develop the Church.

- They do this by spreading the word of God and the Bible and sharing Catholicism's message.

- This takes place within local communities as well as across the world.

## Importance of this work for Catholics

Jesus spread God's redeeming message during his lifetime through his preaching. Catholics believe they should also share their faith through preaching – they follow Bible teachings that suggest God commanded them to share their faith with others to save their souls. Pope Francis in his *Evangelii Gaudium*, an address given on the importance of helping others, promotes missionary work.

## Mother Teresa (1910–1997)

A Catholic nun who had a calling to work for God in 1922, aged 12.

⬇

Worked in a school in Calcutta in India.

⬇

Witnessed first-hand the suffering of the poor and in 1950 founded the Missionaries of Charity – a mixed order of sisters, brothers and priests dedicated to serving the poor.

⬇

Although her main aim was to help others, she also instructed in the Catholic faith if asked.

⬇

She was canonised to become St Teresa of Calcutta by Pope Francis in 2016.

## Sources of authority

A Church which 'goes forth' is a Church whose doors are open. (*Evangelii Gaudium*, Chapter 5)

He said to them, 'Go into all the world and preach the gospel to all creation.' (Mark 16:15)

Therefore go and make disciples of all nations, baptising them in the name of the Father and of the Son and of the Holy Spirit... (Matthew 28:19)

Develop your answers with sources like these.

## Where missionary and evangelical work takes place

| Locally | Nationally | Globally |
| --- | --- | --- |
| • Churches fund projects to spread God's word. <br> • Church events introduce non-believers to Catholicism. <br> • Churches work together to inspire Christians to spread the faith. <br> • Education for local communities. <br> • Provide support for the needy in the community, e.g. food banks, charity work. | • Churches are linked nationally and hold events where they meet and share their faith. <br> • Churches in different areas may work together on community projects. <br> • There may be projects that people can become involved in to educate others. | • Many churches and denominations subscribe to projects for young people to get involved in world aid and missionary work. <br> • People can visit underdeveloped areas to help on projects. <br> • Opportunities may arise to study in different countries or create links with Christians in other countries and spread the message. |

## Now try this

Outline **three** ways that evangelism work is important to Catholics.

**(3 marks)**

Had a look ☐  Nearly there ☐  Nailed it! ☐

Catholic
Christianity
Matters of life
and death
Paper 1

# Origins of the universe

The main scientific explanation for the origin of the universe is the Big Bang Theory. Most Christians today, including Catholics, embrace this theory within traditional Christian teaching about the world's origins and its value as a resource for humans.

The Big Bang Theory states that an explosion from a single point of dense matter started the universe around 14 billion years ago.

Georges Lemaitre is thought to be the first person to write about this idea in 1927. He was a Roman Catholic priest as well as a scientist and he saw no conflict between religion and science.

## Big Bang Theory

The scientific Big Bang Theory suggests that before the universe existed all matter was concentrated into a dense mass, which spontaneously began to expand to form the universe. Everything – planets, stars, matter – is believed to result from the cooling and condensing of matter following the Big Bang.

## Catholic teaching on the Creation

Day 1 — Earth, space, time and light (half light/half dark)
Day 2 — Atmosphere (sky/sea)
Day 3 — Dry land and plants
Day 4 — Sun, moon and stars
Day 5 — Sea creatures and birds
Day 6 — Land animals and man

Catholic teaching supports the idea that the Creation account found in Genesis 1–2 is a **theological myth**. It presents the work of the Creator symbolically. The story reveals truths about God's nature (his power as creator and sustainer of life).

## Catholic response to scientific explanations

Literal readings of the Bible Creation story (that it is true in all detail) and the rejection of evolutionary theories, have not been official Church teachings for a long time.

The current Catholic view, upheld by Pope Francis' teachings, is that there is no conflict between science and religion, as it was all part of God's plan.

## Value of the universe for Catholics

The question about the origins of the world and of man has been the object of many scientific studies which have splendidly enriched our knowledge of the age and dimensions of the cosmos, the development of life-forms and the appearance of man. These discoveries invite us to even greater admiration for the greatness of the Creator. (CCC 283).

## Christian response to the universe as a commodity

Past interpretations of the Bible Creation story that humans have dominion over the world and so can use it as a commodity are today regarded as outdated. Catholics and many other Christians now believe:

- ✓ God created the world and it should therefore be respected
- ✓ God gave humans the task of stewardship, they have a duty to future generations to care for the world
- ✓ they will be judged on how they have cared for the world after death.

## Now try this

Outline **three** Catholic beliefs about the origin of the universe.　　(3 marks)

25

Catholic
Christianity
Matters of life
and death
Paper 1

Had a look ☐   Nearly there ☐   Nailed it! ☐

# Sanctity of life

Catholic Christians believe human life is both special and holy because it is created and given by God, a belief summed up by the phrase, the 'sanctity of life'.

## Human life as holy

Human life is sacred because from its beginning it involves the creative action of God and it remains forever in a special relationship with the Creator, who is its sole end. (CCC 2258)

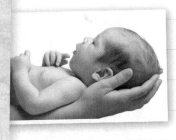

Catholics believe human life is holy and sacred because:

- it was created by God and belongs to him
- God created humans 'in his image' and so they are special
- they believe humans were created to be special and the summit of God's creation.

## All life is special

Some important Bible passages support the idea of the sanctity of life.

Then the Lord God formed a man from the dust of the ground and breathed into his nostrils the breath of life, and the man became a living being. (Genesis 2:7)

…your bodies are temples of the Holy Spirit… (1 Corinthians 6:19)

You shall not murder. (Exodus 20:13)

God gave humans the breath of life.

St Paul refers to the human body as a 'temple', suggesting it is special.

This Bible commandment that ending another's life is not acceptable implies that all human life is special.

## Made in the image of God

So God created mankind in his own image, in the image of God he created them; male and female he created them. (Genesis 1:27)

The Bible (Genesis 1–3) teaches Christians they were made by God – in his image. This implies that humans are different from all of God's other creations and explains why human life is so special and sacred.

Made 'in the image of God' doesn't mean people actually look like God, but that they have characteristics such as goodness that are similar to God, and which allow them to become more like God and enter heaven.

## Importance of sanctity of life

The sanctity of life teaching is still important to Catholics today because:

1. it determines their **beliefs about issues** such as abortion and euthanasia – they will favour the preservation of life
2. they will **value human life** and this will impact on the way they live – they will respect and care for those both close to them and in the wider community
3. it will guide them in **moral decisions** and determine how they treat others
4. it offers **absolute teaching** on the sacred nature of life that is unchanging in the face of modern issues.

## Now try this

1 Explain **two** Catholic teachings about human life being holy. In your answer you must refer to a source of wisdom or authority.
**(5 marks)**

2 'The sanctity of life argument is still important today.'
Evaluate this statement considering arguments for and against. In your response you should:
- refer to Catholic teachings
- reach a justified conclusion.
**(12 marks)**

Ensure you offer **two different** reasons. State the reason first and then develop it by expanding on the point made or adding an example. Remember, you also need to refer to a source of authority by giving a quote from, for example, the Bible.

Had a look ☐   Nearly there ☐   Nailed it! ☐

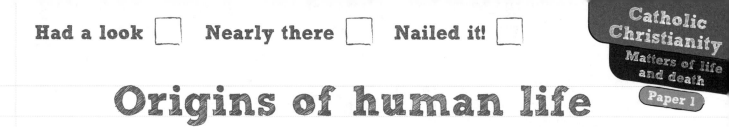

Catholic
Christianity
Matters of life
and death
Paper 1

# Origins of human life

Catholics, like most other Christians, believe that the Bible account of the origins and value of human life are compatible with the scientific explanation outlined in the theory of evolution, so you need to understand this theory.

## Theory of evolution

Charles Darwin's 19th-century theory of evolution argued that the origin of human life was the result of the gradual development of species over millions of years from simple life-forms to more complex ones through a process of 'natural selection'.

## 'Survival of the fittest'

This is another way of describing the process of 'natural selection' from the theory of evolution. Individuals who were better adapted to their environment (fitter) survived to pass on their genes to the next generation – the **'survival of the fittest'**. Over time, this meant life **evolved** so only those beings with the characteristics or features that were strongest survived.

## Catholic responses to evolution

- Catholics see no conflict between religion and science, viewing evolution as part of God's plan for the creation of life and God's existence as necessary to make the world come into being.

- There are a few Catholics and other Christians who still believe evolution is incompatible with the Bible, but that is not the accepted Catholic view.

## Significance for Catholics today

- In today's scientific world, it is hard to deny that evolutionary theory provides a plausible explanation for human existence.

- By accepting scientific explanations alongside religion, Catholics feel they can answer some of life's most important questions.

- It also means their traditional beliefs are still intact.

## Non-religious views

Non-religious people also value human life because:

- it has intrinsic value – it is valuable simply because it exists

- humans are capable of rational thought

- human life is protected by laws reflecting its worth

- it has extrinsic value – it has potential (e.g. humans can achieve, develop and grow).

Catholics would agree with non-religious views as to why life is valuable. They would, however, maintain that the most important reason for this is because it is God's creation.

## Pope Francis and evolution

Pope Francis made a statement about evolution on 27 October 2014 at the Pontifical Academy of Sciences. This accepts scientific theories of evolution as part of God's intention in creating humans, while stressing God's involvement in all Creation.

When we read the account of Creation in Genesis we risk imagining that God was a magician, complete with an all-powerful magic wand. But that was not so. He created beings and he let them develop according to the internal laws with which He endowed each one, that they might develop, and reach their fullness. (Pope Francis)

### Now try this

Outline **three** Catholic responses to scientific explanations about the origins of human life.          **(3 marks)**

# Abortion

Catholics are firm in their views on abortion, using the sanctity of life argument and the *Humanae Vitae* as evidence of why it is wrong. Other Christians may hold different views on abortion that refer to different teachings. All Christians, however, believe that life is sacred.

## What is abortion?

Abortion is the deliberate medical termination of a human pregnancy so that a child is not born. Currently in the UK, it is legal to have an abortion up to 24 weeks with two doctors' consent.

## The *Humanae Vitae*

The *Humanae Vitae* is a circular letter written by Pope Paul VI in 1968, which reinforced the Catholic position on abortion being wrong. This view was reinforced in 1995 by Pope John Paul II, who stated that the Catholic position remained unchanged and unchangeable.

> The transmission of human life is a most serious role in which married people collaborate freely and responsibly with God the Creator. (*Humanae Vitae*)

## Arguments against abortion (pro-life)

Catholics do not support abortion because:

- they believe all life has value and begins at conception, so abortion is seen as murder
- life is a sacred gift from God which humans cannot take away
- Catholics believe God has a plan for everyone – abortion goes against this
- the *Humanae Vitae* states that abortion is wrong.

Some other Christians may hold similar views and also argue for a 'pro-life' perspective.

## Arguments for abortion (pro-choice)

Some Christians agree that, while abortion is not good, sometimes it is the 'lesser of two evils' and say that:

- Jesus taught compassion towards others
- we cannot be sure life begins at conception
- in cases of rape or incest, abortion may be the kindest action
- if medical technology identifies serious problems with the foetus, a termination may be fairer
- abortion is justified if the mother's life or health is at risk.

## Non-religious views

There is no 'one' atheist or Humanist view on abortion. **Atheists** may argue that:

- it is the woman's personal right to decide
- some people may not be ready to have or cannot afford a child
- the rights of the mother outweigh those of the child before it is born
- abortion is wrong, but not for religious reasons.

> **Humanists** do not believe the foetus becomes a 'person' until well after conception. They view life as special, but think abortion should be an option.

## Catholic response

Catholics hold the view that abortion is always wrong. They would reject pro-choice arguments. They would also disagree with other Christian denominations who suggest that, although not a preferred option, it may sometimes be morally preferable.

> **Situation ethicists** argue that the correct action regarding abortion is dependent on the given set of circumstances.

## Now try this

'Abortion is always wrong.'
Evaluate this statement considering arguments for and against. In your response you should:

- refer to Catholic teachings
- refer to non-religious points of view
- refer to relevant ethical arguments
- reach a justified conclusion.

**(12 marks)**

Had a look ☐  Nearly there ☐  Nailed it! ☐

Catholic
Christianity
Matters of life
and death
Paper 1

# Life after death

Catholics believe in life after death – in heaven, purgatory or hell. They use the proof of Jesus' resurrection, his ascension into heaven and Bible teachings to support their views.

## Resurrection

Catholics believe Jesus' resurrection shows death is not the end. They believe Jesus rose from the dead three days after his crucifixion and this gives them hope that if they follow Jesus' teachings and accept him as their saviour, eternal life will be the reward. By living and dying as a human, Jesus made this new 'life after death' (promised by him in the New Testament) possible for all.

I am the resurrection and the life. The one who believes in me will live, even though they die. (John 11:25–26)

## Catholic teachings

The Bible often refers to life after death.

My Father's house has many rooms; if that were not so, would I have told you that I am going there to prepare a place for you? (John 14:2)

Jesus talks of a place for all in heaven where he will go first.

For God so loved the world, that he gave his one and only Son, that whoever believes in him shall not perish but have eternal life. (John 3:16)

Jesus came to Earth as God Incarnate to save humanity.

And God raised us up with Christ and seated us with him in the heavenly realms in Christ Jesus… (Ephesians 2:6)

God has given humans the chance to join him in heaven.

## Other Christian views

Different Christian denominations also believe in Jesus' resurrection and ascension into heaven and refer to the same teachings. They may also offer the following reasons:

- They believe God is just and fair and accept that after death people will be judged according to how they lived their lives.
- They also accept the idea that there is reward or punishment after death.

Non-religious people often don't believe in life after death, but some do for the following reasons.

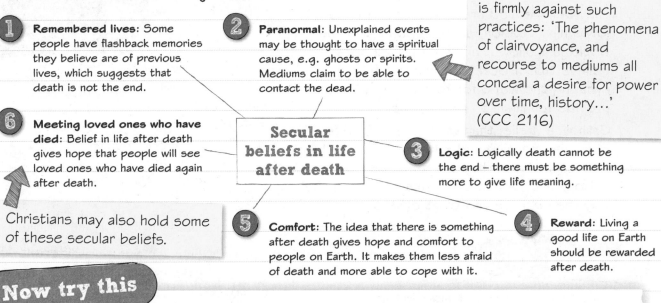

1  **Remembered lives:** Some people have flashback memories they believe are of previous lives, which suggests that death is not the end.

2  **Paranormal:** Unexplained events may be thought to have a spiritual cause, e.g. ghosts or spirits. Mediums claim to be able to contact the dead.

6  **Meeting loved ones who have died:** Belief in life after death gives hope that people will see loved ones who have died again after death.

Christians may also hold some of these secular beliefs.

**Secular beliefs in life after death**

The Catholic Church is firmly against such practices: 'The phenomena of clairvoyance, and recourse to mediums all conceal a desire for power over time, history…' (CCC 2116)

3  **Logic:** Logically death cannot be the end – there must be something more to give life meaning.

5  **Comfort:** The idea that there is something after death gives hope and comfort to people on Earth. It makes them less afraid of death and more able to cope with it.

4  **Reward:** Living a good life on Earth should be rewarded after death.

## Now try this

Explain **two** reasons why Catholics believe in life after death.  **(4 marks)**

# Non-religious arguments against life after death

Counter to Catholic Christian beliefs, many non-religious people will argue that there is no life after death. They think that a person is born, lives and then simply dies.

**1** **Lack of evidence:** No evidence of life after death – no one has ever returned to prove it exists. Many think science disproves religious ideas of an afterlife and claim there is nothing after death.

**2** **False comfort:** Some people think that holding beliefs about an afterlife provides a false sense of comfort, and they consider that is the reason why it is a popular, though misguided, belief.

**3** **Fraudulent accounts:** Some people trick others into believing they can contact the dead and take advantage of vulnerable people. This type of behaviour makes some people reject the idea of an afterlife.

**6** **Humanist beliefs:** Humanists believe that when a person dies their body decays and there is nothing else. Life after death is seen as an impossibility.

**Secular arguments against life after death**

**5** **Social control:** Some believe the Church might pressure individuals to believe in an afterlife.

**4** **Coping mechanism:** Some people think that belief in life after death gives people control over what they fear most. They believe it is a type of coping mechanism.

## Catholic response

✓ Catholics believe there is evidence of life after death, found in the resurrection and ascension of Jesus and Bible teachings.
For more on the resurrection see page 6.

✓ They believe that having faith means accepting things without question – a belief in life after death is part of this. Having belief and faith in God means putting trust in him and his teachings.

✓ They believe God created the world and loves his Creation, so they don't think he would just allow it all to end. Catholics believe that if God took such care in creating the world for humans, he will also provide for them after they die.

✓ Catholics' belief that there is an afterlife gives life meaning and purpose. They believe that after death they will be judged on their actions and faith in God. This influences the way they behave and treat others.

...by the resurrection of Jesus Christ, who has gone into heaven and is at God's right hand – with angels, authorities and powers in submission to him. (1 Peter 3:21–22)

This Bible quote shows Catholics that Jesus died and was resurrected to save the sins of the world. Catholics accept he was sent so they might follow his example and get closer to God in the hope that they can achieve eternal life with God in heaven.

## Now try this

Explain **two** reasons why Catholics reject arguments against life after death. **(4 marks)**

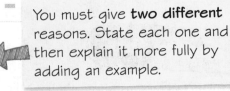

You must give **two different** reasons. State each one and then explain it more fully by adding an example.

# Euthanasia

Euthanasia (or assisted dying) is the act of ending a dying person's life painlessly, or allowing them to die to relieve pain and suffering. It is a controversial issue because Catholic Christians see it as murder, while others may see it as a compassionate act.

## Nature of euthanasia

There are three different types of euthanasia.

1. **Assisted suicide** – where a person is given the means to end their own life.

2. **Voluntary euthanasia** – where a person's life is ended deliberately and painlessly at their request.

3. **Non-voluntary euthanasia** – ending a person's life painlessly when they are unable to ask, but you have good reason for thinking it is what they would want (e.g. by taking a person off life support).

## The sanctity of life and Ten Commandments

Catholics are against euthanasia because:

- Catholics believe humans were made in God's image to be special. For more on the sanctity of life see page 26.

- the Old Testament Commandment 'You shall not murder' (Exodus 20:13) forbids prematurely ending life.

## Catholic teaching

Whatever its motives and means, direct euthanasia consists in putting an end to the lives of handicapped, sick, or dying persons. It is morally unacceptable. (CCC 2277)

The Catechism sums up Catholicism's key belief that euthanasia is never acceptable.

## Other arguments against euthanasia

- The slippery slope argument – if euthanasia was legal, it might be allowed in less serious cases.
- Some people may be pressurised into choosing euthanasia.
- Doctors can make mistakes.
- Hospices can provide palliative care, relieving the symptoms of conditions they cannot cure.

## Non-religious views

Most non-religious people believe human life is valuable for non-religious reasons, and so have different opinions regarding euthanasia.

**Atheists** may argue that the kindest thing is to allow a dying person to die a gentle, pain-free, dignified death and that the wishes of the dying person should be respected.

**Humanists** use reason to make decisions and would support the use of euthanasia if requested by the dying person.

**Situation ethicists** argue that the correct action depends on the circumstances and an absolute rule of euthanasia always being right or wrong cannot be applied.

## Different Christian views

Most Christians believe in the sanctity of life and regard euthanasia as wrong. The Church of England is strongly opposed to euthanasia, stresses the importance of valuing and caring for ill and vulnerable individuals, and supports the concept of good hospice care as an alternative to assisted dying.

## Catholic response

Catholics would respond to non-religious views that support euthanasia by focusing on Bible and Church Catechism teachings that state euthanasia is always wrong. They believe only God can decide when life should end, and that suffering may have a purpose and is not a good enough reason to end a life.

## Now try this

Explain **two** Catholic teachings on euthanasia. In your answer you must refer to a source of wisdom or authority. **(5 marks)**

Catholic
Christianity
Matters of life
and death

Paper 1

Had a look ☐   Nearly there ☐   Nailed it! ☐

# Issues in the natural world

Today's natural world faces many threats, often from humans. Catholics have specific beliefs and teachings about what should be done and how the world should be cared for.

## Threats to the environment

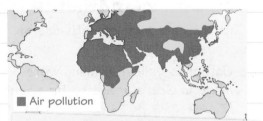

■ Air pollution

The world today is being damaged by pollution, global warming and humanity's excessive use of natural resources, which are running out. Many animal species are threatened with extinction, while the world's fast-growing human population is becoming unsustainable.

## Catholic response

Catholics believe they should care for the world and not waste its resources because:

✓ the Bible teaches that we should care for the world

✓ the world is a gift from God

✓ they are taught that humans will be judged after death on how they treated the Earth

✓ God gave humans the responsibility of stewardship of the Earth – caring for it for future generations.

> God blessed them and said to them, 'Be fruitful and increase in number; fill the earth and subdue it. Rule over the fish in the sea and the birds in the sky and over every living creature that moves on the ground.' (Genesis 1:28)
>
> The Lord God took the man and put him in the Garden of Eden to work it and take care of it. (Genesis 2:15)

## Stewardship

Catholics believe God has given them a duty of stewardship, which means they must look after the world and not destroy it.

> God entrusted animals to the stewardship of those whom he created in his own image. Hence it is legitimate to use animals for food and clothing. They may be domesticated to help man in his work and leisure. Medical and scientific experimentation on animals is a morally acceptable practice if it remains within reasonable limits and contributes to caring for or saving human lives. (CCC 2417)

This Catechism quote supports the use of animals for food and experimentation.

## Use of animals in experimentation

Catholics believe that:

• animals are part of God's creation, so should be cared for – the idea of stewardship supports this

• animals can be used in experiments if it benefits and saves human life – but this should be within reasonable limits and should not cause unnecessary suffering.

## Use of animals for food

Catholics believe that:

• it is acceptable for animals to be used for food, as God gave them to humans for this purpose

• although animals were created by God, humans are more important as they were made 'in the image of God'

• God gave humans dominion and stewardship over animals, so there is nothing wrong with eating them.

## Utilitarianism

Ethical theories such as **utilitarianism** can offer guidance on correct moral action. Utilitarianism states that the 'right' action is that which brings the most benefit to the largest number. In terms of using animals for food and experimentation, this theory seems to suggest that this is acceptable if large numbers of humans benefit.

### Now try this

Outline **three** Catholic responses to the threats to the natural world today.          **(3 marks)**

Make sure you give **three different** examples of things that threaten today's natural world.

# Justice

Justice is important for Catholics and is a key part of Christian teachings.

## The nature of justice

Justice is concerned with moral rightness and fairness in the way people are treated.

## Importance of justice for Catholics

**1** God is understood and seen to be just and expects people to act in the same way.

**2** Jesus taught that everyone should be treated fairly, and Catholics believe we should follow this.

**3** The Catholic Church promotes justice towards others.

**4** God will judge people after death – his justice and mercy will lead to forgiveness for those who truly repent of their wrongdoings.

**5** The Bible teaches about God's justice such as Micah 3:1–12.

Micah talks of the sins committed by those who rule, exhorting them to behave justly and fairly towards others. He warns that those who do not show mercy cannot expect mercy from God. Catholics following Bible teachings try to apply this in their own lives.

## Importance of justice for the victim

☑ To make them feel safe from further harm.

☑ To make it seem fair that a person has been punished for their crime.

☑ To make the victim feel like the criminal has 'paid' for their crime – especially if it involves giving back to society.

Then I said, 'Listen, you leaders of Jacob, you rulers of Israel. Should you not embrace justice, you who hate good and love evil; who tear the skin from my people and the flesh from their bones; who eat my people's flesh, strip off their skin and break their bones in pieces; who chop them up like meat for the pan, like flesh for the pot?' Then they will cry out to the Lord, but he will not answer them. At that time he will hide his face from them because of the evil they have done. (Micah 3:1–4)

Catholics recognise that justice is important for the victim as the wronged person, but stress that criminals should also be treated fairly.

## Non-religious attitudes to justice

**Atheists** see the need for justice in society, recognising that it allows for fair treatment of all involved.

**Humanists** also support the importance of justice because:

- they believe equality and fair treatment of all humans is important
- they make ethical decisions based on reason, empathy and concern for all humans
- they believe people have a right to be happy; justice plays a key role in this.

Catholics and non-religious people hold similar beliefs on justice, both stressing its importance, although the reasons for its importance may differ.

### Now try this

Outline **three** reasons why justice is important for Catholics. **(3 marks)**

# Crime

A crime is an action someone commits against the laws of the state, e.g. murder, theft or drink-driving. Crime is a significant problem in the UK with a statistical increase for certain types of violent crime and other new crimes, including social media crimes.

## Causes of crime

The causes of crime are complex and varied.

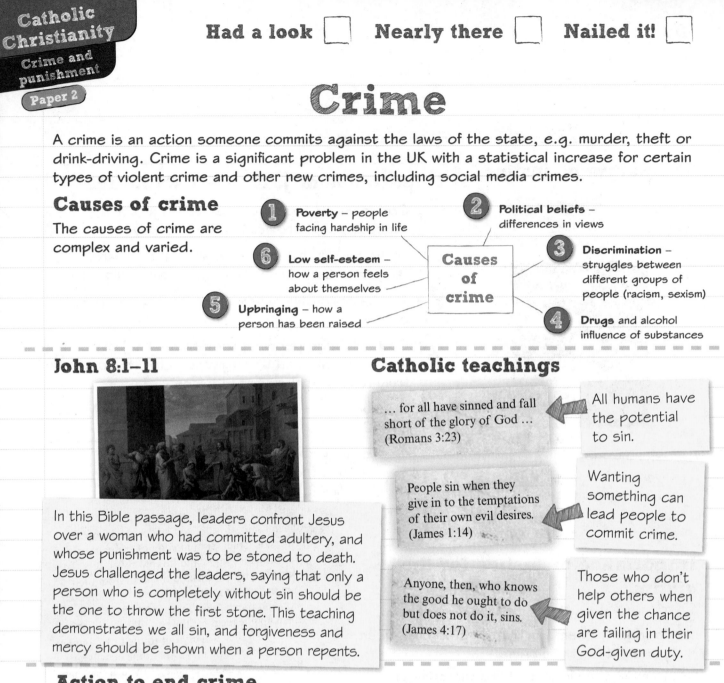

**1** Poverty – people facing hardship in life

**2** Political beliefs – differences in views

**3** Discrimination – struggles between different groups of people (racism, sexism)

**4** Drugs and alcohol influence of substances

**5** Upbringing – how a person has been raised

**6** Low self-esteem – how a person feels about themselves

**Causes of crime**

## John 8:1–11

In this Bible passage, leaders confront Jesus over a woman who had committed adultery, and whose punishment was to be stoned to death. Jesus challenged the leaders, saying that only a person who is completely without sin should be the one to throw the first stone. This teaching demonstrates we all sin, and forgiveness and mercy should be shown when a person repents.

## Catholic teachings

… for all have sinned and fall short of the glory of God … (Romans 3:23)

All humans have the potential to sin.

People sin when they give in to the temptations of their own evil desires. (James 1:14)

Wanting something can lead people to commit crime.

Anyone, then, who knows the good he ought to do but does not do it, sins. (James 4:17)

Those who don't help others when given the chance are failing in their God-given duty.

## Action to end crime

Some Christian individuals and organisations work to reduce crime.

**1 Prison Fellowship**

**Prison** FELLOWSHIP

- Includes volunteers from local churches.
- Money is raised to provide support to prisoners.
- Organises prayer groups and victim awareness programmes (so prisoners understand how their crimes hurt others).
- Supports prisoners' families, so special occasions can be shared.
- Includes letter-writing programmes to prisoners so they don't feel so alone.

**2 Street Pastors**

- Groups of trained volunteers who work on the streets in the UK and abroad.
- Can often be seen on Friday and Saturday evenings providing support and guidance.
- Work in local schools and educational establishments to support young people. Also work in schools and colleges.
- Provide support and care where a crisis has occurred (response pastors).

## Now try this

Explain **two** teachings why Catholics believe it is important to help those tempted to commit crimes. In your answer you must refer to a source of wisdom or authority. **(5 marks)**

# Good, evil and suffering

Catholics have clear teachings on ideas about good, evil and suffering.

## Good and evil actions

**1** **Good actions** – Catholics believe that if a person lives according to God's rules and performs good deeds, God will reward them in the afterlife by sending them to heaven. Catholics also believe in purgatory – a temporary punishment or purification of sin before eventual entry into heaven.

**2** **Evil actions** – Catholics believe that if a person is evil during their lifetime, does wrong and hurts others, God will punish them in the afterlife by sending them to hell.

## Parable of the Sheep and the Goats

Jesus used parables to teach people how they should behave and treat others. An important one is the Parable of the Sheep and the Goats (Matthew 25:31–46), which explains how God will judge people.

For more on the this parable see page 23.

- People will be separated into two categories: those who help and care for others (the sheep) and those who do not (the goats).
- Eternal reward is promised to those who have lived their life as God intended.
- Eternal punishment is given those who ignore God and don't help others.

## Non-religious views

**Atheists:**

- may use the existence of evil and suffering to refute God's existence, suggesting an all-loving, powerful God would not let his Creation suffer.

**Humanists:**

- don't accept evil and suffering is a test, punishment or part of a divine plan
- believe humans have a degree of choice in life and are responsible for their actions
- believe some evils are the result of human action, e.g. war, famine and poverty
- believe some people may suffer through natural causes, e.g. illness or floods.

Take your inheritance, the kingdom prepared for you since the creation of the world. For I was hungry and you gave me something to eat, I was thirsty and you gave me something to drink, I was a stranger and you invited me in, I needed clothes and you clothed me, I was sick and you looked after me, I was in prison and you came to visit me. (Matthew 25:34–36)

## Other Christian views

Most Christians agree with Catholics and believe:

- suffering makes us stronger – we learn from it and it helps us cope in the future
- suffering is a punishment – for 'the Fall' from grace and idea of Original Sin from the story of Adam and Eve
- suffering is a test of faith – it is a challenge to accept that humans suffer but God still exists and loves his Creation.

## Catholic response to evil and suffering

Catholics teach that:

- suffering is part of human life and has a purpose – even if we do not understand it
- God gave humans free will – the choice between good and evil, so humans must accept the consequences of their actions
- people must look to Jesus' Bible teachings to understand evil and suffering.

**Now try this**

Explain **two** reasons why Catholics believe humans suffer.

**(4 marks)**

# Punishment

In order for the law to work for the good of society, those who break the law should be punished. A punishment is the imposition of a penalty or deprivation for breaking the law. Its severity should reflect the seriousness of the offence.

Punishments can range from a fine or community service to imprisonment.

## Catholicism and punishment

**1 Importance of punishment**

- It teaches people that their behaviour is wrong.
- It gives criminals the chance to change.
- God commanded people to follow the laws of the country where they live.
- It seems just and fair for a person to be punished for wrongdoing.

**2 Bible teachings**

- The Bible describes God as a God of justice, suggesting crimes should be punished.
- Jesus taught the importance of forgiveness, mercy and compassion: 'Be merciful, just as your Father is merciful... Do not judge, and you will not be judged. Do not condemn, and you will not be condemned. Forgive, and you will be forgiven' (Luke 6:36–37).
- Jesus told parables concerning punishment: 'The servant who knows the master's will and does not get ready or does not do what the master wants will be beaten with many blows. (Luke 12:47).

**3 Church teachings**

The Church teaches that fair and just punishment for a crime should be in line with basic respect for the person: 'If, however, non-lethal means are sufficient to defend and protect people's safety from the aggressor, authority should limit itself to such means...' (CCC 2267).

**4 Punishment is justice**

Catholics consider fair punishment for a crime to be just. When a crime is committed, appropriate punishment means the victim gets retribution, while the criminal has the opportunity to realise their actions are wrong and change.

**5 Necessity of punishment**

Catholics understand that the threat of punishment encourages individuals to follow society's rules, as well as protecting and keeping them safe.

## Worked example

Outline **three** Catholic beliefs about the importance of punishment.    **(3 marks)**

Punishment is important in helping people learn that their behaviour is wrong. St Paul commanded Christian to follow the country's laws. Jesus taught punishment was important for achieving justice.

## Now try this

1 Explain **two** reasons why Catholics believe punishment is a good thing.    **(4 marks)**
2 Explain **two** Catholic teachings about punishment. In your answer you must refer to a source of wisdom or authority.    **(5 marks)**

Both of these questions are EXPLAIN style questions. Question 2, however, requires you to include a quote from a source of authority such as the Bible, Church Catechism or papal teaching.

# Aims of punishment

## Aims of punishment and Catholic responses

| Type of punishment | Aim of punishment | Catholic response |
|---|---|---|
| ① Protection | To protect society from violent or dangerous criminals by keeping them away from society so they can't hurt others. | The protection of human life is important for Catholics, so they would accept that punishment is necessary in order to provide protection from harm for others. |
| ② Retribution | To make criminals pay for what they have done wrong. | Catholics do not agree with ideas of revenge, but see a purpose in retribution through making the criminal realise and accept that what they have done is wrong, which leads to reform. |
| ③ Deterrence MUGGER GETS FIVE YEARS A serial mugger was sentenced yesterday at Newtown county court to | To discourage someone from breaking the law by showing them the consequences. | Most Catholics accept that if seeing the punishments imposed on some criminals deters others from carrying out the same deed, this is a positive effect. |
| ④ Reformation ABC | To show the criminal they have done wrong and to give them an opportunity to change (through education or provision of skills) so they do not reoffend. | This would be the most important aim of punishment for Catholics. They believe in forgiveness and 'turning the other cheek' (Matthew 5:39). Giving criminals an opportunity to change their behaviour is key to providing future stability to society and can lead to reparation where a criminal makes up for what they did wrong. |

## Teachings on punishment

**Christianity teaches that punishment is necessary when a person has done wrong.**

Anyone who does wrong will be repaid for their wrongs, and there is no favouritism. (Colossians 3:25)

The person who has done wrong will get what they deserve.

Be sure of this: the wicked will not go unpunished… (Proverbs 11:21)

Reward and punishment will be linked to how a person behaves and acts.

Then they will go away to eternal punishment, but the righteous to eternal life. (Matthew 25:46)

Those who deserve it will gain eternal life, but others will suffer eternal punishment.

The defense of the common good requires that an unjust aggressor be rendered unable to cause harm. (CCC 2265)

Society has a right to protect itself from criminals.

Brothers and sisters, if someone is caught in a sin, you who live by the Spirit should restore that person gently. But watch yourselves, or you also may be tempted. Carry each other's burdens, and in this way you will fulfil the law of Christ. If anyone thinks they are something when they are not, they deceive themselves. Each one should test their own actions. (Galatians 6:1–4)

Mercy and understanding alongside punishment are important. Christians should support others who have committed sins, as they themselves are not above committing sins.

## Now try this

Explain **two** reasons why Catholics would oppose some aims of punishment. **(4 marks)**

# Forgiveness

**Forgiveness** means to stop blaming someone for what they have done. **Reconciliation** here means to make and live in peace with others; it is not the same as the sacrament of reconciliation – where Catholics receive absolution for their sins.

## Catholic beliefs and teachings on forgiveness

 Forgiveness is a key Bible teaching: 'Bear with each other and forgive one another if any of you has a grievance against someone. Forgive as the Lord forgave you' (Colossians 3:13).

2 The Lord's Prayer talks about forgiveness: 'And forgive us our debts, as we also have forgiven our debtors' (Matthew 6: 12).

3 Jesus taught about forgiveness and the importance of moving forward.

4 Jesus died on the cross to bring forgiveness and reconciliation between God and humanity.

## Importance of forgiveness by the community

Offenders can be reintegrated in the community by providing them with an education and new vocational skills. They may also be asked to show they are sorry by 'paying back' through community service. It is also important that the community tries to offer them forgiveness.

I'm Sorry

Therefore, if you are offering your gift at the altar and there remember that your brother or sister has something against you, leave your gift there in front of the altar. First go and be reconciled to them; then come and offer your gift. (Matthew 5: 23–24)

## Nature and importance of mercy

Mercy refers to the benevolence, forgiveness and kindness shown to those who repent of their actions.

This passage shows the importance of mercy and reconciliation rather than holding a grudge.

Showing mercy to criminals is important because:

✓ Catholics believe they should show mercy towards others even when it is difficult – God helps them do this

✓ the Bible teaches that it is important to show mercy through forgiveness:

'...if you hold anything against anyone, forgive them...' (Mark 11:25).

Forgiveness allows people to move forward.

'Blessed are the merciful, for they will be shown mercy.' (Matthew 5:7).

This is similar to 'treating others as you want to be treated' – showing mercy to others as you would wish it shown towards you.

✓ kindness and compassion are key ideas linked to forgiveness within Catholic teachings: 'Forgiveness also bears witness that, in our world, love is stronger than sin' (CCC 2844).

## Worked example

Explain **two** reasons why forgiveness is important for Catholics. In your answer you must refer to a source of wisdom or authority. **(5 marks)**

Forgiveness is an important Bible teaching. Jesus taught about forgiveness in the Lord's Prayer: 'And forgive us our debts, as we also have forgiven our debtors' (Matthew 6:12). A second reason is that Jesus died on the cross to bring forgiveness and repair the relationship between God and humanity; this is a key Catholic teaching on the importance of forgiveness.

## Now try this

Outline **three** Catholic beliefs about forgiveness.
**(3 marks)**

Had a look ☐  Nearly there ☐  Nailed it! ☐

Catholic
Christianity
Crime and
punishment
Paper 2

# Treatment of criminals

Catholics believe it is important for criminals to be treated fairly despite their crimes.

## Catholic beliefs

- Punishing criminals provides an opportunity for their rehabilitation and reform.
- Forgiveness can work alongside punishment – offenders are appropriately punished while others involved can move on.
- Justice is important – even criminals deserve just and fair treatment.
- All humans are God's creations deserving dignity and respect – although criminals lose some rights, they still deserve respect as human beings.

Balancing the ideas of punishing criminals alongside giving them respect and dignity as humans can be difficult for many religious believers, including Catholics.

## Catholic teachings

Justice and fairness are important to all Catholics in all circumstances. It is important to stand up for people who cannot stand up for themselves, including criminals whose rights are denied.

> Speak up for those who cannot speak for themselves, for the rights of all who are destitute. Speak up and judge fairly; defend the rights of the poor and needy. (Proverbs 31:8–9)

Church Social teaching promotes work in local communities to give people guidance, comfort or even practical help.

---

### 1 Use of torture
The Bible appears to acknowledge the use of torture ('handed him over to the jailers to be tortured' (Matthew 18:34)), but Catholics today would not support its use.

### 4 Trial by jury
Trials need to be conducted fairly, in front of a panel of objective peers (a jury) who, as a broad and unbiased cross-section of society, can make informed decisions based on the evidence.

**Issues concerning the treatment of criminals**

### 2 Human rights
Although punishment may involve the loss of some human rights (e.g. the right to freedom), Catholics believe that basic human rights (e.g. the right to food and water) should always be upheld.

### 3 Fair trial
Catholics believe justice is important and support the right to a fair trial, where both sides of a case are heard and all have fair, legal representation.

---

## Different Christian views

Most other Christian denominations would agree with Catholic views on the just and fair treatment of criminals. However, some may find this difficult to accept for the most serious crimes, accepting capital punishment as a way of protecting society.

## Non-religious views

There are wide-ranging views among non-believers regarding the treatment of criminals, but **Humanists** and most others would agree that criminals deserve to keep rights, such as fair and humane treatment and a fair trial.

## Ethical theories

**Situation ethics** states that individual situations and circumstances should be considered. In extreme cases, this could be used to support the view that in some circumstances – the use of torture or the deprivation of human rights might be justified.

---

Outline **three** reasons why Catholics believe criminals should be treated fairly.        **(3 marks)**

# Capital punishment

## Nature of capital punishment

Capital punishment (also known as the death penalty) is execution – a condemned prisoner's life is taken away. It has been abolished completely in the UK, although some countries retain it, including many states in the USA. Methods can include: hanging; firing squad; electric chair; and lethal injection.

## Purpose

**1** To provide punishment for the most severe crimes committed.

**Aims of capital punishment**

**2** To act as a deterrent to other criminals.

**3** To make victims feel as though punishment has been carried out.

## Differing Catholic Christian views and reasons

FOR the death penalty:

- the Old Testament teaches that the death penalty is appropriate for some crimes: 'Anyone who strikes a person with a fatal blow is to be put to death' (Exodus 21:12)
- Jesus never taught the death penalty was wrong
- the Christian Church used the death penalty in the Middle Ages; and the Catechism states: '... the traditional teaching of the Church does not exclude recourse to the death penalty, if this is the only possible way of effectively defending human lives against the unjust aggressor' (CCC 2267)

AGAINST the death penalty:

- Catholicism's overall message is to love and forgive – capital punishment goes against this
- Jesus taught revenge was wrong: 'But I tell you, do not resist an evil person. If anyone slaps you on the right cheek, turn to them the other cheek also' (Matthew 5:39)
- it goes against the sanctity of life argument
- the Catechism states that taking another life is wrong and many popes have spoken out against the death penalty, including Pope John Paul II, calling it 'cruel and unnecessary': 'God alone is the Lord of life from its beginning until its end: no one can under any circumstance claim for himself the right directly to destroy an innocent human being' (CCC 2258).

## Bible teachings

The Bible has conflicting arguments:

Whoever sheds human blood, by humans shall their blood be shed. (Genesis 9:6)

This suggests capital punishment is acceptable if someone takes another's life.

You shall not murder. (Exodus 20:13)

God's commandment teaches that killing is always wrong.

## Non-religious views

**Atheists** may think the most severe crimes justify capital punishment. Others may think using the death penalty means the criminal escapes from justice.

**Humanists** generally oppose the use of the death penalty.

**Situation ethicists** advise looking at each situation individually, so might consider capital punishment justified in extreme cases.

## Now try this

'The death penalty should be brought back for the most serious crimes.'
Evaluate this statement considering arguments for and against. In your response you should:

- refer to Catholic teachings
- refer to different Christian points of view
- refer to non-religious points of view
- reach a justified conclusion.

**(12 marks)**

# Peace

Peace is an important idea for Catholics. It is important to know why and how Catholics see Jesus as a peacemaker and call him 'the Prince of Peace'.

## Nature and importance of peace

Peace is understood to be the absence of war or conflict. Catholics also understand it as trust and community among people. It is important for Catholics because:

✓ the Catechism teaches that peace and justice is essential in Catholic lives

✓ they believe all Church members are part of a community – the sign of peace (sometimes denoted by a handshake) is an important part of Mass

✓ there are many examples of peace being promoted in the Bible by Jesus and others.

## Church teachings

- Catholics follow Jesus' example, who taught his disciples to forgive and '... love your enemies and pray for those who persecute you' (Matthew 5:44).

- 'If anyone slap you on the right cheek, turn to them the other cheek also' (Matthew 5:39).

> Jesus' teaching promotes peace and reconciliation rather than war and hatred.

- Catholics believe peace is only possible when people recognise they are all God's creations – this links to teachings on the sanctity of life.

- Although the Church never promotes violence, there have been times when violence has been considered necessary to bring about peace, e.g. defending Christianity in the crusades.

## Jesus as peacemaker

1 Jesus taught and showed through many actions that peace can be achieved through love of others:
'Love your neighbour as yourself' (Mark 12:31).

2 He embraced the worst sinners, cared for the sick and dying, performed miracles to help others and showed that all people are of equal worth and should live in peace with one another.

3 He taught in the Sermon on the Mount 'Blessed are the peacemakers' (Matthew 5:9).

4 Even when the prophecy about his death was coming true and he faced arrest in the Garden of Gethsemane, he continued to preach the importance of peace:

> When Jesus' followers saw what was going to happen, they said, 'Lord, should we strike with our swords?' And one of them struck the servant of the high priest, cutting off his right ear. But Jesus answered, 'No more of this!' And he touched the man's ear and healed him. (Luke 22:49–51)

5 He died on the cross to bring forgiveness and reconciliation between God and humanity, forgiving his enemies even as he was dying.

## 'Prince of Peace'

> For to us a child is born, to us a son is given, and the government will be on his shoulders. And he will be called Wonderful Counsellor, Mighty God, Everlasting Father, Prince of Peace. (Isaiah 9:6)

> This Bible teaching names Jesus as the 'Prince of Peace' alongside his role as God incarnate – God in human form – whose sacrifice repairs the spiritual relationship between God and all of humanity.

## Now try this

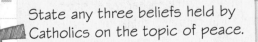

State any three beliefs held by Catholics on the topic of peace.

Outline **three** Catholic beliefs about peace.  **(3 marks)**

# Peacemaking

Peace is important for Catholic Christians. There are many examples of religious organisations working towards peace in today's world.

## Importance of justice, forgiveness and reconciliation

**1** **Justice**: Justice is fair behaviour or treatment. Catholics believe in a direct link between justice and peace. A lack of peace is often seen in places where injustices occur. If justice can be attained, peace will naturally follow.

**Steps to peacemaking**

**2** **Forgiveness**: Catholics believe that to attain peace, they should follow Jesus' Bible teaching on forgiveness. To forgive means moving on from what has happened and attaining peace through working together.

**3** **Reconciliation**: This is the idea of making up after conflict. Catholics believe peace is only possible after talking through issues and reconciling.

## Church beliefs and teachings

- Catholics believe they have a duty to work for peace in areas of conflict in the world.
- They follow Jesus' example and the teachings on peace he provided.
  For more Jesus' teachings on peace see page 41.
- The Catechism teaches that:

> Respect for and development of human life require peace. Peace is not merely the absence of war, and it is not limited to maintaining a balance of powers between adversaries. Peace cannot be attained on earth without safeguarding the goods of persons, free communication among men, respect for the dignity of persons and peoples, and the assiduous practice of fraternity. Peace is 'the tranquillity of order'. Peace is the work of justice and the effect of charity. (CCC 2304)

Catholics believe peace can be attained through mutual respect, justice, forgiveness and reconciliation.

## Why work for peace?

> Blessed are the merciful, for they will be shown mercy. Blessed are the pure in heart, for they will see God. Blessed are the peacemakers, for they will be called children of God. Blessed are those who are persecuted because of righteousness, for theirs is the kingdom of heaven. (Matthew 5:7–10)

Organisations such as Pax Christi aim to promote the characteristics contained in this teaching and help in the world as God intended.

## Pax Christi (the Peace of Christ)

- International Catholic organisation set up in 1945 to work towards peace and justice.
- The organisation is opposed to war and violence.
- It encourages people and governments to solve their conflicts through discussion, reconciliation, and economic and social justice.

Pax Christi:

- ✓ goes into schools and youth groups to promote peace
- ✓ holds interfaith conferences to show unity and pray for those without peace
- ✓ takes part in public demonstrations, e.g. against war, the arms trade or injustice to raise awareness and campaign against oppressive governments
- ✓ educates others about war or injustice and teaches forgiveness
- ✓ helps victims of injustice by supporting their rights and giving practical help
- ✓ encourages peace talks between groups to end conflict and support reconciliation.

**Now try this**

Outline **three** ways in which a Catholic organisation can work for peace.          **(3 marks)**

Had a look ☐   Nearly there ☐   Nailed it! ☐

Catholic
Christianity
Peace and
conflict
Paper 2

# Conflict

Conflict, where an argument or disagreement has led to a breakdown in a relationship, can cause serious problems within society, such as the inability to work together.

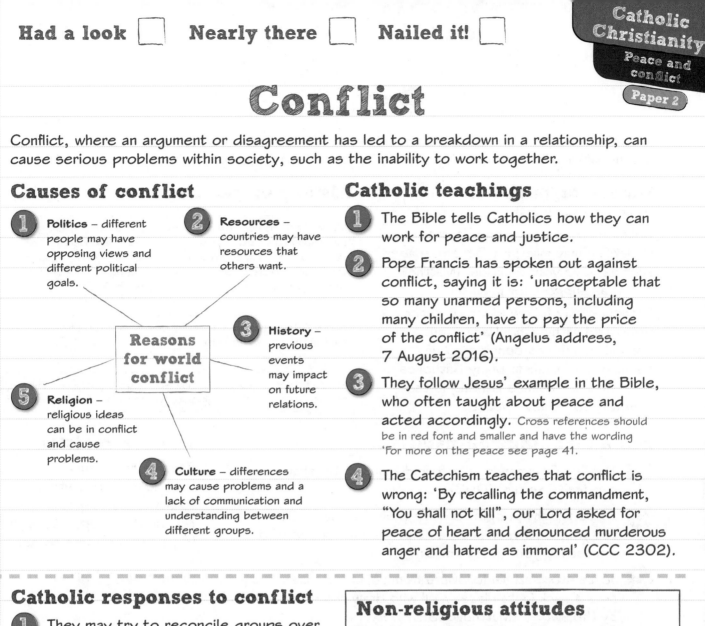

## Causes of conflict

**1** **Politics** – different people may have opposing views and different political goals.

**2** **Resources** – countries may have resources that others want.

**Reasons for world conflict**

**3** **History** – previous events may impact on future relations.

**5** **Religion** – religious ideas can be in conflict and cause problems.

**4** **Culture** – differences may cause problems and a lack of communication and understanding between different groups.

## Catholic teachings

**1** The Bible tells Catholics how they can work for peace and justice.

**2** Pope Francis has spoken out against conflict, saying it is: 'unacceptable that so many unarmed persons, including many children, have to pay the price of the conflict' (Angelus address, 7 August 2016).

**3** They follow Jesus' example in the Bible, who often taught about peace and acted accordingly. Cross references should be in red font and smaller and have the wording 'For more on the peace see page 41.

**4** The Catechism teaches that conflict is wrong: 'By recalling the commandment, "You shall not kill", our Lord asked for peace of heart and denounced murderous anger and hatred as immoral' (CCC 2302).

## Catholic responses to conflict

**1** They may try to reconcile groups over issues of conflict.

**2** They may hold a pacifist position and be against any form of violence or fighting.

**3** They may believe that religion and its teachings can bring people together to end conflict rather than cause it.

**4** They may refer to the example of Jesus' arrest, where his disciples tried to defend him: 'Put your sword back in its place,' Jesus said to him, 'for all who draw the sword will die by the sword' (Matthew 26:52).

This teaches that violence causes more violence rather than dealing with issues.

## Non-religious attitudes

People with non-religious views such as **atheists and humanists** may have divided opinions about the best way to end conflict, some of which may be in line with Catholic thinking.

- They may claim that religion itself is at the root of many conflicts.
- They may believe that as differences in beliefs cause conflict, religion cannot offer a way of achieving peace.
- They may not agree with conflict, but may advocate that sometimes violence is required in order to achieve peace.

**Situation ethicists** argue that each situation should be dealt with separately, rather than applying an absolute rule in all cases.

## Catholic responses to non-religious views

Catholics may recognise that religion can contribute to conflict. They would always, however, look to key Catholic teachings to show that conflict is not the way to resolve differences, and that Christians work for peace.

### Now try this

Outline **three** Catholic responses to the causes of conflict. **(3 marks)**

# Pacifism

The New Testament and Catholic Catechism teach all Christians to seek peace and reconciliation with their enemies. Some Christians hold a pacifist position on war and violence.

## Nature of pacifism

Pacifism is the belief that war and violence are always wrong. Some Christians may interpret Bible passages such as 'love your enemies' (Matthew 5:44) as support for pacifism.

Catholics may follow ideas of peace promoted within Christianity, but Catholicism is not considered as traditionally pacifist. Many Catholics think that sometimes fighting is the only way to achieve peace.

## History of pacifism

Many Christians see Jesus as a pacifist – his many teachings on peace include the Sermon on the Mount: 'Blessed are the peacemakers, for they will be called children of God. Blessed are those who are persecuted because of righteousness, for theirs is the kingdom of heaven' (Matthew 5:9).

▽

Some British pacifists (conscientious objectors) refused to fight in the two world wars.

▽

Martin Luther King and Mahatma Ghandi were pacifists, refusing to use violence in their fights to overcome injustice in the world.

## Bible teachings on pacifism

1. The Ten Commandments forbid killing: 'You shall not murder' (Exodus 20:13).

2. Jesus taught people to 'love their enemies: 'But I tell you, love your enemies and pray for those who persecute you' (Matthew 5:44).

3. Jesus stopped his followers from using violence: 'Put your sword back in its place ... all who draw the sword will die by the sword' (Matthew 26:52). See page 41 and 43 for more on Jesus and how he stopped his followers using violence.

4. As humans were made 'in his [God's] own image' (Genesis 1:27), their life is sacred, violence should not be used.

## Passive resistance

Passive resistance is non-violent opposition to authority, especially a refusal to co-operate with legal requirements to fight.

Peace I leave with you; my peace I give you. (John 14:27)

Some Catholics interpret this as advocating passive resistance.

## Other Christian attitudes to pacifism

The **Quakers** (Religious Society of Friends) are a Christian denomination opposed to violence.

- They believe God is in every person, and oppose anything that harms people.

- They believe they should act peacefully against injustice. Many may be conscientious objectors.

- In the past, some Quakers refused to defend themselves from attack.

## Thomas Merton (1915–1968)

- Thomas Merton was a Catholic monk who supported the peace movement.

- He wrote many letters to the Vatican Council, mainly about Catholics' right to be conscientious objectors and against the use of weapons of mass destruction.

- He took a stance of passive resistance, believing only peaceful means could achieve peace: 'Nonviolence seeks to "win" not by destroying or even by humiliating the adversary, but by convincing [the adversary] that there is a higher and more certain common good than can be attained by bombs and blood.'

## Now try this

'Everyone should be a pacifist.'
Evaluate this statement considering arguments for and against. In your response you should:
- refer to Catholic teachings    • refer to other Christian points of view    • reach a justified conclusion. **(12 marks)**

Catholic Christianity
Peace and conflict
Paper 2

# The Just War theory

A 'just war' is one that Christians think is fought for the right reasons, in the right way and is therefore justified.

## Importance of Just War theory

Just War theory is a largely Christian doctrine providing guidance on whether or not war is right and just. It:

- applies to states, not individuals
- is intended to prevent rather than justify war by showing that going to war in all but a few limited circumstances would be wrong
- provides a framework for discussions about possible actions to be taken.

## History of Just War theory

Originated with Greek and Roman philosophers such as Plato and Cicero.

⇩

Began in the Christian tradition with Augustine (354–430CE), who established a foundation for its principles.

⇩

Developed by St Thomas Aquinas (1225–1274CE).

⇩

Has been used in history in many conflict situations, including in modern-day situations.

## Conditions of Just War theory

1. The war must have a **just cause**, e.g. against invasion or in cases of self-defence, not to acquire wealth or power.

2. War must be declared and controlled by a **proper authority** – the state, government or ruler.

3. War must be fought to **re-establish peace** once the war is over.

4. War must be a **last resort** – all peaceful solutions must have been tried and failed.

5. War should be fought with **proportionality** – just enough force to achieve victory and only against legitimate targets.

6. Any good that the war achieves must be **greater** than the evil which led to it.

7. Innocent civilians must **never** be targeted.

### Other Christian views

There have been many wars where both sides have claimed their cause was 'just'. Hitler claimed the Nazis were right in their fight. It raises the question of whether any war is just. Christians are divided on whether war is ever justified.

### Situation ethics

Both religious and non-religious people may take a situation ethics standpoint, considering action appropriate to each individual situation.

## Catholic teachings

- Modern Catholics believe it is right to have armed forces to protect a country.

- They tend to believe that war is rarely justified, but may support a Just War.

- They believe there are situations where war is the 'lesser of two evils', e.g. Hitler.

- They think violence is sometimes necessary, e.g. if a country is invaded.

- The Just War Doctrine, found in the Catholic Catechism, provides strict conditions for deciding whether a war is in line with the Just War theory: 'all other means of putting an end to it must have been shown to be impractical or ineffective' (CCC 2309).

Some Bible support for the Just War theory.

- Jesus and St Paul taught that obedience should be shown to the government: 'Let everyone be subject to the governing authorities, for there is no authority except that which God has established. The authorities that exist have been established by God' (Romans 13:1).

- The Bible recognises that sometimes war is appropriate: 'a time to love and a time to hate, a time for war and a time for peace' (Ecclesiastes 3:8).

### Now try this

Explain **two** reasons why some Catholics would accept the Just War theory. **(4 marks)**

# Holy war

In a holy war religious believers think God is 'on their side' and fighting is what God wants – for example the 11th–13th-century Christian crusades to 'free' the holy places in Palestine.

## Catholic teachings and responses

1. Jesus was given the title 'Prince of Peace', suggesting war is not the answer.

2. The Catechism teaches: 'All citizens and all governments are obliged to work for the avoidance of war' (CCC 2308).

3. Human life is valuable to Catholics as it is a gift created by God 'in his own image' (Genesis 1:27) – so taking life is always wrong.

4. Catholics sometimes actively fought in wars of religious conflict, e.g. the Thirty Years War. The Catechism seems to support this if all other options have failed: 'However, "as long as the danger of war persists and there is no international authority with the necessary competence and power, governments cannot be denied the right of lawful self-defence, once all peace efforts have failed"' (CCC 2308).

## Bible teachings

Greater love has no one than this: to lay down his life for one's friends. (John 15:13)

This suggests that self-sacrifice for love of friends (as in war) could be honourable.

... for all who draw the sword will die by the sword. (Matthew 26:52)

Jesus' teaching that violence is not the answer.

... love your enemies and pray for those who persecute you. (Matthew 5:44)

Jesus encourages love and compassion towards enemies.

I did not come to bring peace, but a sword. For I have come to turn 'a man against his father, a daughter against her mother, a daughter-in-law against her mother-in-law. (Matthew 10:34–35)

Jesus refers to a 'sword' but is not encouraging violence. Before Christianity was established, Jesus knew that following him could split traditional families. He teaches that people should follow him, even if it means division. When put alongside other teachings, it still suggests peace and love are the way, not violence and war.

## Other Christian teachings

- Christians would generally agree that wars should not be fought in God's name and argue that Christianity teaches about peace, so violence should be used as a last resort, if at all: 'Blessed are the peacemakers, for they will be called children of God.' (Matthew 5:9).

- Some Christians may refer to Old Testament teachings to suggest that war may sometimes be justified: 'The Lord said to Moses, "Take vengeance on the Midianites for the Israelites"' (Numbers 31:1–2), but this is not a mainstream view.

- Other Christians (e.g. Quakers) may be pacifist.
  For more on pacifism see page 4.

## Non-religious attitudes

As non-religious people do not believe in God, they would object that religion is never a justifiable reason for war. Most would also oppose war in general, except in particular cases.

## Catholic response

Most Catholics would respond to non-religious views by pointing to Catechism teachings that if their religion is threatened, war may be justified, if peaceful solutions have failed. However, Catholics do not want war or believe it is acceptable. They work mostly for peace, especially in cases of different religious beliefs.

## Now try this

Explain **two** reasons why many Catholics may be against the idea of holy war.  **(4 marks)**

# Weapons of mass destruction

Weapons of mass destruction (WMD) include nuclear, biological or chemical weapons that can cause widespread devastation and loss of life. Catholics are against their use.

## Perceived benefits of WMD

- ✓ A quicker way to win a war.
- ✓ Minimal losses incurred on the side of the attackers using WMD.
- ✓ A threat to deter other nations from starting a war.

## Perceived problems of WMD

- 👎 Moral question of whether the devastation caused is ever morally justified.
- 👎 Dangers from stockpiling WMD.
- 👎 Conditions of the Just War theory would not be met using WMD.

## Catholic teachings and views on perceived benefits and problems

**1** Catholics accept that the problems of WMD outweigh any benefits.

**2** Catholic teachings focus on peace rather than violence.
For more on these teachings resurrection see pages 41 and 45.

**3** Catholics would oppose the high loss of life caused by WMD.

**4** Catholics recognise that the nature of war today has changed, but would still respond to the benefits and problems of WMD by arguing that their use cannot be justified.

**5** The Catechism opposes their use: 'Every act of war directed to the indiscriminate destruction of whole cities or vast areas with their inhabitants is a crime against God and man, which merits firm and unequivocal condemnation' (CCC 2314).

**6** Pope Francis has spoken out against WMD: 'There is urgent need to work for a world free of nuclear weapons' (Pope Francis to the UN, 2015).

## Catholic attitudes

- All Christians, Catholics included, are against the use of WMD as they do not discriminate between innocent civilians and soldiers and, above all, they do not respect the sanctity of life.
- Weapons on this scale and of this type do not fit conditions of a Just War.

> When you march up to attack a city, make its people an offer of peace... If they refuse to make peace and they engage you in battle, lay siege to that city. (Deuteronomy 20:10–12)

Although this passage seems to condone violence, Catholics would focus on the first part highlighting the importance of peace.

Most Catholics are likely to support non-religious views that the damage caused by WMD is unjustifiable, even if their reasons differ.

## Non-religious attitudes

Atheists, would be unlikely to support the use of WMD as they cause so much damage to life and the environment.

Humanists believe life is special and would also not support the use of WMD due to the immoral destruction and threat to life.

## Utilitarianism

The ethical theory of utilitarianism argues that the right action is that which brings about 'the greatest happiness for the greatest number'. The highly destructive nature of WMD would not justify their use.

### Now try this

'The problems of WMD means their use is not justified.'
Evaluate this statement considering arguments for and against. In your response you should:
- refer to Catholic teachings
- refer to non-religious points of view
- reach a justified conclusion. **(12 marks)**

Had a look ☐  Nearly there ☐  Nailed it! ☐

# Issues surrounding conflict

Today's world contains new threats of war from modern pressures such as new technologies used in the service of violence and terrorism.

**Threats of war**

**1** **Violence:** Violent acts are constantly reported in the media, suggesting that people are not afraid of laws and consequences. So it can be argued that there is a developing fear of violence within society.

**2** **War:** Warfare now involves new, stronger and more damaging weapons that use new technologies.

**3** **Terrorism:** A violent form of protest, often linked to extremist radical groups, e.g. suicide bombers or individuals choosing targets that inflict as much damage and harm as possible.

## Catholic teachings and responses

**1** Catholics look to Church and Bible teachings in response to issues surrounding conflict.

**2** The Bible, Catholic Church and the pope teach ideas of peace, reconciliation and forgiveness.

**3** Catholics do not condone the use of violence and believe in working together to find peaceful ways to resolve conflict.

Terrorism threatens, wounds, and kills indiscriminately; it is gravely against justice and charity. (CCC 2297)

It is a profanation and a blasphemy to declare oneself a terrorist in God's name. (2004 Compendium of the Social Doctrine of the Church No. 515)

Terrorism grows when there is now other option... this is fundamental terrorism, against all humanity. (Pope Francis)

Love your enemies, do good to those who hate you, bless those who curse you, pray for those who ill-treat you. If someone slaps you on one cheek, turn to them the other also. (Luke 6:27–29)

## What did Dorothy Day do?

Dorothy Day, an American journalist, social activist and converted Catholic, campaigned against social injustices and conflict.

- Founded the *Catholic Worker* – a newspaper devoted to Catholic teachings and challenging injustices in the world.
- Inspired and formed the 'Catholic Worker Movement' to challenge injustice.
- Helped the poor and homeless.
- Was arrested for protesting.
- Went on a hunger strike after protesting for women's rights.

As for ourselves, yes, we must be meek, bear injustice, malice, rash judgement. We must turn the other cheek, give up our cloak, go a second mile. (Dorothy Day)

## What did Oscar Romero do?

Oscar Romero, archbishop of San Salvador, stood up for those facing violence and oppression.

- Witnessed numerous violations of human rights and spoke out against injustice.
- Worked in the community, visiting those in prison, providing Catechism classes and helping to feed the poor.
- Wrote to the president to protest and comforted the families of three people killed in his diocese by the army.
- Spoke out against the use of violence and the murder of innocent people.
- Was assassinated, while holding Mass, as a result of his work to overcome conflict.

The ones who have a voice must speak for those who are voiceless. (Oscar Romero)

### Now try this

Explain **two** ways in which Catholics respond to issues of conflict in the world. **(4 marks)**

Include examples such as Dorothy Day or Oscar Romero in your answer.

# Revelation

Many people claim to have experienced God. These types of experiences allow people to feel they 'know' God and are used as 'proof' that he exists.

## Revelation

Revelation is the way in which God reveals his presence to humanity. Catholics believe Jesus is the revelation of God.

> Through an utterly free decision, God has revealed himself and given himself to man. This he does by revealing the mystery, his plan of loving goodness, formed from all eternity in Christ, for the benefit of all men. God has fully revealed this plan by sending us his beloved Son, our Lord Jesus Christ, and the Holy Spirit. (CCC 50)

**People experience God through...**

**Jesus:** as the Son of God he reveals God's nature and purpose

**the Bible:** reveals what God is like as it is considered the 'Word of God'

**visions:** messages for humanity that reveal God's nature and purpose

**Catholic teachings and leaders:** interpret God's teachings for humanity

**miracles:** God acting within the world

**the natural world:** revelation of God through his Creation

**prayer:** communication with God through answers to prayers

## Significance of Jesus

Jesus is at the centre of Catholicism. Catholics believe he is the second part of the Trinity – God incarnate (God in human form). They believe God is revealed through Jesus because he sent his son to Earth to redeem humanity's sins by dying on the cross; Jesus is the culmination – the final and highest part – of God's revelation.

## Jesus and the nature of God

The revelation of Jesus shows that God is:

- ✓ **omnipotent** (all-powerful) – he is able to send his son to save the world
- ✓ **omniscient** (all-knowing/seeing) – he knows everything that happens
- ✓ **benevolent** (all-loving) – he loves his Creation, which is why he sent Jesus
- ✓ wishing to **communicate** with humanity – Jesus is one way he achieved this
- ✓ both **transcendent** (beyond human understanding) and **immanent** (close to the world) – although apparent opposites, the revelation of Jesus shows how God can be both in heaven and acting within the world.

In the past God spoke to our ancestors through the prophets at many times and in various ways, but in these last days he has spoken to us by his Son, whom he appointed heir of all things, and through whom also he made the universe. The Son is the radiance of God's glory and the exact representation of his being, sustaining all things by his powerful word. After he had provided purification for sins, he sat down at the right hand of the Majesty in heaven. (Hebrews 1:1–4)

Catholics believe prophets conveyed messages from God, but that Jesus, his own son, is the greatest of his revelations. As Jesus represents God and his nature, Catholics can 'know' God through him. They believe Jesus' sacrifice to save the world's sins is proved through his resurrection and position at God's right hand.

## Now try this

1. Outline **three** Catholic beliefs on what the revelation of Jesus shows about the nature of God. **(3 marks)**
2. Explain **two** reasons why Jesus is important as a form of revelation for Catholics. **(4 marks)**

Give two reasons **why** Jesus is important, not just information about him.

# Visions (1)

A vision is something a person sees, possibly in a dream. Often, angels, saints or messengers appear, although some claim to have seen God himself. Catholics believe visions are evidence of God communicating with humanity.

## Importance of visions

Visions are an important form of religious experience because:

- people often only believe things they can see, so experiencing a vision may be considered more reliable than other religious experiences and is seen as direct contact with God
- they can help to strengthen faith by reinforcing Catholics' beliefs
- many famous Catholics have received visions, especially of the Virgin Mary (e.g. Bernadette Soubirous), who is important to Catholics
- there are many examples of visions in the Bible, showing God communicating with humanity.

## Examples of visions

 **Abraham's vision and covenant with God**

The Bible describes God appearing to Abraham through a vision and promising Abraham a son and heir, as well as land for his descendants in return for obeying him. This is the first covenant made between God and Abraham, and Abraham is recognised as a prophet who brought an important message to humanity of God's caring and protective nature.

After this, the word of the Lord came to Abram in a vision: 'Do not be afraid, Abram. I am your shield, your very great reward'. (Genesis 15:1)

**2 The transfiguration of Jesus**

In this Bible account, Jesus and three of his disciples climb a mountain to pray. At the summit, Jesus begins to shine with bright rays of light. Then the prophets Moses and Elijah appear beside him and he speaks to them. Jesus is then called 'Son' by God's voice. The disciples fall face down on the ground, terrified. Jesus is shown to be the connection between heaven and Earth.

There he was transfigured before them. His face shone like the sun, and his clothes became as white as the light. Just then there appeared before them Moses and Elijah, talking with Jesus. (Matthew 17:2–3)

**3 Joan of Arc**

Joan of Arc was made a Roman Catholic saint. She had many visions of St Margaret, St Catherine and St Michael delivering God's message. First she was told to attend Church and live a pious life, but later visions instructed her to deliver France from the invading English. She was eventually put on trial on a number of charges including heresy and was burnt at the stake.

I was in my thirteenth year when I heard a voice from God to help me govern my conduct. And the first time I was very much afraid. (Joan of Arc)

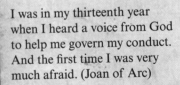
These are the three examples you need to know. You may also use other examples such as Paul's vision on the road to Damascus, Joseph's dreams or St Bernadette's visions of the Virgin Mary at Lourdes (page 52).

## Now try this

State **three** examples of visions used as revelations of the nature of God.                    **(3 marks)**

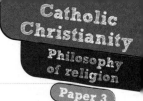

# Visions (2)

Visions are considered to be evidence that God exists.

## Role of visions in belief

Visions might lead to belief in God because...

- people may believe God is contacting them directly with a message
- people think visions connect them to God and help them get closer to him
- they help people to understand God better and develop a relationship with him.

## Different interpretations of visions

Some Catholics believe visions are evidence of God's nature and a sign of his omnipotence and benevolence, as they show his power and love in wanting to reveal himself. Other Catholics accept visions happen, but place more importance on other ways in which God reveals himself, e.g. through the Bible or Jesus' example.

## Non-religious arguments about visions

Non-religious people (e.g. atheists and Humanists) may say visions are not 'proof' of God's existence because:

- they may believe the visions are not 'real' – they could be hoaxes or illusions
- they may offer alternative explanations for visions, such as people experiencing hallucinations or dreams
- they may only believe things they can verify scientifically.

## Catholic response

Catholics would argue visions provide real evidence of God, for example the healing miracles at Lourdes resulting from the vision received by Bernadette Soubirous. They claim that religious believers are unlikely to be under the influence of stimulants or necessarily experiencing mental illness, and even though they may face ridicule because of visions, they remain true to their experience and argue that they have nothing to gain by lying.

## Worked example

Explain **two** reasons why visions may lead to belief in God. **(4 marks)**

People tend to believe what they see and experience; therefore, a vision may be a more believable experience. Visions tend to reveal truths or messages that are believed to come from God. Also, there are examples of visions in the Bible. This means that humanity has learnt information about what God is like from these experiences and Christian teachings are based on them.

## Now try this

Explain **two** beliefs about what visions reveal of the nature of God. In your answer you must refer to a source of wisdom or authority. **(5 marks)**

State each reason and then develop it, perhaps using an example to show you understand the point. Remember, you must also link one reason to a quote from a source of authority such as the Bible.

# Miracles

Miracles are amazing events that cannot be explained by the laws of nature or science. They are believed to prove God's power and presence in the world.

## Importance of miracles

- Miracles show God exists and cares for his Creation.
- They provide people with comfort that God is close and active in the world.
- They can help to strengthen faith as they provide evidence of God's existence.
- Miracles always have a positive benefit, e.g. healing.

## Examples of miracles

 **St Bernadette of Lourdes (1844–1879)**

Bernadette Soubirous was a child best known for her visions of Mary. In her visions, Bernadette was told to drink and wash in the water of the spring but no water was found. The following day, water appeared where Bernadette had claimed the vision had told her it would. Millions of pilgrims come to Lourdes to bathe in the water and, to date, there have been 69 confirmed healing cases accepted by the Catholic Church as 'miracles'.

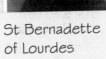

St Bernadette of Lourdes

Jesus heals an official's son.

When he inquired as to the time when his son got better, they said to him, 'Yesterday, at one in the afternoon, the fever left him.' Then the father realised that this was the exact time at which Jesus had said to him, 'Your son will live.' So he and his whole household believed. (John 4:52–53)

 **Miracles of Jesus**

The Bible describes Jesus performing many miracles, including walking on water, turning water into wine, feeding large crowds of people, as well as healing and bringing people back to life.

## Role of miracles in belief

Miracles might lead to belief in God because:

- people are amazed by what has happened
- people cannot explain events any other way
- they are proof of God's existence and his love for and involvement in the world.

## Different interpretations

Some Catholics believe miracles show God's omnipotence and benevolence; his power and love. Other Catholics accept miracles happen, but place less importance on them, instead focusing on other ways in which God reveals his nature, e.g. through the Bible or Jesus' example.

## Non-religious arguments

Non-religious people (e.g. atheists and Humanists) may say miracles are not 'proof' of God's existence because:

- there could be other scientific explanations that do not involve God
- people can experience and interpret events differently
- they may not believe miracles actually happen or that God is not the cause.

Catholics believe science and religion can both be used to explain events, but do accept that miracles happen. They would argue that people have no reason to invent them, and that many religions including Christianity are based on religious experiences.

## Now try this

Explain **two** reasons why Catholics may believe miracles are proof of God's existence.    **(4 marks)**

Had a look ☐     Nearly there ☐     Nailed it! ☐

Catholic
Christianity
Philosophy
of religion
Paper 3

# Religious experiences

Although religious experiences may confirm Catholics' belief in God, many other people do not accept they are real. Even some Catholics place less importance on them, and focus instead on other ways they believe God is revealed.

## Nature of religious experience

A religious experience is when a person undergoes revelation of God in some form – a communication from him. It could be a miracle, a vision, hearing a voice or even in dreams. Through this experience Catholics believe they get to 'know' God better.

## Not approved?

The Catholic Church does not approve all religious experiences.

> Yet even if Revelation is already complete, it has not been made completely explicit; it remains for Christian faith gradually to grasp its full significance over the course of the centuries. (CCC 66)

Faith is about understanding God's revelation; if religious experience adds nothing new, not all experiences are accepted.

## Non-religious arguments against religious experience

**1 Lack of evidence**
- There is not enough evidence to suggest religious experiences actually happen and 'prove' that God exists.
- Individual experiences are subjective and so are open to challenge and interpretation.
- Any experience could be claimed to be 'religious'.

Religious experiences do not prove God exists

**2 Use of stimulants**
Those who have a religious experience may be under the influence of drugs or alcohol, so their experiences may be inaccurate and cannot be trusted.

**3 Hallucinations**
Mental health issues or illness may cause a person to hallucinate and interpret normal events as religious experiences.

Sigmund Freud and Karl Marx were two famous thinkers from the world of psychoanalysis and philosophy, respectively, who both challenged the value of religious experience.

**4 Wish fulfilment**
Some people may be so desperate for a message from God that they interpret normal events as religious experiences.

## Catholic response to non-religious arguments

Religious experiences are real to those people who experience them and many religions, including Christianity of which Catholicism is a denomination, are based on and around religious experiences. Religious experience is only one way of God revealing himself and others – such as the Bible – help to confirm belief in God's existence.

## Now try this

'There is no real proof that God exists.'
Evaluate this statement considering arguments for and against.
In your response you should:
- refer to Catholic teachings
- refer to non-religious points of view
- reach a justified conclusion.                    **(12 marks)**

Include both the Catholic point of view and non-religious perspectives in your answer. State each argument and develop it using evidence and reasoning to support your points.

# The design argument

The design argument tries to prove the existence of God by arguing that the universe was **designed**. Its **designer** must be God as the only being powerful and knowledgeable enough to do this. This leads some people to believe in or confirm their faith in God.

## Overview of the design argument

Design is the result of intelligent thought. ⟹ The universe shows evidence of being designed (e.g. gravity, ozone layer). ⟹ This suggests that a being with intelligence designed the universe. ⟹ The universe is too complex to have happened by chance or be designed by any being other than God. ⟹ Therefore, God exists.

## Paley's watch

**1** William Paley compared the world to a watch.

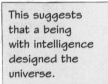

**2** If a person saw a watch for the first time they would immediately know it had been designed because it is so complex.

**3** A watch has many parts that have been carefully made and put together to work successfully, so it must have been planned and designed.

**4** Paley argued the same of the universe, saying it could not have happened by chance and must have had a clever designer.

**5** The only being capable of designing the universe is God.

**6** Therefore God exists.

## Catholic interpretations

Catholics believe God's nature is demonstrated in the world's design:

- **omnipotent** – all-powerful, as he designed the world to suit humans
- **benevolent** – as he cared enough for his Creation to take time to plan it
- **unknowable** in some ways, as he is transcendent (beyond human understanding).

> For since the creation of the world God's invisible qualities – his eternal power and divine nature – have been clearly seen, being understood from what has been made, so that people are without excuse. (Romans 1:20)

This is in line with the design argument, as humans cannot fully understand the design of God's Creation.

## Non-religious views

People with non-religious views may be critical of the design argument for the existence of God:

**1** Design may be the result of evolution, and not God. For more on evolution see page 27.

**2** It is impossible to 'prove' that God designed the world.

**3** The world may not be planned and designed – the argument that it happened by chance is equally strong.

**4** Science offers explanation of the world, and belief that God designed it is outdated.

**5** There is evidence of 'bad' design in the world, e.g. volcanoes and earthquakes; if God does exist, why did he design these?

Catholics would respond by arguing that. Genesis describes how the world was created, suggesting some planning or design. Some Catholics may argue that science and religion work together, and that evolution was part of God's plan.

## Now try this

Explain **two** beliefs the design argument shows about the nature of God for Catholics. **(4 marks)**

Had a look ☐    Nearly there ☐    Nailed it! ☐

Catholic
Christianity
Philosophy
of religion
Paper 3

# The cosmological argument

The cosmological argument tries to prove God's existence using the idea of **cause** and **effect**.

## Overview of the cosmological argument

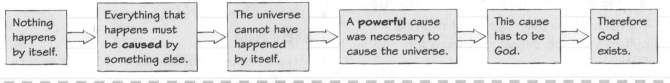

| Nothing happens by itself. | → | Everything that happens must be **caused** by something else. | → | The universe cannot have happened by itself. | → | A **powerful** cause was necessary to cause the universe. | → | This cause has to be God. | → | Therefore God exists. |

## St Thomas Aquinas (1225–1274)

The Catholic priest Thomas Aquinas put forward a version of the cosmological argument, summarised in the first three Ways of his 'Summa Theologicae':

Thomas Aquinas

### Motion

- Everything that moves is put in motion by something else.
- Chain of movers cannot be infinite.
- There must be a **first mover**, which is God.

### Cause

- Every effect has a cause.
- Chain of causes cannot be infinite.
- There must be a **first cause**, which is God.

### Contingency

- Everything that is contingent relies on something else to exist.
- All things must have been brought into existence by a **necessary being**.
- This necessary being doesn't rely on anything else for its existence, so must be God.

## Further Catholic interpretations

Catholics believe the cosmological argument confirms God's existence and his nature as:

- omnipotent, benevolent and unknowable.

Catholics would respond by maintaining that God created the universe, supported by the Creation story. Some may argue that science and religion can work together.

## Non-religious views

People with non-religious views may be critical of the cosmological argument:

1. We cannot 'prove' that God caused the world – an alternative, scientific explanation for the creation of the world is the Big Bang Theory.

2. Even if we accept everything within the universe has a cause, this doesn't mean that the universe itself has a cause.

3. If everything has a cause, what caused God?

4. If God created the world, why did he create bad things such as earthquakes and volcanoes?

## Now try this

'The cosmological argument proves the existence of God.'
Evaluate this statement considering arguments for and against. In your response you should:
- refer to Catholic teachings • refer to non-religious points of view • reach a justified conclusion.

**(12 marks)**

Paper 3

# The existence of suffering

Evil and suffering are a problem for people who believe in God, as well as non-believers. It may lead some to question their faith in God or even reject God's existence altogether.

## Types of evil and suffering

There are two main types of evil and suffering which cause problems for Catholics.

**1** **Moral evil/suffering** – actions carried out by humans who cause suffering, e.g. murder, rape, war and theft.

**2** **Natural evil/suffering** – things that cause suffering but have nothing to do with humans, e.g. famine, disease and natural disasters.

### Issues that evil raises for Catholics

- Makes people ask why God doesn't stop evil and suffering.
- Makes people question whether evil and suffering are a punishment.
- Evil and suffering are often unfair, which doesn't make sense to some people.
- Questions Bible teachings that there is only One God.
- Calls the nature of God into question.
- May make them challenge God's existence.

## The problem of evil and suffering

If God is **all-good**, he would want to remove evil and suffering as he cares for his Creation.

omnibenevolent

GOD

If God is **all-knowing**, he would know how to remove evil and suffering.

omniscient

If God is **all-powerful**, he would be able to remove evil and suffering.

omnipotent

Turn to me and be saved, all you ends of the earth; for I am God, and there is no other. By myself I have sworn, my mouth has uttered in all integrity a word that will not be revoked: before me every knee will bow; by me every tongue will swear. They will say of me, 'In the Lord alone are deliverance and strength.' (Isaiah 45 :22–24)

God declares that he is the only God. It shows how people may blame a bad situation on God rather than putting their trust in him as they should.

## How the existence of evil and suffering can affect a person's faith

- They may question their faith when something bad happens; they may ask why God doesn't help.
- They could turn away from faith – the existence of evil and suffering is often the most convincing philosophical argument used by non-believers to suggest God doesn't exist.
- Their faith could be strengthened – Catholics believe God is transcendent (beyond human understanding), so the presence of evil and suffering could be a test of their faith.

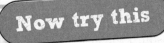
**Now try this**

Explain **two** reasons why the presence of evil and suffering could test the faith of a Catholic.  **(4 marks)**

# Solutions to the problem of suffering

The existence of evil and suffering in the world challenges Christian belief in an all-loving and all-powerful God. Catholics respond to this challenge differently, with some looking to the Bible for guidance and others offering theoretical or practical solutions.

## What does the Bible say about evil and suffering?

> Free will – the idea that humans are free to make their own choices.

- Genesis says that God created a perfect world.
- Adam and Eve used their free will in the Garden of Eden to disobey God (the Fall), which allowed evil and suffering to enter the world.
- Christians believe God sent Jesus to Earth to overcome the evil in the world and die for the sins of humanity on the cross.

---

 **Book of Psalms** – Catholics believe this offers reassurance that evil and suffering have a purpose in the world, even if they do not fully understand it, and gives people the opportunity to follow Jesus' example and live as God intended: 'Let me live that I may praise you, and may your laws sustain me. I have strayed like a lost sheep. Seek your servant, for I have not forgotten your commands' (Psalm 119:175–176).

Psalm 119 talks of God helping his followers to cope with life's struggles if they follow his rules.

2 **Job** – Job endured much suffering, including losing his family and enduring physical pain, yet he trusted in God and believed that suffering was part of God's plan for him. Christians believe they may not understand why they suffer, but they need to trust in God and will be rewarded: 'In all this, Job did not sin by charging God with wrongdoing' (Job 1:22).

Job didn't blame God for his suffering or question it – he accepted it as a test of his faith.

### Catholic responses to the problem of evil and suffering

3 **Free will** – God gave people free will and humans sometimes choose to turn away from God, to commit acts of moral evil. Theories such as this are contained in St Augustine's 'theodicy'.

6 **Charity** – many Christians are inspired by suffering in their own lives to try to help others. For example, Chad Varah established The Samaritans as a result of the suffering he witnessed as a priest working in London.

5 **Prayer** – many Catholics respond to evil and suffering in the world by prayer, so that God will give them strength to cope with problems they are facing. Christians believe that even if their prayers are not answered the way they want, God still has a plan for everyone.

4 **Human development** – St Irenaeus wrote that evil and suffering are needed for humans to become more like God.

## Other Christian views

Christians may hold different views on overcoming evil and suffering. They may believe:

- practical solutions such as prayer and charity work have a more direct impact
- Bible teachings such as the example of Job provide hope and comfort when people are facing difficulties
- explanations as to why people suffer may help people to cope with problems.

### Now try this

Outline **three** ways in which Catholics may respond to the problem of evil and suffering.    **(3 marks)**

State **three different** ways to successfully answer this question. Remember, you are not required to explain them.

# Human rights

Human rights are the basic rights and freedoms to which all people are entitled. They are very important to Catholics.

## Nature and history

- Human rights are protected by law in the UK.
- The UN Universal Declaration of Human Rights says all humans are born free and equal in dignity and rights.
- All UK citizens are entitled to life, liberty, free speech, racial, sexual and religious equality, education and privacy.
- The UK 1998 Human Rights Act allows people to defend their rights in the courts and ensures that public organisations (e.g. the police) treat everyone fairly.

## Purpose

Human rights exist to:

- ✓ ensure certain freedoms are upheld for all humans by protecting them
- ✓ bring law and order to society by making sure people know what their rights are
- ✓ protect individuals, especially where there is the possibility of unfair treatment
- ✓ ensure fair and just treatment for all.

## Catholic teachings

1. Catholics believe all humans are created in God's image and deserve equal treatment: 'So God created mankind in his own image' (Genesis 1:27).

2. They believe God loves everyone equally and so should be treated equally: 'There is neither Jew nor Gentile, neither slave nor free, nor is there male and female, for you are all one in Christ Jesus' (Galatians 3:28).

3. Bible teachings support human rights, e.g. the Ten Commandments.

4. The Church teaches that all humans have the right to respect, dignity and religious freedom: 'Social justice can be obtained only in respecting the transcendent dignity of man' (CCC 1929).

## Catholic response

Catholics support and uphold human rights as they mirror Christian principles; this is set out in a document on social teaching by Catholic bishops from England and Wales.

> These rights are universal. The study of the evolution of the idea of human rights shows that they all flow from the one fundamental right: the right to life. From this derives the right to those conditions which make life more truly human: religious liberty, decent work, housing, health care, freedom of speech, education, and the right to raise and provide for a family. (The Common Good and the Catholic Church's Social Teaching, 37)

## Non-religious responses

**Atheists** are likely to uphold human rights, believing life is special, although not for religious reasons. **Humanists** are fully committed to upholding human rights, which represent the key issues of equality and dignity.

Catholics would agree with these views, but would have the additional religious reasons of having a God-given duty to promote equality.

## Other Christian views

Some Christians such as Desmond Tutu and Martin Luther King Jr felt that if the law was in conflict with their conscience over human rights, it was right to challenge the law.

Some Catholics may feel there is sometimes a conflict between Catholic principles and human rights, particularly if teachings are not always clear on modern-day issues.

Desmond Tutu

## Now try this

Explain **two** reasons why Catholics believe human rights are important. In your answer you must refer to a source of wisdom or authority.   **(5 marks)**

# Equality

Equality is a key idea promoted within Catholic Christianity. Inequality in society can cause bad feeling among people and lead to the breakdown of communities.

## Causes of inequality

**1** **Experiences**
People don't always treat others the same because of prior experiences.

**2** **Poverty**
People are born into different situations, which leads to inequality.

**3** **Selfishness**
Some people feel they are more important than others.

**4** **Global influences**
Events in other parts of the world, e.g. political unrest or natural disasters, can lead to inequality.

**5** **Ignorance**
Some people do not care about inequality.

## Catholic response to inequality

- Catholics follow Jesus' teachings and example: 'As I have loved you, so you must love one another' (John 13:34).

- They value ideas of justice, equality and people working together.

> This tells Catholics they should show love and kindness to all, which involves treating people equally.

- They work to try to reduce inequality through Christian organisations, charity work and individuals.

## Catholic teachings on equality

Catholics believe all people are equal because:

**1** humans are made in God's image and so are all of value: 'So God created mankind in his own image' (Genesis 1:27)

**2** they believe God does not show favouritism: 'As for those who were held in high esteem – whatever they were makes no difference to me; God does not show favouritism' (Galatians 2:6)

**3** the story of the Good Samaritan teaches Christians to care and love everyone

**4** Jesus taught that everyone should treat others as fairly as they would treat themselves. For more on this story see page 62.

**5** Catholics believe they will be judged after death on how they helped others.

## Possible solutions to inequality

- **Charity work** – organisations such as CAFOD work to tackle the causes of inequality in the world. They try to improve people's lives by providing emergency aid and relief after disasters or educating others about the difficulties some people face in their daily lives.

- **Individuals** – people such as Martin Luther King Jr, Desmond Tutu and Mother Teresa have worked to challenge the inequalities in society.

Martin Luther King Jr

---

**Now try this**

Outline **three** Catholic beliefs about equality.      **(3 marks)**

# Religious freedom

Religious freedom means that a person is free to choose what religion they belong to, to change their religion or to have no religion at all.

## Catholic teachings

Catholics and the Church believe:

- people have the right to religious freedom: 'This Vatican Council declares that the human person has a right to religious freedom' (Declaration on Religious Freedom 'Dignitatis Humanae' by Pope Paul VI, 1965)

- freedom in all areas is important.

> The right to the exercise of freedom, especially in moral and religious matters, is an inalienable requirement of the dignity of the human person. (CCC 1738)

This Church teaching shows its commitment to the rights of individuals.

## Catholic response to a multi-faith society

Catholics accept and respect the existence of a multi-faith society, believing people can come to God in many ways. However, they still believe Christianity offers the 'full and complete truth'. While some Catholics may fear that Christianity is in decline, most recognise that people should have the choice of whether or not to be religious and, if so, which religion to choose.

## Benefits and challenges of living in a multi-faith society

### Benefits

👍 Ability to interact with and learn from people of different faiths.

👍 Greater tolerance and understanding of others' beliefs.

👍 Varied and enriching events from different faith backgrounds, e.g. services, religious observances and celebrations.

👍 Improved communication between different faith groups.

👍 A more peaceful society as different faiths live and work alongside each other.

### Challenges

👎 Some difficulties in openness and understanding towards other viewpoints.

👎 Examples of discrimination and religious persecution such as hate speech.

👎 Religious tension between different faith groups or across same-faith denominations.

👎 Beliefs and values of some minority groups may be dismissed or ignored.

👎 Lack of community spirit and peaceful co-operation due to mistrust, lack of communication and prejudice.

## Non-religious arguments against aspects of religious freedom

Some non-religious people may argue that:

- religion plays too big a role in society

- religious views have too much political influence

- people don't want to upset religious believers, so avoid saying things that could be misinterpreted

- there can be conflict between religion and the laws of a country.

Catholics would argue that religious freedom is important and people can choose to belong, or not belong, to any faith. They believe religious faith should be respected and protected.

### Now try this

Explain **two** ways in which Catholics can benefit from living in a multi-faith society.

**(4 marks)**

# Religious prejudice and discrimination

Catholic Christian teachings warn against religious prejudice and discrimination. Make sure you know what 'prejudice' and 'discrimination' mean – be careful not to get them confused!

## Prejudice and discrimination

- **Prejudice** is making a judgement about someone before you actually know them.
- **Discrimination** is an action – when a person is actually treated differently as a result of a prejudice.

## Problems this may cause

- Poor relationships between religious and non-religious groups.
- Increase in crime and hate attacks.
- Increase in physical and mental health issues.
- Lack of cohesion in society.
- Reduced opportunities in education, employment and housing.

## Catholic response

Catholics believe religious prejudice and discrimination are wrong, but that each problem situation needs to be considered individually – it is a situation ethics viewpoint. Catholics believe it is important to try to reconcile people, finding common ground between them.

In a 1965 declaration on the Catholic Church's stance on non-Christian religions ('Nostra aetate'), Pope Paul VI stated: 'The Church reproves, as foreign to the mind of Christ, any discrimination against men or harassment of them because of their race, colour, condition of life, or religion.'

## Catholic teachings on prejudice and discrimination

 **1** All humans are of equal value as all are created by God – irrespective of the religion they choose to follow.

> Catholics believe God made humans 'in his own image' (Genesis 1:27) and gave them a soul, making them special.

**2** Christians teach agape love, believing this should be shown towards all people regardless of their religion: 'A new command I give you: love one another. As I have loved you, so you must love one another' (John 13:34).

> Agape love is the highest form of love – unconditional love. Jesus taught that love should transcend all barriers and be open to everyone.

**3** The Catholic Church Catechism teaches that all humans deserve equal treatment.

**4** Christians follow the example of Jesus, who did not discriminate and treated everyone with the same love and respect.

> Created in the image of the one God and equally endowed with rational souls, all men have the same nature and the same origin. Redeemed by the sacrifice of Christ, all are called to participate in the same divine beatitude: all therefore enjoy an equal dignity. The equality of men rests essentially on their dignity as persons and the rights that flow from it. (CCC 1934–1935)

## Now try this

Outline **three** reasons why Catholics believe it is wrong to discriminate against people because of their religion.   **(3 marks)**

 Remember to state **three different** reasons – each as a different sentence.

# Racial harmony

Racial harmony is when all races live peacefully together. Catholics believe racism is wrong.

## Catholic teachings and responses

**1** All humans are equal: 'There is neither Jew nor Gentile, neither slave nor free, nor is there male and female, for you are all one in Christ Jesus' (Galatians 3:28).

**2** Jesus taught the Parable of the Good Samaritan (Luke 10), which tells people to help one another regardless of their race or faith. It puts the teaching of Jesus to love others into practice: 'A new command I give you: love one another. As I have loved you, so you must love one another' (John 13:34).

**3** Jesus also taught: 'do to others as you would have them do to you' (Luke 6:31).

**4** St Paul taught that: 'From one man he made all the nations, that they should inhabit the whole earth' (Acts 17:26).

**5** Christians believe putting these teachings into action will achieve racial harmony in society.

## Catholicism and racial harmony

- Bible teachings and the Church believe humans of all races are of equal value.
- The Catholic faith has members from all over the world.
- The Catholic faith has an ethnically diverse leadership.
- It is believed that Jesus was brought up in a multi-ethnic and multi-faith society and there are examples of Jesus treating people of different races equally, e.g. healing a servant belonging to a Roman soldier who showed faith in Jesus (Luke 7) and speaking to a Samaritan woman as an equal, when this would have been frowned upon (John 4).

## Benefits of a multi-ethnic society

- ☑ Encourages racial harmony – helps people of different cultures, races and religions to understand one another.
- ☑ Allows people insight into all religions and improves communication and tolerance.
- ☑ Reduces discrimination towards Christians.
- ☑ Provides a wide variety of music, food, clothes and culture.
- ☑ Brings together people with fresh new ideas – Catholics can learn from those who have different faiths and backgrounds, as well as sharing their own faith and backgrounds.
- ☑ Allows all believers to explore their own beliefs and faith.

## How Catholics work for racial harmony

**1** Leaders are ethnically diverse and work at local and international levels to promote unity between all races.

**2** Welcomes believers from all races: 'In the Church, God is "calling together" his people from all the ends of the earth' (CCC 751).

**3** Educates about equality, tolerance and understanding.

**4** Prays for those who are persecuted or treated unfairly due to their race.

**5** CARJ (Catholic Association for Racial Justice) work to break down barriers between different races.

> **Now try this**
>
> Explain **two** ways in which Catholics work for racial harmony.    **(4 marks)**

# Racial discrimination

Racial discrimination is when a person is treated unfairly because of their race. Issues of race can include colour, nationality, citizenship and ethnic origins.

## Catholic teachings and responses to racial discrimination

**1** Catholics believe humans are all made equal by God as they are created 'in his own image' (Genesis 1:27) – all are special none should face discrimination.

**2** They believe God loves everyone equally and does not distinguish between races.

**3** They believe God does not favour any one race above another, meaning all races should be treated equally: 'God does not show favouritism' (Galatians 2:6).

**4** Jesus often taught about fair treatment for all and led by example. Catholics try to live as Jesus instructed and do not condone racial discrimination: 'As I have loved you, so you must love one another' (John 13:34).

## What the Bible says

From one man he made all the nations, that they should inhabit the whole earth; and he marked out their appointed times in history and the boundaries of their lands. (Acts 17:26)

This quote states that although humans were made different, they were all created by God from one individual, Adam. Differences between peoples can cause problems in society, but Christianity teaches that all races should work together.

## Historical racial discrimination

Open racial discrimination in the USA, including the segregation of black and white people, continued up until the mid-1950s, when the

social unrest it caused resulted in the US civil rights movement successfully fighting to be treated equally in the Civil Rights Act, 1965.

## Problems in society

Racial discrimination leads to:

- people feeling they are not being treated fairly or with respect
- a lack of trust
- negative feelings of self-worth
- feeling isolated
- a lack of access to resources.

This answer offers two different reasons and both are developed using new information. The first reason also includes a quote from the Bible to reinforce it.

## Worked example

Explain **two** reasons why Catholics believe racial discrimination is wrong. In your answer you must refer to a source of wisdom or authority. **(5 marks)**

One reason why Catholics believe racial discrimination is wrong is because Bible teachings suggest God made humans different but equal. Galatians 3:28 says, 'There is neither Jew nor Gentile, neither slave nor free, nor is there male and female, for you are all one in Christ Jesus', suggesting that God made no distinction between people of different races and all humans he created should be treated fairly.

Another reason is because of Jesus' Bible teachings. Jesus told stories such as the Good Samaritan, which criticised the way Jews discriminated against Samaritans. He also told people to 'love one another', meaning that everyone should be treated with justice and without racial or other discrimination.

## Now try this

Explain **two** reasons why Catholics might feel racial discrimination causes problems in society. **(4 marks)**

# Social justice

Social justice is equal distribution of wealth, opportunities and privileges in society.

## The distribution of wealth and opportunity

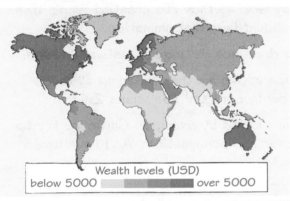

Wealth levels (USD)
below 5000 ▬▬▬ over 5000

Wealth is not distributed equally in the UK or the wider world. Small numbers of people hold large amounts of wealth, while many others live in poverty. People living in poverty have fewer opportunities in life.

## Church Catechism

Church Catechism verses 1928–1933 outline Catholic teachings on social justice.

- They focus on every person being deserving of dignity and respect.
- Catholics believe that inequality should be addressed and that they have a duty to do what they can to make society fair.

> The duty of making oneself a neighbour to others and actively serving them becomes even more urgent when it involves the disadvantaged, in whatever area this may be. 'As you did it to one of the least of these my brethren, you did it to me.' (CCC 1932)

This teaches Catholics that helping others is a duty, and a 'neighbour' is understood as anyone around you.

## Catholic teachings and beliefs

 **1** Catholics believe they have a duty to work for social justice as God gave them the responsibility of stewardship, which includes caring for other people.

**2** The Catholic Church and the pope both teach the importance of social justice:

> Society ensures social justice when it provides the conditions that allow associations or individuals to obtain what is their due, according to their nature and their vocation. Social justice is linked to the common good and the exercise of authority. (CCC 1928).

> Essential to the attainment of these national goals is the moral imperative of ensuring social justice and respect for human dignity. The great biblical tradition enjoins on all peoples the duty to hear the voice of the poor. It bids us to break the bonds of injustice and oppression which give rise to glaring, and indeed, scandalous social inequalities. (Pope Francis, 2015)

**3** Catholics believe all humans are made in God's image and deserve equal respect: 'So God created mankind in his own image' (Genesis 1:27).

**4** Catholics believe that all human beings are entitled to fundamental human rights.

 **5** Many Catholics support charity work to help those less fortunate.

## How the Catholic Church works for social justice

 **1** By promoting ideas of social justice in communities and Catholic leaders highlighting these issues in their sermons.

 **2** Limiting social inequality by providing food banks.

**3** Being involved in charity work to fight social injustice. Charities such as CAFOD work to end world poverty and injustice.

 **4** Educating others about social injustice and raise awareness of specific campaigns.

**5** Tackling issues of social injustice e.g. Caritas.

### Now try this

Outline **three** ways in which the Catholic Church works for social justice.  **(3 marks)**

# Wealth and poverty

Poverty causes great suffering in the world. Its causes and effects are of great concern for Catholics – their teachings speak of a duty to help those facing poverty.

## Nature of poverty

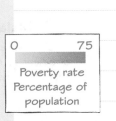

0      75
Poverty rate
Percentage of population

- **Absolute poverty** was defined by the United Nations in 1995 as 'severe deprivation of basic human needs including food, safe drinking water, sanitation facilities, health, shelter, education and information'.
- **Relative poverty** is the standard of poverty defined in terms of the country it refers to, so may vary from one country to another.

## Causes of poverty

1. **inequality in wages** – some people do not earn enough to survive

2. **provision of services** – some people do not have access to services in order to meet their needs

3. **population growth** – puts further demand on services and provisions

4. **war** – can cause shortages, destruction and loss of life

5. **unemployment** – puts some people in a spiral of debt

6. **homelessness** – leads to people being unable to earn and provide.

## Catholic teachings on and responses to poverty

- Many teachings from Jesus and the Bible state that people have a responsibility to care for the world, including those in poverty.
- Catholics try to reduce poverty – through practical help, donating money or time, or through prayer, or educational help, by raising awareness.

## Virtue ethics

This is an ethical theory that focuses on a person's virtues or moral character rather than concentrating only on actions. It can be applied in line with Catholic principles, e.g. to avoid blaming those in poverty and to show them compassion and understanding.

## Catholic teachings on wealth and poverty

1. Jesus often taught that wealth should be shared and compassion shown to others.

2. Catholics believe they will be judged after death by God, and their afterlife will be determined by the way they acted in life. For more on the Parable of the Sheep and the Goats see page 35.

3. All Christians, including Catholics, want a fairer distribution of wealth. Many Catholics donate money regularly to charity or organisations working to support the poor.

4. Catholics support charities such as CAFOD, which works to eradicate poverty.

5. Catholics do not believe it is wrong to be wealthy, but that it is important to gain wealth honestly and use it to help others.

> Anyone who has two shirts should share with the one who has none, and anyone who has food should do the same. (Luke 3:11).
>
> Go, sell everything you have and give to the poor, and you will have treasure in heaven. (Mark 10:21)

### Now try this

Explain **two** reasons why Catholics work to reduce poverty. **(4 marks)**

# The Six Beliefs of Islam

There are many schools of Islam. These schools agree on most beliefs and practices within the Islamic faith, although there are differences. One of the main schools is Sunni. The **Six Beliefs of Islam** are accepted by **Sunni Muslims**. **Shi'a Muslims** accept many of the ideas of the Six Beliefs but refer to them differently – some are part of the Five Roots of 'Usul ad-Din.

For more on 'Usul ad-Din', see page 69.

**1 Tawhid – the belief in the oneness of Allah**

Islam is monotheistic, meaning Muslims accept there is only one God (Allah).

**2 Malaikah – the belief in angels**

Muslims accept the existence of angels who are obedient to Allah's commands. It is through them that messages are given to prophets.

**3 Authority of kutub (holy books)**

The main holy book for Muslims is the Qur'an, but they also recognise Sahifah (the scrolls of Abraham and the scrolls of Moses), the Tawrat (Torah), Zabur (Psalms) and Injil (the Gospel).

The Six Beliefs of Islam

**6 Akhirah – teachings about life after death**

Muslims believe that there is an afterlife after death. They accept a Day of Judgement when every human will be judged by Allah on their actions on Earth.
For more on 'Akhirah', see page 75

**5 Belief in al-Qadr**

Muslims believe that Allah knows everything and, although humans have freewill, Allah knows what will happen.
For more on 'al-Qadr', see page 74

**4 Nubuwwah (prophethood) – following the prophets of Allah**

Muslims recognise prophets or messengers of Allah. These include: Adam; Ibrahim (Abraham); Isma'il; Musa (Moses); Dawud (David); Isa (Jesus); and Muhammad. The nature and importance of prophethood for Muslims is called Risalah.

## Purpose and importance of the Six Beliefs of Islam

✓ To unite all Sunni Muslims.
✓ To help Sunni Muslims understand their religion better.
✓ To support Sunni Muslims in how they should live their lives.
✓ To support what beliefs they should have.

The Six Beliefs of Islam are contained in the Kitab al-Iman or 'Book of Faith'. They are important for Sunni Muslims as they are the fundamental beliefs of the faith that they hold to be true.

## How the Six Beliefs of Islam are expressed today

Muslims will recite the belief in the oneness of **Allah** in their prayers each day. They will also look to the Qur'an for advice to help them understand their faith better and follow Allah. They will live their lives always aware of Allah and the fact that Islam teaches that he will **judge** them on their actions after death. This will make them more aware of their behaviour.

Person praying in a mosque

**Now try this**

Remember that this question asks you to state **three** different ways. Try to write three sentences with a different idea in each one.

Outline **three** ways in which Sunni Muslims will express the Six Beliefs of Islam in their lives today. **(3 marks)**

# The five roots of 'Usul ad-Din in Shi'a Islam

Another major branch of Islam is **Shi'a**. Shi'a Muslims believe in the Six Beliefs of Islam, but also accept the **Five Roots of 'Usul ad-Din** based on the Qur'an.

## The Five Roots of 'Usul ad-Din (foundations of faith)

**1** **Tawhid** – the oneness of Allah
The idea of one God called Allah.

**2** **Adl** – divine justice
Allah is understood to be fair and just in the way he treats everything.

**3** **Nubuwwwah** – prophethood
The belief that Allah appointed prophets or messengers to pass his message on to humanity.

**4** **Imamah** – successors to Muhammad
The belief that Allah appointed imams or leaders to guide humanity and be a source of authority.

**5** **Mi'ad** – the **Day of Judgement** and the **Resurrection**
The belief that all humans will be judged by Allah on their actions after death.

Most Shi'a believe there were 12 imams after the death of Muhammad, known as **Twelvers**. Some believe there were seven, known as **Seveners**.

## Worked example

Explain **two** reasons why the Five Roots of 'Usul ad-Din are important in Shi'a Islam. **(4 marks)**

They are important to Shi'a Muslims because they unite them as Muslims. They are the key beliefs all Muslims hold to be true. For example, all Shi'a Muslims believe in Allah as the only God – Tawhid.

A second reason is that by holding these beliefs, Shi'a Muslims can understand their faith better. They help to identify the beliefs such as Mi'ad or the Day of Judgement.

This student has stated two different reasons and developed them.
Your answer could also explain how the teachings come from the Qur'an 'Allah, is One' Surah 112 and that they are beliefs Muslims must hold if their practices and teachings are to be correct.

## Now try this

'Tawhid is the most important Muslim belief.' Evaluate this statement considering arguments for and against. In your response you should:
• refer to Muslim teachings
• reach a justified conclusion. **(15 marks)**

You must make sure you refer to teachings within Islam, as well as explain why other beliefs may be just as important. Remember that there are also 3 extra SPaG marks available on this question.

## The basis of the Five Roots of 'Usul ad-Din

Say: He is Allah, [who is] One, Allah , the Eternal Refuge. He neither begets nor is born, Nor is there to Him any equivalent (Surah 112:1–4)

The Five Roots are all based around the central idea – Tawhid, the oneness of Allah. This is explained in the Qur'an.

# The nature of Allah

Islam is a **monotheistic religion**, which means Muslims believe in one God, Allah. Beliefs about what he is like are described in many places including the Muslim holy book, the Qur'an.

## The eight characteristics of Allah shown in the Qur'an

**2 Immanence**

The idea that Allah is close and involved within the world.

**3 Transcendence**

The idea that Allah is above and beyond human understanding. It can be difficult for Muslims to fully understand Allah.

**1 Tawhid**

The Islamic word used to describe the idea that Muslims only accept one God. This is the most fundamental belief of the religion of Islam as all other principles relate to it.

**4 Omnipotence**

The idea that Allah is more powerful than anything in existence. He is seen to have created the world and is in control of everything.

And We certainly sent into every nation a messenger, [saying], 'Worship Allah and avoid Taghut.' (Surah 16:36)

**5 Beneficence**

The idea that Allah is caring and loves his creation.

**8 Adalat**

Allah is equitable and just. He created the world in a fair way and will judge humans in this way too.

**7 Fairness and justice**

The idea that Allah is fair and just and will judge humans after death in this way. Muslims believe Allah judges people in a fair and unbiased way.

**6 Mercy**

The idea that Allah forgives people for the wrong things they do.

This is only in Shi'a Islam.

---

Muslims believe Allah is the designer and creator of the world. He is given 99 names to help Muslims understand what he is like because they believe he is transcendent (above human experience). These include names such as Al-Rahman (the Compassionate) and Al-Hakam (the Judge).

The most beautiful names belong to Allah: so call on him by them. (Surah 7:180)

## Importance of the characteristics

Muslims believe that by knowing what Allah is like they can:

- ✓ understand him better
- ✓ follow the way he wants them to live their lives
- ✓ strengthen their relationship with Allah
- ✓ encourage Muslims to strive to be better as this is what they believe Allah wants.

---

You need to give **two different** ways and explain each one fully.

## Now try this

1 Explain **two** ways in which Allah is described by Muslims. **(4 marks)**

2 Explain **two** reasons why the characteristics of Allah are important for Muslims. In your answer you must refer to a source of wisdom or authority. **(5 marks)**

This style of question requires you to mention a quote from a source of authority (for example the Qur'an) to explain the point you have presented.

# Risalah

**Risalah** is the Islamic word for prophethood or **messengers** of Allah. These messengers are the channel of communication that links Allah to humanity.

Allah → Angel → Prophet → Humans

Rasul → Book

Prophets are important to Muslims as they enable Allah to communicate with humankind.

## Prophets

Islam teaches that there have been many **prophets** who have acted as messengers of Allah, such as Isma'il, Muhammad and Adam. It is thought there have been as many as 124,000 but only 25 are named in the Qur'an. Prophets whose message has been written down are called **rasuls**.

| Rasuls | Where their message has been written |
|--------|--------------------------------------|
| Ibrahim | Sahifah |
| Musa | Tawrat |
| Dawud | Zabur |
| Isa | Injil |

### Adam

He was the first prophet (and human) to be created. His task was to look after the world (to be a **khalifah**), which teaches Muslims today that they, too, should look after and care for Allah's creation.

### Ibrahim

Ibrahim is mentioned many times in the Qur'an. It is believed that he tried to encourage the worship of Allah. The story of Ibrahim having his faith tested by Allah by being willing to sacrifice his son teaches Muslims to submit to Allah in their lives.

### Isma'il

Isma'il is the son of Ibrahim and was associated with the construction of the Ka'bah in Makkah. He is praised for characteristics such as patience and kindness, showing Muslims that they too should develop these sorts of characteristics.

### Muhammad

Muhammad is called by Muslims 'the Seal of the Prophets' as he was the last prophet and received the final message from Allah – the Qur'an. Muslims are taught from a young age that they should follow the example set by Muhammad. He is very important as Muslims believe he brought the final and perfect message in the form of the Qur'an.

**Prophets in the Qur'an**

### Musa

The Qur'an states that Musa was sent by Allah to the Pharaoh of Egypt and the Israelites for guidance and warning. His presence is also seen to confirm the message and authority of the prophets before him.

### Isa

Isa is more often associated with Christianity (Jesus), but is recognised in Islam as the messenger of Allah and who received the Injil (Gospel). Muslims do not accept his resurrection or that he was the Son of God.

### Dawud

Dawud is recognised by Muslims as being a lawgiver of Allah and the King of Israel, as well as a prophet. He is best known for defeating Goliath.

Say (O Muslims): 'We believe in Allah and that which is revealed unto us and that which was revealed unto Abraham, and Ismael, and Isaac and Jacob, and the tribes and that which Moses and Jesus received and that which the Prophets received from their Lord.' (Surah 2:136)

## Now try this

1 Outline **three** beliefs about the role of prophets in Islam. **(3 marks)**
2 'Risalah is the most important belief in Islam.'
 Evaluate this statement considering arguments for and against.
 In your response you should:
 • refer to Muslim teachings
 • reach a justified conclusion. **(15 marks)**

Make sure you consider the statement carefully. You need to think about how important prophets are in Islam, and also consider other beliefs which may be equally or even more important.

# Muslim holy books

Muslims accept five holy books (**kutub**), although the **Qur'an** is given the most importance. Muslims are commanded in the Qur'an to believe in the books also revealed to Christians and Jews, which is why Muslims are often called 'People of the Book'.

## The Qur'an

The most important holy book for Muslims is the Qur'an, which was revealed to Muhammad by Allah.

**1** Muslims believe that the Qur'an was revealed to Muhammad over a period of 23 years.

**2** The Qur'an is written in **Arabic**.

**3** The word 'Qur'an' means 'recitation' because when it was revealed to Muhammad it was spoken, as Muhammad was illiterate.

**4** The Qur'an is divided into Surah (chapters) and Ayats (verses).

**5** Muslims believe the holy Qur'an came from Allah.

**6** Muslims use the Qur'an in prayer and to help them when they need guidance in their lives.

> It is not but a revelation revealed, Taught to him by one intense in strength. (Surah 53:4–5)

**1** The Qur'an mentions other holy books. Muslims believe these were also revealed by Allah, but that their meaning changed or became corrupted over time.

**5** Tawrat (Torah)
Muslims believe this holy book was given by Allah to Musa (Moses). Tawrat means 'instruction' and Muslims recognise there are important laws contained within it.

> We sent down the Torah, in which was guidance and light. (Surah 5:44)

**4** Zabur (Psalms)
The holy book of Dawud (David), which some Muslims today believe is still relevant.

**Kutub**

**2** Sahifah (Scrolls)
An early scripture believed to have been revealed to Ibrahim and used by his sons Ishma'il and Ishac. The scrolls are believed to be lost, having perished over time.

… and to David We gave the book [of Psalms]. (Surah 4:163)

**3** Injil (Gospel)
The Gospel of Isa (Jesus), believed to have been revealed by Allah, contained in the books Matthew, Mark, Luke and John.

> We sent, following in their footsteps, Jesus, the son of Mary…; and We gave him the Gospel….

Or has he not been informed of what was in the scriptures of Moses. (Surah 53:36)

## Now try this

1 Outline **three** reasons why the Qur'an is important in Islam. **(3 marks)**

2 Explain **two** reasons why Muslims recognise a number of holy books as sources of authority in Islam. **(4 marks)**

> Make sure you explain each reason fully before you move on to the next. Try to give examples where possible.

# Malaikah

Malaikah are beings that are believed to be **angels** or messengers of Allah.

There can be no images of Allah or Muhammad in Islam.

Muslims believe angels act as messengers between Allah and humans. They are not thought to have **free will** or physical bodies, but can take on human shape when needed. Belief in angels is contained in the Six Beliefs of Islam for Sunni Muslims.

## Importance of the angels

| Angel | Why are the angels important? | What do they teach Muslims today? |
|---|---|---|
| Jibril, or Gabriel as he is known in Christianity and Judaism, is an important angel as it was through him that Allah revealed the Qur'an to Muhammad over 23 years. It is believed that Jibril also taught Muhammad how to pray.<br><br>… then We sent her our angel, and he appeared before her as a man in all respects. (Surah 19 (Maryam):17) | Without Jibril the message of the Qur'an would not have been received. | To live around the teachings of the holy book, often reading it every day to understand how they should live their lives. |
| Izra'il is the Angel of Death and is responsible for signalling the coming of the Day of Judgement (when all Muslims will be judged by Allah) by blowing a trumpet. It is believed that he will return human souls to Allah.<br><br>The angel of death will take you who has been entrusted with you. Then to your Lord you will be returned. (Surah 32:11) | Izra'il is important in helping Muslims to understand that they need to live their lives how Allah wants them to, following his rules, so that they may be rewarded and not punished in the afterlife. | To live their lives in the knowledge that they will one day be judged by Allah on their actions on Earth. |
| Mika'il is often understood to be the Angel of Mercy or Sustenance, given the role of rewarding those who have led good lives. He is believed to bring rain and thunder to Earth.<br><br>Whoever is an enemy to Gabriel – for he brings down the (revelation) to thy heart by Allah's will, a confirmation of what went before, and guidance and glad tidings for those who believe, – Whoever is an enemy to Allah and His angels and messengers, to Gabriel and Michael, – Lo! Allah is an enemy to those who reject Faith. (Surah 2:97–98) | Muslims wish to be rewarded in the afterlife and not punished so the teaching of Mika'il reassures them that it is possible. | Reassurance that it is possible to be rewarded in the afterlife. |

Make sure you link one of your reasons to a source of wisdom and authority. For example, give a quote from the Qur'an that links to the point you have made.

## Now try this

1 Outline **three** beliefs about angels in Islam.  **(3 marks)**
2 Explain **two** reasons why angels are important in Islam. In your answer you must refer to a source of wisdom or authority.  **(5 marks)**

# Al-Qadr

Muslims believe in **al-Qadr** or **predestination**. This is the concept of fate or destiny – the idea that Allah is able to know and control everything that happens. Sunni Muslims recognise this as one of the Six Beliefs, although Shi'a Muslims do not fully accept al-Qadr.

## Day of Judgement

Muslims believe that on the Day of Judgement Allah will judge them on how they lived their life and behaved. There is a direct link between al-Qadr and the Day of Judgement as Muslims believe that once this day comes, it is too late to beg forgiveness for wrongdoing. Al-Qadr teaches Muslims that everything is the will of Allah and, although Muslims may not understand it, the important thing is how they react to it. Reacting the right way will mean a reward on the Day of Judgement. Sahih al-Bukhari 78:685 describes how people are responsible for their own sins, as they have decided what action to take and will be judged on this.

## Implications of al-Qadr

1. Muslims will want to live their lives according to the beliefs of the Day of Judgement and al-Qadr to ensure they gain reward in the afterlife

2. they will constantly be aware of their thoughts, beliefs and actions in order to ensure they behave how Allah wants them to – they will try to follow the duties given to them by Allah (e.g. the Five Pillars)

3. they will try to help others, as they believe this is what the Qur'an and Muhammad teaches them.

## Worked example

This answer offers reasons that both agree and disagree with the statement. The student also correctly gives an overall conclusion to bring their argument to a close.

'Predestination is not important to Muslims.'
Evaluate this statement considering arguments for and against.
In your response you should: • refer to Muslim teachings    • reach a justified conclusion.    **(15 marks)**

Some Muslims, especially Sunni Muslims, would disagree with this statement as predestination, or al-Qadr, is important to them. They believe that Allah controls and knows everything, which affects their beliefs about the afterlife for Muslims. Allah is believed to judge them after death on their actions in life. However, Sunni Muslims also accept the idea that Allah gave humans free will, therefore they are free to make their own decisions. This does not detract from the importance of predestination as Sunni Muslims believe that these ideas are not in conflict, but that Allah knows when a human will use their free will to turn away from him. Predestination is shown as being important to Sunni Muslims as it is contained in the Six Beliefs of Islam.

Another reason why Sunni Muslims might disagree is because the concept of predestination demonstrates the power that Allah is seen to have in being able to control and decide what happens in the world. He is able to know everything that a person will choose to do.

In contrast, Shi'a Muslims would agree with the statement as they do not fully accept the idea of predestination. It is further supported by their acceptance of the idea of Bada', which suggests Allah has not predetermined a set course for each Muslim and they are free to make their own choices and decisions.

In conclusion, I would argue that the strongest side of the argument is put forward by the Sunni Muslims. Their recognition of predestination as one of their key beliefs and application to their lives demonstrates it is important. They are also the larger group of Muslims in the world, showing that more would probably disagree with the statement than support it.

## Now try this

Explain **two** ways in which the belief of al-Qadr impacts on Muslims today.    **(4 marks)**

# Akhirah

Muslims believe in **akhirah** (life after death). It is considered to be one of the most important beliefs in Islam and will affect the way a Muslim lives their life.

## Muslim beliefs about akhirah

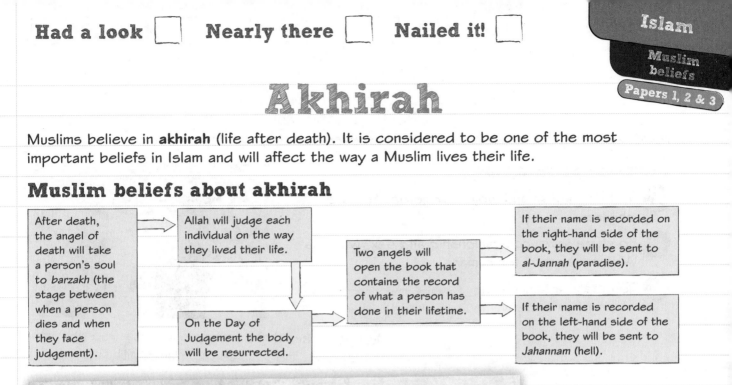

After death, the angel of death will take a person's soul to barzakh (the stage between when a person dies and when they face judgement). → Allah will judge each individual on the way they lived their life. → On the Day of Judgement the body will be resurrected. → Two angels will open the book that contains the record of what a person has done in their lifetime. → If their name is recorded on the right-hand side of the book, they will be sent to al-Jannah (paradise). / If their name is recorded on the left-hand side of the book, they will be sent to Jahannam (hell).

[Mention, O Muhammad], the Day We will call forth every people with their record [of deeds]. Then whoever is given his record in his right hand – those will read their records, and injustice will not be done to them, [even] as much as a thread [inside the date seed]. (Surah 17:71)

## Paradise in the Qur'an

## Hell in the Qur'an

This Qur'anic quote describes **Jahannam** or hell as a place where unbelievers are punished and face dreadful torments such as fires of hell.

And fear the Fire which has been prepared for the disbelievers. (Surah 3:131)

The Qur'an describes **al-Jannah** (paradise) as a reward for believers. It is described as a garden full of flowers and birds.

## Divergent ways that life after death affects Muslims today

1. Makes them more aware that Allah is always watching.

2. Makes them realise the importance of asking for forgiveness.

3. They view every action they perform as a way of worshipping Allah.

4. They try to live life as good Muslims: read the Qur'an; perform the Five Pillars; go to the mosque; help others, etc.

For more about the Five Pillars, see pages 85–89.

## Similarities and differences between Christianity and Islam about life after death

| Similarities | Differences |
|---|---|
| • Life is a test<br>• Places of eternal reward and eternal punishment<br>• Resurrection | • Christians accept sacrifice of Jesus to atone for sins of the world – Muslims believe only sinner can ask for forgiveness<br>• Purgatory in Christian Catholicism is not the same as barzakh in Islam<br>• Christians don't have angels recording deeds of a person like Muslims do |

### Now try this

Outline **three** beliefs about life after death for Muslims.                    **(3 marks)**

# Marriage

Marriage is very important in Islam. It is believed to bring stability to society.

## Purpose of marriage

**1** To bring a man and woman together to have children.

**2** To share love, companionship and sex, which is Allah's intention for humans.

**3** To create a family and strengthen society.

> Marry those among you who are single. (Surah 24:32)

> Muslims believe that marriage is important so they can have children and pass on the Islamic faith to them.

## Muslim beliefs about marriage

**1** Marriage in Islam is intended to be for life.

**2** Many Muslims will help their children to find the right partner – **arranged marriages**.

**3** Muslim women are expected to marry within the Islamic faith so children will be raised as Muslim.

**4** Muslim men can marry, for example, a Christian, as children will follow the faith of the father.

**5** Marriage is seen as a legal contract.

**6** Muslim men may have up to four wives but Muslim women can only have one husband.

**7** Islam encourages people to marry, following the example of Muhammad.

**8** Allah is believed to have created man and woman for each other.

### Worked example

Explain **two** reasons why marriage is important to Muslims. **(4 marks)**

One reason why marriage is important to Muslims is because it is seen as the joining of a couple who want to make a commitment to each other. The Qur'an instructs those who are single that it is their duty to marry.

A second reason why marriage is important is because Muslims believe marriage and the family provide stability for children and society. It is believed to provide a secure basis for children to be raised, as they can be taught about Islam, raised within the Islamic faith and be shown how to be good citizens in society.

This answer gives two good reasons and developed explanations.

## Cohabitation

**Cohabitation** is where a couple live together without being married. Muslims do not believe this is acceptable and would not cohabit. Muslims have very traditional views about members of the opposite sex meeting up prior to marriage and, generally, the woman would be **chaperoned** by a member of her family.

## Non-religious attitudes to marriage

> Being an **atheist**, I would have a **secular** marriage ceremony – I still believe that marriage is the best environment to raise children. I would happily cohabit though, too.

> Being a **humanist**, I too would have a secular marriage ceremony to show my commitment to my partner. I also would happily cohabit.

> **Muslim response:** As a Muslim, I recognise society is changing but I still value marriage in the traditional Islamic sense.

### Now try this

Outline **three** beliefs about the purpose of marriage in Islam. **(3 marks)**

# Sexual relationships

Attitudes towards different types of sexual relationships have changed as society has changed. Muslims have teachings about sexual relationships outside of marriage and homosexuality.

## Sexual relationships and marriage

Muslims believe that sexual relationships should only take place within the correct context of marriage. They believe that sex is an important part of a married relationship as it is a bond between the couple and is the opportunity to start a family.

> When a husband and wife share intimacy it is rewarded, and a blessing from Allah; just as they would be punished if they had engaged in illicit sex. (Hadith)
>
> Nor come nigh to adultery: for it is a shameful (deed) and an evil, opening the road (to other evils). (Surah 17:32)

## Islamic teachings

Muslims teach that:

**1** sex is an act of worship – Muslims believe it has the purpose of **procreation**, which is what Allah intended, and they will be rewarded for it

**2** sex fulfils physical, emotional and spiritual needs

**3** sex is a gift from Allah intended so that a couple can procreate

**4** sex should only take place within marriage and both partners have a duty to fulfil each other's sexual needs

**5** **adultery** is not acceptable – there are strict rules for married men and women, and there are strict punishments for adulterers

**6** homosexuality is forbidden in Islam and in some countries it is punishable by death – sex is intended for a husband and wife.

## Worked example

Explain **two** reasons why Muslims believe sexual relationships fulfil physical, emotional and spiritual needs. **(4 marks)**

One reason why Muslims believe sexual relationships fulfil physical, emotional and spiritual needs is that Muslims believe sex is natural and a marriage is the correct context for a sexual relationship to take place. It is important for a couple to satisfy each other's needs and sex is seen to allow this.

A second reason is that sex is seen in Islam as an act of worship. Muslims believe it is what Allah intended for them to do and they will be rewarded in the afterlife, therefore fulfilling their spiritual needs.

## Sex before marriage, homosexuality and adultery

The Muslim response to these issues is generally different from that of humanists and atheists.

| Belief | Sex before marriage | Homosexuality | Adultery |
|---|---|---|---|
| Humanists | ✓ | ✓ | ✗ |
| Atheists | ✓ | ✓ | ✗ |
| Muslims | ✗ | ✗ | ✗ |

This answer has provided two different reasons, both of which are developed and explained.

## Now try this

'Sex is a gift from Allah.'

Evaluate this statement considering arguments for and against. In your response you should:

- refer to Muslim teachings
- refer to non-religious points of view
- reach a justified conclusion.

Make sure you include both Muslim teachings and contrasting non-religious views about this statement.

**(12 marks)**

# Families

The family is very important in Islam. Muslims believe it is the creation of Allah and provides security and stability within society.

## Muslim teachings about family

The mother and father have a **responsibility** to raise their children as Muslims.

The family is the **foundation** of the Muslim community.

The family is where many religious activities take place, e.g. prayer and festivals.

**Muslim families**

Muslims believe it is important to marry and have a sexual relationship so they can procreate.

Family life is the first level of community in Islam.

The family provides a healthy and loving environment for children.

Children are taught to show love, kindness, mercy and compassion to one another in the family.

The worldwide Muslim family is the ummah that all Muslims are part of.

## Teachings in the Qur'an

The Qur'an contains teachings about the purpose of family:

> And We have enjoined upon man, to his parents, good treatment. His mother carried him with hardship and gave birth to him with hardship, and his gestation and weaning [period] is thirty months. [He grows] until, when he reaches maturity. (Surah 46:15)

Quotes such as these demonstrate the importance of family encouraging each person to respect their parents and treat them well, remembering all the sacrifices they have made.

### Worked example

Outline **three** purposes of family in Islam. **(3 marks)**

One purpose is for Muslim parents to raise their children as Muslims. A second purpose is that the family gives stability to society. A third purpose is that the Muslim community – the ummah – is strengthened.

The student has correctly identified and listed three purposes of the family in Islam.

## Different types of family

There are different types of family in society:

1. Nuclear – two parents (man and woman) with children.

2. Single parent – one parent and children.

3. Same-sex parents – two parents of the same sex and children.

4. Extended – parents, children, grandparents, aunts, uncles, cousins, etc.

5. Blended – stepfamilies who have joined together through remarriage.

## Divergent Muslim responses to different types of family

Traditional Muslim families are often extended, enabling them to care for both young and old. However, today some Muslims live in nuclear families because:

- issues such as **migration** make it impossible to keep everyone together

- Muslims in Western countries become used to the nuclear family as normal.

Many Muslims recognise other types of family, but prefer more traditional family structures.

### Now try this

'Family is not important today.'

Evaluate this statement considering arguments for and against. In your response you should:

- refer to Muslim teachings
- reach a justified conclusion.

**(12 marks)**

# The family in the ummah

Muslims believe that family has such an important role that, when conflict arises, they believe it is their duty to do all they can to help. The **ummah** is the worldwide family of Muslims showing the unity there is between all Muslims.

## Support for families

**2 Rites of passage**

Muslims will celebrate events such as Bismillah, weddings and funerals as a family together with Muslims from their local community.

**3 Classes for parents**

Parenting classes provide an opportunity for parents to prepare before the birth of a child or share their issues while raising children. They can gain help, advice and support.

**1 Worship**

Muslim families will attend prayer at the mosque together as a family or they will pray together at home.

**How the ummah supports family life**

**4 Groups for children**

The local Muslim community runs the **madrassah** – mosque school. Children attend to learn more about the faith, as well as their role within their family.

**6 Supporting each other**

And hold fast, all of you together, to the cable of Allah, and do not separate. (Surah 3:103)

**5 Counselling**

Muslims will provide support such as counselling if families are struggling. They will also turn to their extended families for support, as often the parents of a couple were involved in the arranging of the marriage.

This demonstrates the importance of supporting each other through the ummah as it is seen to strengthen it.

Muslims believe that family is important as it is where good Muslim children can be raised or support can be given when they may face personal problems. Family is what Allah intended, so providing support is the community's way of following this.

## Divergent understandings of the ummah

Most Muslims believe that the support offered by the ummah to the family unit is of vital importance. It helps them to unite and brings them together, strengthening their bond within the ummah. Some Muslims, however, may feel that in today's world this support can also be gained in other ways, including through social systems in place in society. They may feel that in the Western world this support must be balanced with the idea of 'fitting into society'. Some Muslims may also feel that they do not need support from the ummah as their individual family unit or local community is sufficient.

## Now try this

Make sure you give two different reasons. Each one needs to be developed by using examples.

1 Outline **three** ways the Muslim community tries to support family.  **(3 marks)**

2 Explain **two** reasons why it is important for the Muslim community to support families.  **(4 marks)**

# Contraception

**Contraception** is the intentional prevention of pregnancy. There are many different types of contraception and different Muslims hold differing views about whether or not they are acceptable.

## Guidance from the Hadith Sahih al-Bukhari

Sahih al-Bukhari is a collection of books (**Hadith**) compiled by Imam Muhammad al-Bukhari and gives some guidance on contraception.

> 'What is your opinion about coitus interruptus?' The Prophet said, 'Do you really do that? It is better for you not to do it. No soul that which Allah has destined to exist, but will surely come into existence. (Sahih al-Bukhari 34:432)
>
> We used to practice coitus interruptus during the lifetime of Allah's Apostle while the Quran was being Revealed. (Sahih al-Bukhari 62:136)

Muslims may hold different views about the use of contraception as there is no single approach to this issue. The first quote suggests Prophet Muhammad did not support the use of natural forms of contraception such as the withdrawal method. The second quote, however, appears to contradict this, saying that it was a common practice during the time of Muhammad. Many Muslims believe that in matters such as contraception, if Allah wills for a new life to be created, it should be his decision.

## Differing opinions on contraception

Some Muslim authorities may accept the use of contraception to:

- preserve the life of the mother if her life would be under threat through having another pregnancy
- protect the well-being of the current family unit if having another child would put too much strain on the family in terms of money or support
- plan when to have their family using non-permanent methods because this still allows for procreation in the future.

Some may not accept contraception because:

- only natural methods are allowed – this is what many Muslims feel sources of authority promote
- there is no possibility of procreation, which is the purpose of a sexual relationship, if permanent methods are used
- some methods could be considered an early abortion and, therefore, infanticide
- having children is what Allah intended for humans and using contraception prevents this.

## Muslim response to non-religious views

| Why couples might use contraception in non-religious communities | The Muslim response |
|---|---|
| They can plan when to have a family | Some agree this is OK, others do not |
| Pregnancy could be harmful to the mother | OK if to preserve the life of the mother |
| Lifestyle not compatible with having children | OK if having another child would put a strain on the current family unit |
| Safe from sexual transmitted infections (STIs) | Shouldn't be an issue as Muslims do not believe in sex outside of marriage |
| Avoid genetic disorders being passed on | Most agree that it is OK in this case |

Make sure you read the question carefully to ensure you present the correct arguments for what the question is asking. State each reason and then develop it by using examples or quotes to support the reason you have given.

## Now try this

Explain **two** reasons why Muslims will accept the use of contraception. **(4 marks)**

# Divorce

**Divorce** is the legal termination of a marriage and it has become more acceptable in today's society. In Islam, divorce is allowed but should only be a last resort because marriage is a contract.

## Muslim teachings on divorce

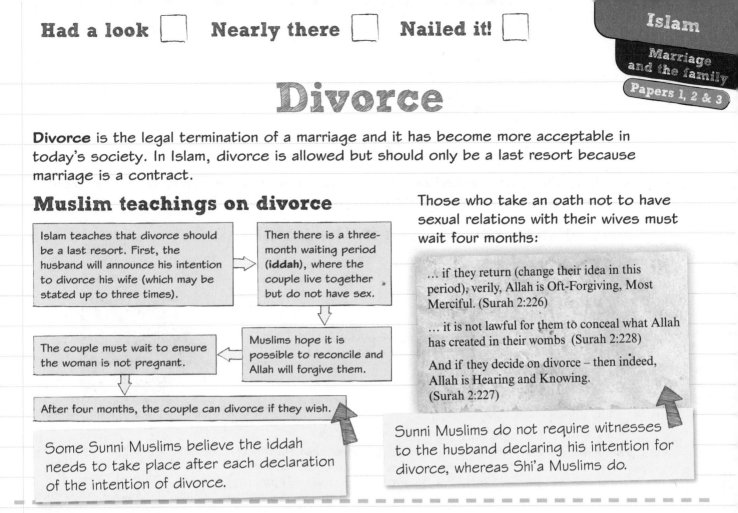

Islam teaches that divorce should be a last resort. First, the husband will announce his intention to divorce his wife (which may be stated up to three times).

Then there is a three-month waiting period (**iddah**), where the couple live together but do not have sex.

Muslims hope it is possible to reconcile and Allah will forgive them.

The couple must wait to ensure the woman is not pregnant.

After four months, the couple can divorce if they wish.

Some Sunni Muslims believe the iddah needs to take place after each declaration of the intention of divorce.

Those who take an oath not to have sexual relations with their wives must wait four months:

... if they return (change their idea in this period), verily, Allah is Oft-Forgiving, Most Merciful. (Surah 2:226)

... it is not lawful for them to conceal what Allah has created in their wombs (Surah 2:228)

And if they decide on divorce – then indeed, Allah is Hearing and Knowing. (Surah 2:227)

Sunni Muslims do not require witnesses to the husband declaring his intention for divorce, whereas Shi'a Muslims do.

## Muslim beliefs and attitudes

Although divorce is allowed by Allah, Muslims believe it is detestable – it is hated by Allah as it is disrespectful to him and the gift of marriage. Although Islam does not encourage divorce, it is recognised as being available as guidelines are given in sources of authority. Most Muslims would maintain that marriage is intended to be for life and is a contract, but if the marriage has broken down and reconciliation is not possible, then divorce may be the only answer. When a couple experience problems in their marriage they are expected to attempt to reconcile. The extended family, as well as the local community, may be involved in trying to resolve their issues.

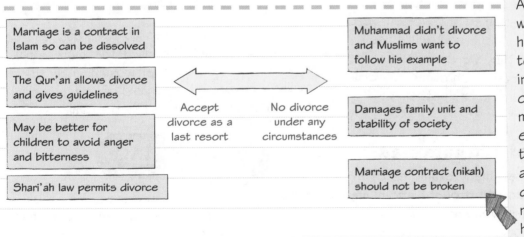

Marriage is a contract in Islam so can be dissolved

The Qur'an allows divorce and gives guidelines

May be better for children to avoid anger and bitterness

Shari'ah law permits divorce

Accept divorce as a last resort ⟷ No divorce under any circumstances

Muhammad didn't divorce and Muslims want to follow his example

Damages family unit and stability of society

Marriage contract (nikah) should not be broken

Although a Muslim woman may, perhaps, have more reasons to seek a divorce – including desertion, cruelty and a lack of maintenance – it is far easier for Muslim men to obtain divorces. If a woman wishes to divorce, she usually needs the consent of her husband.

## Now try this

Use any relevant quotes from Muslim teachings, such as the Qur'an or Hadith to support the points you make.

Explain **two** reasons why some Muslims may dislike divorce. In your answer you must refer to a source of wisdom and authority.

**(5 marks)**

# Men and women in the family

Muslims believe that Allah created all humans as equal but not the same. Therefore, men and women are identified as having different roles and responsibilities within the family.

## The role of men and women in the family

Women are expected to help raise children as good Muslims

Women are free to work and have a career, if they wish

Women are required to have children

Women are expected to look after the home

Men are seen to be the 'protectors of women'

Men provide for their family, helping to raise children as good Muslims

Abu Huraira narrated The Prophet (saw) said, 'The righteous among the women of Quraish are those who are kind to their young ones and who look after their husband's property.' (Sahih al-Bukhari 64:278)

## Divergent Muslim beliefs

O mankind! Be careful of your duty to your Lord Who created you from a single soul and from it created its mate and from them twain hath spread abroad a multitude of men and women. (Surah 4:1)

All people are equal … as the teeth of a comb. (Hadith)

These quotes from Islamic sources of authority seem to suggest ideas of equality between the roles of men and women. The first quote suggests men and women were created equally from one soul, while the second suggests they were created to be together and support each other, meaning their roles complement each other.

Men are in charge of women by [right of] what Allah has given one over the other and what they spend [for maintenance] from their wealth. So righteous women are devoutly obedient … But those [wives] from whom you fear arrogance – [first] advise them; [then if they persist], forsake them in bed; and [finally], strike them. But if they obey you [once more], seek no means against them. Indeed, Allah is ever Exalted and Grand. (Surah 4:34)

The Qur'an, however, also contains quotes that suggest inequality. This gives the impression that men have power over women within the family and women have a role of obedience towards their husband within the family.

## In the time of Muhammad

Muhammad witnessed many examples of poor treatment of women. He brought about improvement in the conditions for women:

👍 the ability for women to own property

👍 the right for women to be able to divorce their husbands

👍 improvements in the provision of education for women.

These changes, which are attributed to the vision of Muhammad in seeing more equality between the genders, helped to shape the future of Islam.

## Now try this

1 Explain **two** ways in which the roles of men and women are understood in Islam. **(4 marks)**

2 'Men and women should be treated the same.'

Evaluate this statement considering arguments for and against. In your response you should:
- refer to Muslim teachings
- reach a justified conclusion. **(12 marks)**

# Gender prejudice and discrimination

Many people believe men and women should be treated equally, although this is not always practised. When a person is treated unfairly and unequally, it is known as **discrimination**.

## Prejudice and discrimination

Gender prejudice (or **sexism**) is when a person is judged on their gender to be superior or inferior. It is an opinion or judgement being made, not an action.

Gender discrimination is when a person is treated differently from another as a direct result of their gender. It is an action rather than just an opinion.

## Muslim attitudes

Muslims believe gender prejudice and discrimination are wrong because:

**1** Islam teaches everyone was created by Allah and is therefore equal

**2** Muslims believe men and women will be treated equally and judged in the same way by Allah after death

**3** men and women are both expected to marry and they have the same rights in terms of religion and education.

However, although Muslims hold the above beliefs and accept men and women are equal before Allah, they accept that men and women are physically and psychologically different and suited to different roles and responsibilities.

## Teachings about gender prejudice and discrimination

For Muslim men and women – for believing men and women, for devout men and women, for true men and women, for men and women who are patient and constant, for men and women who humble themselves, for men and women who give in Charity, for men and women who fast (and deny themselves), for men and women who guard their chastity, and for men and women who engage much in Allah's praise – for them has Allah prepared forgiveness and great reward. (Surah 33:35)

This quote teaches Muslims that there should be equality between men and women in Islam. It supports the idea of gender prejudice and discrimination being wrong because regardless of who a person is – male or female – they will be judged equally by Allah and have the same opportunities and abilities to be rewarded.

Inspirational Muslims, such as Nadiya Hussain, who won 'The Great British Bake Off' competition, have raised the importance of gender equality in promoting that all people can achieve.

Sisters in Islam work to empower women with a voice to challenge mistreatment and gender discrimination through challenging laws that appear to make women inferior, including: polygamy; child marriage; dress in Islam; and violence against women.

Malala Yousafzai stood up to the Taliban to achieve equality in education.

### Gender equality in action

The Inclusive Mosque Initiative campaigns for more equality when praying in mosques.

Make sure you read each question carefully to understand what it requires. The trigger words in these questions ('Outline' or 'Explain') instruct you on what you are required to do.

## Now try this

1 Outline **three** beliefs in Islam about gender prejudice and discrimination. **(3 marks)**
2 Explain **two** ways in which Muslims respond to gender discrimination. **(4 marks)**

# The Ten Obligatory Acts of Shi'a Islam

The **Ten Obligatory Acts of Shi'a Islam** are important for Shi'a Muslims. Sunni Muslims believe in the **Five Pillars of Islam**. Four of the Five Pillars of Islam are also included in the Ten Obligatory Acts, so are important beliefs for all Muslims.

## Nature and purpose of the Acts

The Ten Obligatory Acts are duties that all Shi'a Muslims must perform. Their purpose is to:

- ✓ guide them in how they should live their lives
- ✓ allow them to get closer to Allah in performing the actions he wants
- ✓ help them achieve the reward of paradise after death by following the rules of Allah
- ✓ help them continually focus actions in their lives towards Allah
- ✓ unite all Shi'a Muslims and give meaning to their lives.

## History of the Acts

The Ten Obligatory Acts were given by the 'Twelvers', who Shi'a Muslims believe were chosen by Allah to lead after the death of Muhammad – they are also known as 'the Twelve Imams'.

↓

After the death of Muhammad, Shi'a Muslims believe it was Ali Talib, Muhammad's cousin and son-in-law, who was the successor to Muhammad.

↓

The Ten Obligatory Acts were established as the foundational practices in Islam for Shi'a Muslims.

## The Ten Obligatory Acts

1. **Salah** – compulsory prayer five times a day. Shi'a Muslims combine some of the prayers and pray three times.

2. **Sawm** – fasting during daylight hours in the ninth Islamic month (Ramadan).

3. **Zakah** – donating 2.5 per cent of wealth to help the needy.

4. **Hajj** – pilgrimage to Makkah made by every Muslim once in their lifetime.

5. **Khums** – annual taxation was the historical obligation of Muslims in the army to pay one-fifth of the spoils of war. Today, this money is given to the descendants of Muhammad and Shi'a Muslims, but is also used to help the needy and Shi'a Islamic leaders.

6. **Jihad** – striving to overcome evil, e.g. defending an individual, holy war and personal struggles to resist daily temptations.

7. **Amr-bil-Maroof** – commandment from the Qur'an that instructs Shi'a Muslims on how they should act and behave.

8. **Nahi Anil Munkar** – forbidding what is evil – the need to resist temptation and not sin against Allah.

9. **Tawalla** – expressing love towards what is good, following the examples of the prophets.

10. **Tabarra** – moving away from evil, such as staying away from those who choose to turn away from Allah.

You can find out about the Five Pillars of Islam on pages 85–89.

## The Qur'an and the Acts

The believing men and believing women are allies of one another. They enjoin what is right and forbid what is wrong and establish prayer and give zakah and obey Allah and His Messenger. Those – Allah will have mercy upon them. Indeed, Allah is Exalted in Might and Wise. (Surah 9:71)

## Now try this

Explain **two** reasons why the Ten Obligatory Acts are important to Shi'a Muslims.

**(4 marks)**

# The Shahadah

The **Shahadah** is the first Pillar of Islam – the statement of belief or declaration of faith that is accepted by all Muslims, both Sunni and Shi'a. It is believed to uphold all other beliefs of Islam and shows acceptance of both Allah and Muhammad.

There is no God but Allah and Muhammad is his Messenger.

The Shahadah contains the basic beliefs of Islam that every Muslim holds to be true – namely that they believe in Allah (God) and that Muhammad is the prophet of Allah. Muslims will recite this daily to remind them of the importance of these beliefs.

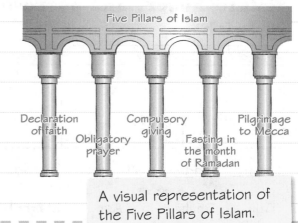

Five Pillars of Islam

Declaration of faith    Obligatory prayer    Compulsory giving    Fasting in the month of Ramadan    Pilgrimage to Mecca

A visual representation of the Five Pillars of Islam.

## The Shahadah in the Qur'an

The patient, the true, the obedient, those who spend [in the way of Allah], and those who seek forgiveness before dawn. Allah witnesses that there is no deity except Him, and [so do] the angels and those of knowledge – [that He is] maintaining [creation] in justice. There is no deity except Him, the Exalted in Might, the Wise. (Surah 3:17–18)

The key belief in Allah of the Shahadah is mentioned in the Qur'an. This demonstrates its importance for Muslims and is considered to be at the centre of the Islamic faith.

Another point is that it recognises the importance of Muhammad in bringing the unaltered word to humanity from Allah.

## Nature of the Shahadah

The Shahadah is the basic statement of Islamic faith and Muslims consider that anyone who cannot recite this is not a Muslim. Muslims believe it demonstrates their loyalty to Allah, the Prophet Muhammad and the religion of Islam.

## Worked example

Explain **two** reasons why the Shahadah is important to Muslims.    **(3 marks)**

The Shahadah is important to Muslims because it contains the basic beliefs central to Islam and being a Muslim, which are acceptance of the oneness of Allah and Muhammad being the messenger of Islam. Everything else in the religion is seen to centre around these key beliefs.

Shahadah is also important to Muslims because all other pillars and practices in Islam are based around the key concept of belief in Allah.

## Role of the Shahadah today

Recited out loud in front of witnesses to profess the Muslim faith.

Whispered into the ears of newborn babies so it is the first thing they hear.

**Shahadah**

Said before death to demonstrate a commitment to the religion of Islam.

Recited throughout the day to remind Muslims of the basic beliefs of Islam. It forms part of Salah as it is contained in the **adhan**, call to prayer.

## Now try this

'The Shahadah is the most important pillar for Muslims.'
Evaluate this statement considering arguments for and against. In your response you should:
- refer to Muslim teachings
- reach a justified conclusion.    **(12 marks)**

See pages 86–89 to find out about the other pillars.

# Salah

Salah is the second of the Five Pillars of Islam and it is the compulsory prayer that takes place five times a day.

## Nature, history and purpose of Salah

| Nature | History | Purpose |
|---|---|---|
| Demonstrates unity | Prophets of Allah performed daily prayers and it was commanded by Muhammad | Brings Muslims closer to Allah |

| Dawn | Midday | Afternoon | Sunset | Night |
|---|---|---|---|---|
| Fajr | Dhuhr | Asr | Maghrib | Isha'a |

## Ablutions (wudu)

Before prayer, Muslims perform wudu, which is a ritual cleansing. This is done to ensure they are spiritually and physically clean for Allah. It also gives them time to be in the correct frame of mind to be able to pray to Allah.

## The Qur'an and Salah

So exalt [Allah] with praise of your Lord and be of those who prostrate [to Him]. And worship your Lord until there comes to you the certainty (death). (Surah 15:98–99)

This quote highlights the importance of worshipping Allah and mentions the idea of prostrating, which is when a Muslim submits to Allah. This can be seen within Salah in the rakahs – prayer positions.

Recite, [O Muhammad], what has been revealed to you of the Book and establish prayer. Indeed, prayer prohibits immorality and wrongdoing, and the remembrance of Allah is greater. And Allah knows that which you do. (Surah 29:45)

## Divergent understandings

| Shi'a | Sunni |
|---|---|
| Combine five daily prayers into three | Five daily prayers |
| Raise hands three times at end of prayers | Move head from right to left |
| Touch foreheads directly to the floor when prostrating | May rest their head while prostrating on a piece of wood |

Other differences are the wording of prayers and Sunni believe that anyone who doesn't pray five times a day is an unbeliever.

This quote demonstrates the importance of prayer as regular communication with Allah and the significant role it has in the life of every Muslim.

## How prayer is performed

Muslim men are expected to attend the mosque to pray, women are not. Prayer can happen anywhere that is clean and if wudu has been performed. On a Friday, all Muslim men are expected to attend the **Jummah** service as part of Salah. Women may also attend.

bowing

standing    prostrating

When praying, Muslims face the direction of **Makkah** and recite verses and prayers. They follow a set pattern of movements.

## Now try this

Outline **three** reasons why Muslims pray.

(3 marks)

# Sawm

**Sawm** (fasting) is the fourth Pillar of Islam. The main period of fasting is during **Ramadan** – the ninth month of the Islamic calendar when all Muslims are required to not eat or drink during daylight hours, as well as avoid evil thoughts and deeds. There are other times when Muslims fast, but these times are not compulsory. There are also times when it is forbidden to fast.

## Nature, role and purpose of Sawm

> : O ye who believe! Fasting is prescribed for you … (Surah 2:183)

Muslims believe the Qur'an was first revealed to Muhammad during the month of Ramadan, which gives Sawm importance. Fasting is an act of worship of Allah and has a long history. It is completed because it is a duty in Islam, but it also helps Muslims to develop discipline and understand the problems others may face.

## Significance of Sawm

Sawm is important to Muslims because:

- ✓ It is one of the Five Pillars and is compulsory for most healthy adult Muslims – it shows a Muslim is obeying God
- ✓ It helps Muslims to learn self-discipline
- ✓ It helps Muslims to appreciate what Allah has provided, develop sympathy with the poor and realise the importance of charity
- ✓ It helps Muslims to remember the importance of the Qur'an, which was first revealed during Ramadan
- ✓ It brings the Muslim community (ummah) together and strengthens their unity.

## What is forbidden in daylight hours during Sawm?

No food    No smoking    No sexual activity    No bad thoughts or deeds

## Who is exempt from Sawm?

The elderly, young children, pregnant women, those travelling and Muslims who are physically or mentally unwell do not have to take part, as it could be considered harmful if they did.

> If a Muslim adult does not fast, they should carry out the fast at another time or make a donation to the poor.

## Nature and history of Laylat al-Qadr

Sawm is performed to commemorate the moment when Muhammad received a religious experience while meditating in a cave on Mount Nur during Ramadan. The Angel Jibril appeared to him and revealed the Qur'an from Allah. This event is known as the Night of Power or Laylat al-Qadr.

Cave on Mount Nur

## Purpose of Laylat al-Qadr

- To remember the gift of the Qur'an being given to humanity.
- To give Muslims the opportunity to ask for forgiveness for the things they have done wrong and worship Allah.
- To commemorate Muhammad receiving revelation from Allah.

> Worshipping Allah in that night is better than worshipping Him a thousand months. (Surah 97:3)

Muslims believe that they will be rewarded for marking this important occasion.

## Now try this

Explain **two** reasons why some Muslims do not have to fast.

**(4 marks)**

# Zakah and khums

**Zakah** is the third Pillar of Islam and involves the obligatory giving of money to charity. **Khums** is a religious tax.

## Zakah

**Nature:** Zakah is a type of worship or self-purification involving obligatory almsgiving.

**Role:** It involves giving 2.5 per cent of one's wealth each year to benefit the poor.

**Significance:** This duty is contained in the Qur'an and has a long history within Islam.

**Purpose:** Benefits of Zakah are to obey Allah, to show that everything a Muslim owns comes from Allah, and to support the idea of sharing and charitable actions.

## Khums

**Nature:** In Shi'a Islam, khums is one of the Ten Obligatory Acts.

**Role:** Khums is paying 20 per cent of one's surplus income – half to the ummah and the to the poor.

**Significance:** This form of giving is mentioned in the Qur'an.

**Purpose:** Traditionally, the recipients of khums have been the descendants of Muhammad and those within the Shi'a Islamic faith.

## The Qur'an and Zakah and khums

> Zakah expenditures are only for the poor and for the needy and for those employed to collect [zakah] and for bringing hearts together [for Islam] and for freeing captives [or slaves] and for those in debt and for the cause of Allah and for the [stranded] traveler – an obligation [imposed] by Allah. And Allah is Knowing and Wise. (Surah 9:60)

> And know that anything you obtain of war booty – then indeed, for Allah is one fifth of it and for the Messenger and for [his] near relatives and the orphans, the needy, and the [stranded] traveler, if you have believed in Allah and in that which We sent down to Our Servant on the day of criterion – the day when the two armies met. And Allah, over all things, is competent. (Surah 8:41)

This talks about the uses and purpose of Zakah in helping others. It recognises that it is commanded by Allah.

This demonstrates the use of khums and who it is intended to benefit.

## Importance of khums for Shi'a Muslims

- It gives special recognition to Muhammad, his descendants and leaders within Shi'a Islam.
- It is used to help build Islamic schools or Islamic projects.
- It is used to help the poor or those who may be suffering.
- It is used to promote the religion of Islam through education.
- It is one of the Ten Obligatory Acts.

Sunni Muslims also recognise the historical importance of khums, but do not attribute it the same significance

## Importance of Zakah for Sunni Muslims

- It is one of the Five Pillars, so is a duty.
- Wealth is believed to be a gift from Allah that should be shared.
- Muslims believe it is what Allah wants them to do and they will be judged on their actions and the way they helped others after death.
- It is a sign of unity and supports the ummah.
- It helps a Muslim to grow spiritually and frees them from greed and selfishness.
- It helps those who need it most – some Zakah money is used by Islamic charities such as Islamic Relief or Muslim Aid to respond to disasters around the world.

Shi'a Muslims also perform Zakah

## Now try this

Explain **two** benefits for Muslims of receiving Zakah. **(4 marks)**

# Hajj

**Hajj**, the fifth Pillar of Islam, is the annual Muslim pilgrimage that takes place in and around Makkah. All Muslims are obligated to make this journey once in their lifetime if they are physically fit and can afford to do so.

## Nature

Hajj is a holy journey that Muslims are expected to make to Makkah, Saudi Arabia. It is held annually in the month of Dhul-Hajjah, lasts five days and over two million Muslims attend. Makkah is the holy city for Muslims as it is where Muhammad was born and lived, and where Muslims face when they pray.

## Role

Hajj is intended to allow Muslims to get closer to Allah, as well as follow the example of Muhammad, who began the ritual.

## Significance

Hajj is important to Muslims as it is one of the Five Pillars. It reminds them of the importance of recognising that all Muslims are equal and equally part of the ummah. It is a struggle to complete Hajj, but Muslims believe it teaches them to be patient and gives them time to reflect on Allah and their faith.

## Origins

Hajj is built around many events and people who hold importance in Islam. The rituals completed during Hajj were established by the Prophet Muhammad, who demonstrated the actions to his followers shortly before his death.

## The Qur'an

Surah 2:124–127 talks about the story of Ibrahim, who, it is believed, built the first **Ka'bah** (House of Allah) – the sacred shrine in Makkah. Surah 22:27–29 also talks of proclaiming the Hajj to followers.

## How Hajj is performed

- Put on ihram (white, seamless robes).
- Perform Tawaf – circling of the Ka'bah seven times.
- Complete the sa'y – running between the hills of Safa and Marwa in remembrance of Hagar searching for water in the desert.
- Stand on Mount Arafat and pray and read from the Qur'an.
- Throw stones at pillars to symbolise rejecting the devil.
- Celebrate the festival of Id-ul-Adha on the last day to remember the sacrifice Ibrahim was willing to make of his son, Ishma'el.
- Perform Tawaf – circling of the Ka'bah seven times again.

## Benefits of Hajj

👍 Shows commitment to Allah – Muslims believe they will be rewarded in al-Jannah.

👍 Strengthens the ummah and the faith of individual Muslims.

👍 Gives an opportunity to focus on Allah, ask for forgiveness and get closer to him.

## Challenges of Hajj

👎 Muslims have to be physically fit and financially stable.

👎 Over two million Muslims attend Hajj every year, making it difficult to have a personal experience due to large numbers.

👎 There have been incidences due to the large volume of people.

## Now try this

Develop each benefit by adding extra information that links to the reason.

1 Outline **three** actions completed on Hajj. **(3 marks)**

2 Explain **two** benefits of attending Hajj for Muslims. **(4 marks)**

# Jihad

**Jihad** means 'struggle' and has its origins in the Qur'an. It is used to describe the personal struggle of every Muslim to follow the teachings of Islam. There are two types of jihad (greater and lesser).

## Greater and lesser jihad

| Greater jihad | Lesser jihad |
|---|---|
| **Inner struggle** to be a better Muslim and closer to Allah by:<br>• studying the Qur'an<br>• doing good deeds<br>• attending mosque regularly<br>• resisting temptation, greed and envy. | **Outer struggle** to defend Islam:<br>• Can be non-violent and in some cases violent<br>• Fought for a just cause<br>• Fought as a last resort<br>• Authorised and accepted by Muslim authority<br>• The minimum amount of suffering should be caused<br>• Ends when enemy surrenders<br>• Innocent civilians not attacked<br>• Aims to restore peace and freedom. |

## Worked example

Explain **two** reasons why greater jihad is important to Muslims. **(4 marks)**

Greater jihad is important to Muslims as it is viewed as an act of sacrifice for Allah. It involves Muslims giving up time, money, skill or even their life in order to resist any temptations they may face and overcome them through moral actions.

Greater jihad is also important to Muslims because it shows how Muslims should live life as Allah intended. Muslims believe struggling against evil and temptation in the world helps them to develop characteristics such as self-discipline, compassion and honesty.

## Lesser jihad and the Qur'an

Fight in the cause of Allah those who fight you, but do not transgress limits; for Allah loveth not transgressors. (Surah 2:190)

Permission [to fight] has been given to those who are being fought, because they were wronged. And indeed, Allah is competent to give them victory. (Surah 22:39)

The Qur'an makes it clear that there are strict conditions when lesser jihad can be declared and therefore justified.

This answer gives two reasons, which are both developed successfully. The explanation given is accurate and shows the knowledge of the student about this topic.

## Divergent understandings of jihad

• Most Muslims agree that greater jihad is the most important as this is stressed in the Qur'an.

• Greater jihad is a personal battle, which many Muslims understand to be the true meaning of the term.

• Even though Muhammad was involved in military battles, he supported greater jihad as being more important.

• There may be occasions when the religion of Islam or the name of Allah is threatened and it would be appropriate to defend Islam, but Islam does have set conditions for this.

Make sure you state the reason and then develop it by adding an example or indicating more knowledge about your reason.

## Now try this

1 Outline **three** conditions needed for the declaration of lesser jihad. **(3 marks)**

2 Explain **two** reasons why greater jihad is seen as more important to some Muslims than lesser jihad. **(4 marks)**

# Celebrations and commemorations

Muslims celebrate or commemorate special days and events throughout the year. For example, **Id-ul-Fitr** celebrates the end of Ramadan. A commemoration, like **Id-ul-Adha**, is a reminder of an important event that has happened in the past.

## Why Muslims have celebrations and commemorations

**1** To remember past events and important people within Islam.

**2** To strengthen the ummah and unite Muslims together.

**3** To share beliefs that they have in common.

**4** To have a cycle of special days and events that are marked throughout the year.

> This day I have perfected for you your religion and completed My favor upon you and have approved for you Islam as religion. (Surah 5:3)

Quote from the Qur'an citing Id-ul-Ghadeer.

> Whomsoever to him I am master (Maula), Ali is also his/her master (Maula). O God, love those who love him, and be hostile to those who are hostile to him. (Hadith)

Quote from the Hadith citing Id-ul-Ghadeer.

| Festival | Sunni | Shi'a |
|---|---|---|
| **Id-ul-Adha** End of Hajj | • Known as the 'Festival of Sacrifice'. • Remembers Ibrahim's willingness to sacrifice his son when God asked him to. This story is found in the Qur'an 37:100–111 and reminds Muslims of the test of faith faced by Ibrahim and how they should apply this to their own lives, as well as the mercy shown by Allah. • Signifies the end of Hajj. • Muslims remember their own willingness to sacrifice anything to God's wishes. They celebrate with the sacrifice of an animal, which is shared among family, friends and the poor. • Prayers, cards and presents are given. | |
| **Id-ul-Fitr** End of Ramadan | • A time to celebrate and thank Allah for his help in getting through the month of fasting. • Begins when first new moon is seen. • The first Id is believed to have been celebrated by Muhammad, so it commemorates this event in Islamic history. • Homes are decorated. There will be special services and a celebratory meal is shared. | |
| **Ashura** Tenth day of Muharran, the first month of the Islamic calendar | • A day of fasting and mourning to remember how Nuh (Noah) left the Ark and how Musa (Moses) and the Israelites were saved from the Egyptians. • People wear black and no music is allowed. | • As Sunni, but the event is also one of mourning to remember the martyrdom at Karbala in 680CE of Hussain, who was a grandson of Prophet Muhammad. |
| **Id-ul-Ghadeer** Occurs eight days after Id-ul-Adha | • Sunnis do not celebrate this festival as they do not recognise Iman Ali as the successor to Muhammad. | • To celebrate the appointment of Imam Ali as successor to Muhammad. |

## Now try this

Outline **three** ways Id-ul-Adha is celebrated. **(3 marks)**

Had a look ☐    Nearly there ☐    Nailed it! ☐

# Origins of the universe

The main scientific explanation for the origin of the universe is the **Big Bang theory**. There are also other theories.

## The Big Bang theory

The Big Bang theory is the belief that the universe started around 14 billion years ago when matter was concentrated into a great mass and began to expand. This expansion continues today, but at a slower rate, with everything moving away from everything else. The stars and planets are thought to have formed by the cooling of matter and more diverse kinds of atoms forming and eventually condensing.

## Muslim beliefs about the origin of the universe

☑ Everything was created by Allah.

☑ He created balance in the universe – e.g. night and day, sea and land.

☑ It took periods of time to create the universe.

☑ Creation was intended, planned and designed by Allah.

☑ After creating the Earth, Allah created all living things, including humans.

## Muslim responses to scientific explanations

Most Muslims believe science does not affect their beliefs in Allah's creation of the universe because:

- the explanation of the Big Bang helps to fill in gaps of what is not explained in the Qur'an
- they believe scientific explanations give them a better understanding of Allah and his creation.

They believe the Qur'an has an account of the creation of the universe similar to that offered by science:

> And the heaven We constructed with strength, and indeed, We are [its] expander. (Surah 51:47)

However, some Muslims may view the Big Bang theory as contradicting the Islamic creation story, as it appears to question whether a loving God planned the creation of the universe.

> Blessed is He in whose hand is dominion, and He is over all things competent – [He] who created death and life to test you [as to] which of you is best in deed – and He is the Exalted in Might, the Forgiving – [And] who created seven heavens in layers. You do not see in the creation of the Most Merciful any inconsistency. So return [your] vision [to the sky]; do you see any breaks? Then return [your] vision twice again. [Your] vision will return to you humbled while it is fatigued. And We have certainly beautified the nearest heaven with stars and have made [from] them what is thrown at the devils and have prepared for them the punishment of the Blaze. (Surah 67:1–5)

The Qur'an is the source for beliefs about the universe.

## The universe – gift or commodity?

Some Muslims believe humans are the most important part of Allah's creation. The universe was created for them and they can take what they need.

Some Muslims believe the universe is a gift from God and that they should carry out the task given by Allah to be kalifahs (stewards) who care for the universe. To avoid being judged in the afterlife, they must look after the universe and not take what they want.

### Now try this

"The Qur'an and science are in conflict over how the world was created.' Evaluate this statement considering arguments for and against. In your response you should:

- refer to Muslim teaching
- reach a justified conclusion. **(12 marks)**

# Sanctity of life

Muslims believe that life is special and holy. This will determine how they act or behave, as well as their views and beliefs about some issues.

**Sanctity of life** is the belief that life is holy and special.

Muslims will have views on issues such as abortion, euthanasia and murder that agree with their view that life is special and holy.

Muslims believe:

**1** life is special and holy as all life is created by Allah

**2** they should respect all life and not harm any living thing

**3** that, as all life is holy, every human life is worth the same value as any other

**4** that, as Allah is the creator of life, only he can take it away.

See pages 95 and 98 for more information on abortion and euthanasia.

Because of that, We decreed upon the Children of Israel that whoever kills a soul unless for a soul or for corruption [done] in the land – it is as if he had slain mankind entirely. And whoever saves one – it is as if he had saved mankind entirely. And our messengers had certainly come to them with clear proofs. Then indeed many of them, [even] after that, throughout the land, were transgressors. (Surah 5:32)

This suggests that it is wrong to take a life away as it is holy. Preserving and recognising that life is special benefits the whole of mankind.

O you who have believed, do not consume one another's wealth unjustly but only [in lawful] business by mutual consent. And do not kill yourselves [or one another]. Indeed, Allah is to you ever Merciful. (Surah 4:29)

It is clear from this verse that life should not be taken and the reason for this is because it was created by Allah.

---

## Worked example

Explain **two** divergent Muslim understandings about the importance of the sanctity of human life. You must include a source of wisdom and authority in your answer. **(5 marks)**

Some Muslims believe that life starts at conception as it was created by Allah. They believe it is holy and intended to be special and, therefore, would not accept life being taken away in cases of abortion, euthanasia or capital punishment.

Other Muslims may recognise that life is holy as it was created by Allah, but believe that some teachings in the Qur'an indicate it can be ended in some circumstances. The Qur'an teaches that, if Islam is threatened, it may be acceptable to use violence to end life in order to protect the religion even though life is sacred. The Qur'an states: whoever 'kills a soul unless for a soul or for corruption [done] in the land – it is as if he had slain mankind entirely.' (Surah 5:32)

This question requires you to give and develop two different reasons and link one of them to a source of authority, which this student has done.

You must make sure you offer two clear and different reasons in your response.

## Now try this

Explain **two** reasons why Muslims believe life is holy.                **(4 marks)**

# The origins of human life

Within Islam, there are different responses to scientific explanations about the origins of human life. You will need to understand the scientific **theory of evolution** to understand Muslims' responses.

## The theory of evolution

The ascent of man

In his book 'On the Origin of the Species' published in 1859, Charles Darwin put forward a scientific and non-religious theory of evolution. He argued that the origin of human life was a gradual development of the species over millions of years from simple life forms to more complicated life forms. The characteristics or features that are strongest survive, while weaker ones die out and disappear. This is known as **natural selection**. Darwin also used the term 'survival of the fittest' to describe the species best suited to the environment.

## Muslim responses to the theory of evolution

The majority of Muslims and other religious people, as well as non-religious people, in today's world hold that science offers more believable explanations for the world than religion. Therefore, it is important for religious believers such as Muslims to try to adapt their beliefs to be able to accept both what religion and science tell them.

> Who perfected everything which He created and began the creation of man from clay. Then He made his posterity out of the extract of a liquid disdained. (Surah 32:7–8)

This is what the Qur'an says about humans being created by Allah from clay, which appears to be in conflict with ideas of evolution.

> Have those who disbelieved not considered that the heavens and the earth were a joined entity, and We separated them and made from water every living thing? Then will they not believe? (Surah 21:30)

This reinforces the view that Allah is the origin of human life.

## Worked example

Explain **two** ways in which Muslims respond to scientific explanations about the origins of human life.    **(4 marks)**

One way in which Muslims respond to scientific explanations about the origins of human life is that some traditional Muslims would believe that evolution is in conflict with Qur'anic teachings about the origin of humans. Evolution suggests it was through natural selection and adaptation, whereas the Qur'an teaches that Allah made humans from clay and gave life.

A second way would be for some Muslims to accept ideas from Islam being compatible with scientific ideas of evolution. They would argue that evolution was part of Allah's plan for how humans were created. Adaptation and survival of the strongest characteristics are how humans came about, but were Allah's intentions.

This answer has offered two different ways in which Muslims can respond to ideas of evolution. Further information has then been added.

## Now try this

'There is no way of accepting Muslim ideas about the origins of humans along with scientific views about evolution.' Evaluate this statement considering arguments for and against. In your response you should:
- refer to Muslim teachings
- refer to different Muslim points of view
- reach a justified conclusion.    **(12 marks)**

Show awareness of different Muslim views within your answer, as some may accept evolution while others may reject it.

# Muslim attitudes to abortion

Muslim teachings about the sanctity of life affect Muslim views on **abortion**. Many Muslims do not agree with abortion, using the sanctity of life argument as evidence for their views.

## Nature of abortion

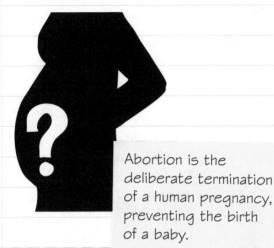

Abortion is the deliberate termination of a human pregnancy, preventing the birth of a baby.

## The value and sanctity of life

Muslims are divided over the issue of abortion, so some traditional teachings may not apply. Some may view allowing abortion as 'the lesser of two evils' as both options in cases where abortion is being considered may be disliked. Some may believe that by allowing abortion, it offers a 'slippery slope' to allowing other actions (such as infanticide), which are not accepted within Islam.

Some Muslims, however, would hold to traditional teachings such as the sanctity of human life, maintaining that life is holy as it was created by Allah and should never be threatened or taken away.

## Non-religious views on abortion and Muslim responses

| Non-religious arguments about abortion | Muslim responses to arguments |
|---|---|
| Abortion is a personal decision and it is the woman's right to decide what is best. | Abortion is wrong as all life is created by Allah (sanctity of life) and only he can decide when life should end. |
| Some parents might neither be ready to have a child nor be able to afford one. | The Qur'an teaches: 'And do not kill your children for fear of poverty.' (Surah 17:32). This quote recognises the sanctity of human life. |
| Abortion is always wrong as the foetus is a human life. | An unplanned pregnancy, worry about providing for a child and pregnancy as a result of adultery are not acceptable reasons for abortion. |
| Individual circumstances should be taken into account and the best decision decided based on these (**situation ethics**). | Some Muslims believe abortion is acceptable if the life of the mother is at risk, or in the case of rape, because it upholds the sanctity of the mother's life. |

## Ensoulment

Allah's Apostle, the true and truly inspired said, '(as regards your creation), every one of you is collected in the womb of his mother for the first forty days, and then he becomes a clot for another forty days, and then a piece of flesh for forty days. Then Allah sends an angel to write four words: He writes his deeds, time of his death, means of his livelihood, and whether he will be wretched or blessed (in religion). Then the soul is breathed into his body.'
(Sahih al-Bukhari 55:549)

This passage describes the point 120 days after conception when the soul enters the body – this is called ensoulment. Sunni Muslims forbid abortion before and after this time, preserving the sanctity of life. Under certain circumstances, others might agree to an abortion taking place before ensoulment, for example if the life of the mother is affected.

## Now try this

Outline **three** Muslim teachings about abortion.      **(3 marks)**

# Death and the afterlife (1)

Muslims believe in akhirah (life after death). It is considered to be one of the most important beliefs in Islam and will affect the way a Muslim lives their life.

## Muslim teachings about death and the afterlife

**1** Allah has full control over life and death.

**2** The world will end when Allah chooses and at this time people will face judgement.

**3** Good deeds and bad deeds will be judged.

**4** People will either be sent to al-Jannah as a reward for a good life or Jahannam for a bad life.

Barzakh is viewed as the barrier between the physical and spiritual worlds – it is where the soul waits after death before resurrection on Judgement Day.

## The Qur'an and death and the afterlife

Then is he whom We have promised a good promise which he will obtain like he for whom We provided enjoyment of worldly life [but] then he is, on the Day of Resurrection, among those presented [for punishment in Hell]? (Surah 28:61)

This shows ideas of reward and punishment after death.

And to every soul will be paid in full (the fruit) of its Deeds; and Allah knoweth best all that they do. (Surah 39:70)

This teaches that Allah is aware of every action and thought of humans.

... those who have believed and worked righteous deeds shall be made happy ... those who have rejected faith and falsely denies our Signs ... shall be brought forth to Punishment. (Surah 30:15–16)

This identifies the reward for those who deserve it and recognises that those who don't will be punished after death.

## Significance of life after death for Muslims

It is important to me because it affects how I live my life. I am constantly aware that Allah is watching me.

I want to go to al-Jannah after death so need to live my life as Allah wants.

The Qur'an teaches me that this life is a test and prepares me for the afterlife. Death is the gateway to life after death.

Believing in akhirah gives my life meaning and purpose.

A Muslim funeral

**1** **Memories of previous lives**

Muslims recognise the afterlife, but Islam does not teach that people have had past lives.

**2** **Paranormal, e.g. ghosts and spirits**

Muslims do not accept ideas of the paranormal.

**3** **Logically death cannot be the end**

Muslims agree that having a reward and punishment after death and a belief in the afterlife gives life meaning and purpose.

**6** **Meeting loved ones who have passed on**

Meeting loved ones again is not of primary importance in Islam.

### Muslim responses to non-religious arguments for life after death

**4** **Reward for living a good life**

Muslims agree that those who have lived a good life deserve to be rewarded after death.

**5** **Makes people less afraid of death**

Ideas of the afterlife give Muslims comfort.

## Now try this

Explain **two** reasons why Muslims support the existence of life after death. **(4 marks)**

# Death and the afterlife (2)

Many people who are not religious will argue that there is nothing after a person dies. They suggest that death is the end.

## Life after death?

| Non-religious arguments against life after death | Muslim responses to non-religious arguments against life after death |
|---|---|
| Holding beliefs about an afterlife offers a false sense of hope as there is no proof that it exists. The psychoanalyst Freud suggested that religion is an illusion that is used to provide comfort to those who need it. | But the teachings from the Qur'an give evidence that there is an afterlife. They offer proof. |
| There is no evidence of an afterlife – no one has ever returned to prove it exists. | But my faith means putting trust in the teachings. Allah teaches in the Qur'an that there is an afterlife (akhirah) and he doesn't lie, so this is sufficient evidence for me that the afterlife exists. |
| Some people have tricked others into believing they can contact people who have died. This takes advantage of vulnerable people. | I recognise that this can happen, but believe it should not detract from the importance of accepting belief in the afterlife. |
| Believing in an afterlife gives people control over what they fear the most. Look at the philosopher Karl Marx, who believed that religion is a way of controlling and managing people. | But my belief in the afterlife gives meaning and purpose to my life. It helps to guide me in how I should behave and act as I know Allah is watching me and will judge me after I die. |
| I am a humanist. I believe that when a person dies their body decays and there is nothing else. Life after death is impossible. | I disagree. Although the body may decay in the ground, it will be reunited with the soul on the Day of Judgement. The Qur'an teaches there is life after death and death is not the end. |

## Worked example

Explain **two** ways Muslims respond to non-religious arguments against life after death. In your answer you must refer to a source of wisdom and authority. **(5 marks)**

Muslims would respond to non-religious arguments claiming that there is no proof or evidence of an afterlife by saying that the Qur'an is evidence. As it was written by Allah and states that life after death exists, Muslims believe that it is real and they will be judged by Allah for the afterlife on how they have lived their lives.

And they say, 'There is not but our worldly life; we die and live, and nothing destroys us except time.' And they have of that no knowledge; they are only assuming. And when Our verses are recited to them as clear evidences, their argument is only that they say, 'Bring [back] our forefathers, if you should be truthful.' (Surah 45:24–25)

In this reference, the Qur'an, which is a source of wisdom and authority, teaches that there is a life after death and Muslims believe this. They think that people who deny this do so because they have no faith.

This student has given one reason that has been developed by adding new information to explain it. It needs a source of wisdom and authority to be linked to it and a second reason now to be added.

## Now try this

Complete the answer to the question in the Worked example.

# Euthanasia

The word **'euthanasia'** literally means 'good death' and is understood as the painless killing of a person – it is also referred to as 'assisted dying'. Muslims view euthanasia as always wrong and offer no reasons to support it.

## Nature of euthanasia

There are different types of euthanasia:

1. Voluntary euthanasia – where a person's life is ended deliberately and painlessly at their request.

2. Assisted suicide – where a person is given the means to end their own life.

3. Non-voluntary euthanasia – ending a person's life painlessly when they are unable to ask, but you have good reason for thinking it is what they would want.

## Non-religious arguments in favour of euthanasia

Many atheists would argue that the kindest thing may be to let a person end their life if it is what they want and they are in pain. Humanists would support the use of euthanasia if a person has made this decision for themselves without any persuasion. They believe a person should have the right to make decisions for themselves, especially if they are suffering from a **terminal illness**. Principles of situation ethics may be applied as many people feel the action that should be taken is whatever is most loving in the given situation – even if this means ending life early. Muslims, however, would argue that life is special and sacred and only Allah can decide when it should end.

## Muslim response to euthanasia

These posters reflect the strong views Muslims have on upholding the sanctity of life in responding to the issue of euthanasia. They believe euthanasia is murder and is wrong under all circumstances.

> Indeed we belong to Allah , and indeed to Him we will return. (Surah 2:156)

The Qur'an teaches the sanctity of life, which is the idea that life has value and is holy as it was created by Allah.

## Muslim teachings about the nature and use of euthanasia

E

U

**T**EST OF FAITH: Suffering is a test and part of life – it is not a person's decision to end their life.

**H**OSPICES: There are alternatives to euthanasia and they include hospices. These are places where a person with a terminal illness can spend their final days and receive palliative care. Hospice care will not cure the illness but will manage its symptoms, making the end of life more bearable.

**A**LL LIFE IS SACRED: Therefore, it is important to care for the elderly as much as anyone.

**N**O SOUL: can ever die except by Allah's leave and at a term appointed (Surah 3:145).

**A**LLAH: Only Allah can decide how long a person's life is.

**S**ANCTITY OF LIFE: Euthanasia is suicide and does not respect the sanctity of life.

**I**S ALWAYS WRONG: Because life is sacred and holy.

**A**

### Now try this

1 Outline **three** Muslim teachings about euthanasia. **(3 marks)**

2 Explain **two** reasons why Muslims will not support the use of euthanasia. **(4 marks)**

# Issues in the natural world

Today's natural world faces many threats, often from humans. Muslims believe they have a responsibility to care for the world as it was created by Allah.

The world is being damaged by humans in many ways.

## Threats to the natural world

Muslims believe they should care for the world and not waste the world's resources because:

- ✓ Allah created the world and humans are its trustees
- ✓ they have been given a duty by Allah to be khalifahs – stewards who care for the world
- ✓ after death they will be called to answer for any ill-treatment of the planet
- ✓ Allah created the world with love and they should show respect by treating it in the same way.

Allah's Apostle said, 'There is none amongst the Muslims who plants a tree or sows seeds, and then a bird, or a person or an animal eats from it, but is regarded as a charitable gift for him.' (Sahih al-Bukhari 3:513)

And the earth He has laid (out) for creatures. (Surah 55:10)

The Earth is green and beautiful, and Allah has appointed you his stewards over it. (Hadith Bukhari)

These quotes from teachings are used by Muslims to either support ideas of animals having rights because they are creations of Allah, or to suggest that animals should not be seen as equal to humans.

Caring for our environment.

## Use of animals for food

- Animals were created by Allah and given to humans so Muslims can eat meat.
- Animals exist for the benefit of humans, but should be treated with respect and kindness as a creation of Allah.
- The Qur'an says: 'It is Allah who made for you the grazing animals upon which you ride and some of them you eat.' (Surah 40:79)
- Some Muslims may choose to be vegetarian, believing that animals should not be eaten.
- Some Muslims may use ethical theories such as utilitarianism, which states that 'the greatest happiness for the greatest number'. This may refer to using animals to benefit humans through food or experimentation.

## Worked example

Explain **two** ways in which Muslims may respond to the use of animals in experimentation. **(4 marks)**

One way in which Muslims would respond to the use of animals in experimentation is to only allow animals to be used for medical research that would benefit or hopefully save human life, as humans are at the top of Allah's creations.

A second way that Muslims may respond is to reject all animal experimentation as they have a duty to care for the creation of Allah. Muslims believe they will be judged on their actions in the afterlife.

This answer gives two developed and specific responses.

## Now try this

Use specialist language where you can.

'Everyone should care for the natural world.'

Evaluate this statement considering arguments for and against. In your response you should:

- refer to Muslim teachings
- reach a justified conclusion.

**(12 marks)**

# Justice

Muslims recognise the importance of **justice** because the Qur'an and the law of Allah teaches that Muslims should act with fairness. Many Muslims campaign for peace and justice.

## The nature of justice for Muslims

Justice is fair treatment or behaviour. In terms of punishment, Muslims would understand justice to be the fair treatment of a person according to the crime they have committed.

O you who have believed, be persistently standing firm in justice, witnesses for Allah. (Surah 4:135)

This quote from the Qur'an demonstrates the importance of justice in Islam by setting down the requirements of what it means to be a Muslim. This includes standing up for justice and acting in a just and fair way within their lives.

| Non-religious attitudes to justice | Muslim response to non-religious attitudes to justice |
|---|---|
| • It means fairness has been applied. <br> • Everyone involved feels the appropriate action has been taken in response to what has happened. <br> • Ideas of equality can be upheld that are important to all people, regardless of religion. | • Muslims would agree, although they would refer to Islamic teachings or key beliefs in Islam as reasons why they are significant. |

## The importance of justice for Muslims

1. Justice is a key idea promoted in the Qur'an.

2. Shari'ah law has strict rules about justice and acting fairly.

3. The Five Pillars support ideas of justice (e.g. Zakah – sharing wealth makes society fairer).

4. Muslims believe that justice is important to Allah and this is what he intended for his creation.

5. Muslims will be judged in the afterlife on how they treated others, so they should always act fairly and in a just way.

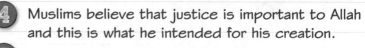

## Worked example

Explain **two** reasons why justice is important for Muslims. In your answer you must refer to a source of wisdom and authority.     **(5 marks)**

Justice is important to Muslims because it is what they believe Allah intended. The Qur'an teaches this and Muslims will try to stand up for justice so they can please Allah and follow his teachings. The Qur'an says: 'O you who have believed, be persistently standing firm in justice, witnesses for Allah' (Surah 4:135).

Justice is also important to Muslims because Shari'ah law (Islamic code of behaviour) supports ideas of justice. Shari'ah law is considered to be the laws of Allah and Muslims want to follow them to be rewarded in the afterlife. Therefore, they want to behave and act in a just way in their lives.

The student has correctly mentioned and explained a source of authority for the first reason, which is required by this style of question.

## Now try this

Outline **three** Muslim teachings about justice.     **(3 marks)**

# Crime

A crime is an action someone commits against the state – for example, murder, theft or drink-driving. Crime is always considered to be a problem in society.

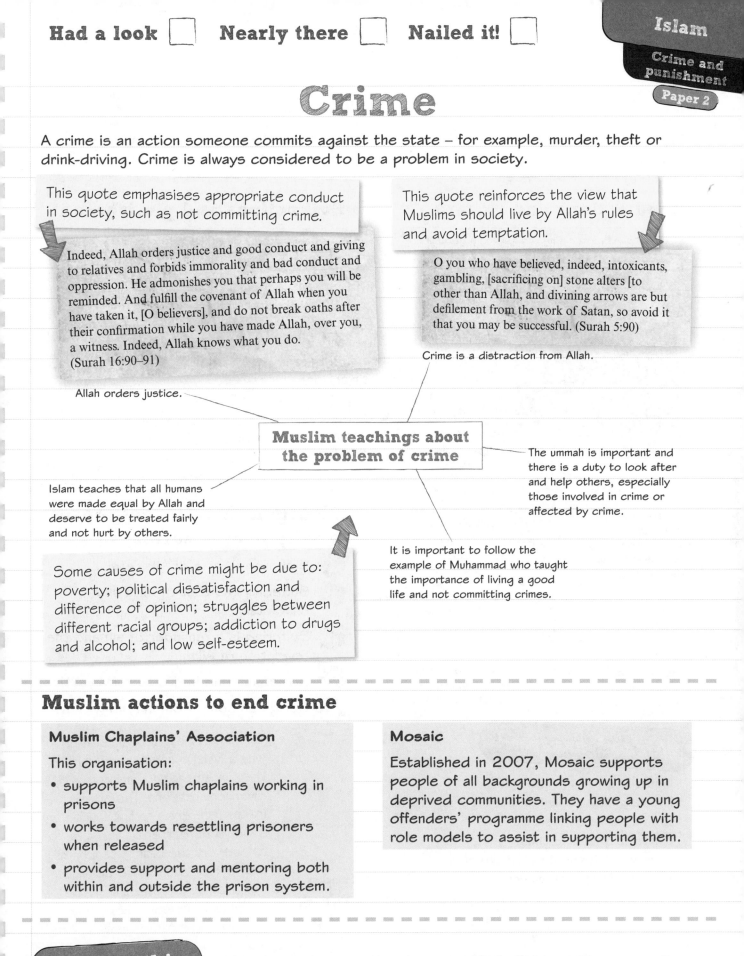

This quote emphasises appropriate conduct in society, such as not committing crime.

Indeed, Allah orders justice and good conduct and giving to relatives and forbids immorality and bad conduct and oppression. He admonishes you that perhaps you will be reminded. And fulfill the covenant of Allah when you have taken it, [O believers], and do not break oaths after their confirmation while you have made Allah, over you, a witness. Indeed, Allah knows what you do. (Surah 16:90–91)

This quote reinforces the view that Muslims should live by Allah's rules and avoid temptation.

O you who have believed, indeed, intoxicants, gambling, [sacrificing on] stone alters [to other than Allah, and divining arrows are but defilement from the work of Satan, so avoid it that you may be successful. (Surah 5:90)

Crime is a distraction from Allah.

Allah orders justice.

**Muslim teachings about the problem of crime**

The ummah is important and there is a duty to look after and help others, especially those involved in crime or affected by crime.

Islam teaches that all humans were made equal by Allah and deserve to be treated fairly and not hurt by others.

It is important to follow the example of Muhammad who taught the importance of living a good life and not committing crimes.

Some causes of crime might be due to: poverty; political dissatisfaction and difference of opinion; struggles between different racial groups; addiction to drugs and alcohol; and low self-esteem.

## Muslim actions to end crime

### Muslim Chaplains' Association

This organisation:

- supports Muslim chaplains working in prisons
- works towards resettling prisoners when released
- provides support and mentoring both within and outside the prison system.

### Mosaic

Established in 2007, Mosaic supports people of all backgrounds growing up in deprived communities. They have a young offenders' programme linking people with role models to assist in supporting them.

## Now try this

1 Outline **three** Muslim responses to crime.    **(3 marks)**
2 Explain **two** reasons why Muslims work to end crime.    **(4 marks)**

# Good, evil and suffering

Muslims have clear teachings on good, evil and suffering. These ideas are seen to be related to each other through the ideas of reward for good behaviour and the infliction of suffering for evil behaviour.

## Good actions and reward

Helping and caring and leading a good life

⬇

Reward is an afterlife in al-Jannah

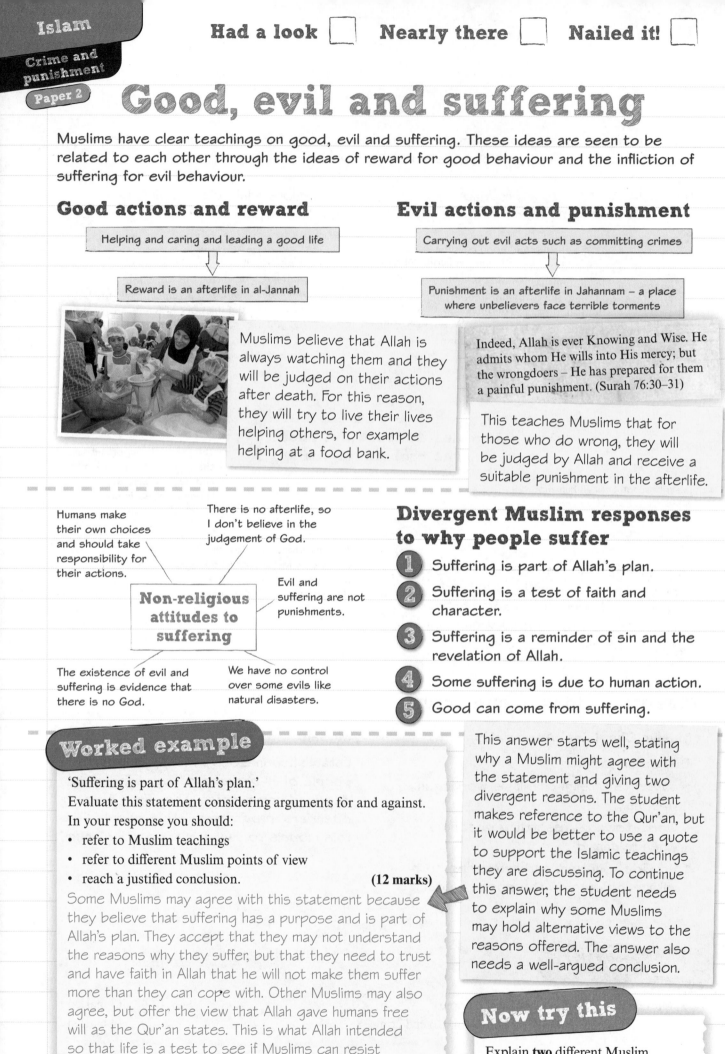

Muslims believe that Allah is always watching them and they will be judged on their actions after death. For this reason, they will try to live their lives helping others, for example helping at a food bank.

## Evil actions and punishment

Carrying out evil acts such as committing crimes

⬇

Punishment is an afterlife in Jahannam – a place where unbelievers face terrible torments

Indeed, Allah is ever Knowing and Wise. He admits whom He wills into His mercy; but the wrongdoers – He has prepared for them a painful punishment. (Surah 76:30–31)

This teaches Muslims that for those who do wrong, they will be judged by Allah and receive a suitable punishment in the afterlife.

Humans make their own choices and should take responsibility for their actions.

There is no afterlife, so I don't believe in the judgement of God.

**Non-religious attitudes to suffering**

Evil and suffering are not punishments.

The existence of evil and suffering is evidence that there is no God.

We have no control over some evils like natural disasters.

## Divergent Muslim responses to why people suffer

1. Suffering is part of Allah's plan.
2. Suffering is a test of faith and character.
3. Suffering is a reminder of sin and the revelation of Allah.
4. Some suffering is due to human action.
5. Good can come from suffering.

## Worked example

'Suffering is part of Allah's plan.'
Evaluate this statement considering arguments for and against.
In your response you should:
- refer to Muslim teachings
- refer to different Muslim points of view
- reach a justified conclusion.    **(12 marks)**

Some Muslims may agree with this statement because they believe that suffering has a purpose and is part of Allah's plan. They accept that they may not understand the reasons why they suffer, but that they need to trust and have faith in Allah that he will not make them suffer more than they can cope with. Other Muslims may also agree, but offer the view that Allah gave humans free will as the Qur'an states. This is what Allah intended so that life is a test to see if Muslims can resist temptation and earn their place in al-Jannah.

This answer starts well, stating why a Muslim might agree with the statement and giving two divergent reasons. The student makes reference to the Qur'an, but it would be better to use a quote to support the Islamic teachings they are discussing. To continue this answer, the student needs to explain why some Muslims may hold alternative views to the reasons offered. The answer also needs a well-argued conclusion.

## Now try this

Explain **two** different Muslim teachings on suffering.    **(4 marks)**

# Punishment

In order for the law to work properly, those who break the law should be punished.

## Nature of punishment and divergent opinion

In the UK, law is made by parliament and crimes are judged in courts of law. In many Islamic countries, the law is derived from the Qur'an and the courts refer to Shari'ah law, which is based on the teachings of the Qur'an.

Shari'ah law was established when society was very different from what it is today. For example, the punishment for theft in Shari'ah law is by amputation of the hand. Western law and society would say this is totally inappropriate. This can lead to differences of opinion.

## The Qur'an and punishment

O you who have believed, prescribed for you is legal retribution for those murdered – the free for the free, the slave for the slave, and the female for the female. But whoever overlooks from his brother anything, then there should be a suitable follow-up and payment to him with good conduct. This is an alleviation from your Lord and a mercy. But whoever transgresses after that will have a painful punishment. (Surah 2:178)

This quote shows the idea of punishment being justice for the crime that has been committed. It seems to suggest that it is appropriate for there to be a punishment.

## Importance of punishment to Muslims

In order to:

- build a peaceful society as Allah intended
- create a stable society and prevent further crimes
- give offenders the chance to change their behaviour
- make some amends for the crime committed.

**Islam and punishment**

## Punishment is justice

This enables the victim to gain retribution.

Some Muslims believe principles of situation ethics should be applied and the punishment should fit the crime and circumstances of the people involved. For example, the crime might have been carried out because of poverty and this should be taken into account.

## Why punishment is needed in society

In order to:

- maintain law and order
- set expected behaviour for society
- give a chance for offenders to mend their ways
- make victims safe
- give a chance for offenders to reflect on the impact of their crime on others.

## Now try this

When referring to the source of authority, explain what it says.

1 Explain **two** reasons why punishment is important for Muslims. **(4 marks)**

2 Explain **two** reasons why Muslims believe punishment is needed in society. In your answer you must refer to a source of wisdom and authority. **(5 marks)**

# Aims of punishment

Punishment has a number of key aims: protection, retribution, deterrence, and reformation. Muslims may have divergent views about which of these aims is most important.

| Type of punishment | What is it? | Muslim response |
|---|---|---|
| Protection | To protect society from dangerous criminals by keeping them away from society so they can't hurt others. | Strongly support this idea, believing that the protection of people in society is of paramount importance. This could be seen as justice (see Surah 4:135). |
| Retribution | Punishment should make criminals pay for what they have done wrong. | Muslims believe they should strive to achieve this by giving a punishment that enables justice to be achieved (see Surah 57:25). |
| Deterrance | To discourage someone from doing something against the law. Punishment may stop someone committing the same crime or seeing someone else punished for a crime might put someone off doing that action. **MUGGER GETS FIVE YEARS** A serial mugger was sentenced yesterday at Newtown county court to | Deterring others from committing the same crime again reduces crime in society and maintains order and justice. Some punishments suggested in the Qur'an may encourage others not to commit the same crime (see Surah 5:41). |
| Reformation | Punishment should show the criminal what they have done wrong and give them time to change so they do not repeat the offence. This could mean education or providing skills or a job so they become a law-abiding citizen. | Forgiveness is important and Islam teaches that just as Allah is forgiving, his followers should also try to apply this within their lives. To give someone a chance to change their behaviour and become a better person is important (see Surah 4:26– 28). |

## Qur'anic teachings about punishment

- The Qur'an gives specific instructions for particular crimes. This shows the use of punishment as a means of reforming the criminal, as they will not want the punishment to happen to them again. Stricter punishments are considered to be last resorts.

- Muslims believe that punishment establishes peace and justice on Earth as Allah intended.

> Allah wants to make clear to you [the lawful from the unlawful] and guide you to the [good] practices of those before you and to accept your repentance. And Allah is Knowing and Wise. Allah wants to accept your repentance, but those who follow [their] passions want you to digress [into] a great deviation. And Allah wants to lighten for you [your difficulties]; and mankind was created weak. (Surah 4:26–28)

This Qur'anic quote shows that Islam teaches that fair punishment is important, but that those who do wrong need to be given the opportunity to repent and change.

Remember to consider all the aims of punishment. Evaluate what a Muslim would say about why punishment is important. Give two views and a conclusion.

### Now try this

1 Outline **three** aims of punishment for Muslims.    **(3 marks)**

2 'The most important aim of punishment is reformation.'
Evaluate this statement considering arguments for and against. In your response you should:
- refer to Muslim teachings
- refer to different Muslim points of view
- reach a justified conclusion.    **(12 marks)**

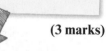

Look at Muslim attitudes to punishment on page 103 to help you.

# Forgiveness

Forgiveness is accepting someone's apology for their misdeed and moving on. It is an important idea in Islamic life.

## Nature and importance of forgiveness

Muslim teachings say that:

- Allah is compassionate and merciful and forgives people so Muslims should too
- if a person truly repents, then they should be forgiven
- people should try to forgive those who have wronged, as Muhammad taught
- Islam is a religion of peace
- a killer may be forgiven if they pay compensation to the family (Qur'an)
- on the Day of Judgement people will be judged on their behaviour and those who repent will be forgiven.

## Being forgiven by the community is important for offenders

Gain skills and education from the punishment

Reintegrated into the community

Carry out community service to make amends for wrong

A way of protecting the ummah

Ease tensions in the community because victims can see justice has been done

> O you who have believed, indeed, among your wives and your children are enemies to you, so beware of them. But if you pardon and overlook and forgive – then indeed, Allah is Forgiving and Merciful. (Surah 64:14)

## Restorative justice

Restorative justice is an attempt to bring together the offender and victim of a crime to try to restore peace and allow a community and individuals to heal.

## Worked example

Explain **two** reasons why restorative justice is important to Muslims. **(4 marks)**

1. Restorative justice is important as it brings peace. It is also important as it is following the teachings of Muhammad.

2. Restorative justice is important as it gives the offender and victim the opportunity to restore peace, which is important. Islam teaches the importance of forgiveness and Muslims should follow Allah's example of being forgiving.

   A second reason why restorative justice is important is that Muhammad taught that people should forgive others when they do wrong and are sorry. Muslims believe they should follow the example of Muhammad and forgiving an offender allows everyone to move forward with their lives.

The first answer offers two reasons, but neither is developed or explained. The second answer shows how the reasons can be explained more fully.

## Now try this

Explain **two** reasons why forgiveness of offenders is important for Muslims. **(4 marks)**

# Treatment of criminals

Muslims believe that it is important for criminals, even though they have committed crimes, to be treated in a fair way.

## Muslim teachings about the treatment of criminals

> And they give food in spite of love for it to the needy, the orphan, and the captive … (Surah 76:8)

The Qur'an teaches that even someone who has done wrong and is being kept captive deserves to be treated in the correct, humane way. Muslims believe in justice and believe that criminals should be given the chance to reform.

Some Muslims, however, may believe that if someone has done wrong, their freedoms and human rights should be limited. Shari'ah law is very clear about those who have been convicted being given punishments, and some Muslims may accept appropriate retaliation against those whose guilt has been proven.

## Fair trial

Barrister addressing a jury in court. A jury assesses the case for the prosecution and defence and makes a decision on whether the person on trial is guilty or innocent. This makes for a fair trial.

---

### Use of torture

To inflict any pain is wrong. Even though criminals have done wrong, they are still human and deserve fair and respectful treatment. As all humans were created by Allah, they should be treated respectfully.

There might be instances, however, where situation ethics could be applied and questions are asked: What is the best course of action for the greater good? Is torture justifiable for this reason?

### Human rights

Muslims believe all humans have equal rights, although they do accept that criminals deserve punishment for their crimes. This may involve the removal of some human rights (e.g. freedom if put in prison), which would be fair treatment for the crimes committed.

Human rights are the fundamental rights of every person whatever their age, gender, colour or religious beliefs to basic necessities such as water, food and shelter and the right to a fair trial.

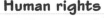

**Muslim beliefs about the treatment of criminals**

### Trial by jury

Trials need to be conducted fairly so a jury would work to achieve this.

### Fair trial

Muslims believe justice is important and criminals have the right to a fair trial where both sides of the case are considered. They believe it is important that the laws of the state are recognised and upheld and punishment is given when a person is found guilty of a crime.

---

Consider developing some of these ideas as reasons: Allah is just and merciful; the Quran teaches that justice is important; all humans were created by Allah.

## Now try this

Explain **two** reasons why fair treatment of criminals is important to Muslims.     **(4 marks)**

# The death penalty

**Capital punishment** is also known as the death penalty. There are many arguments, both religious and non-religious, that support or are against capital punishment.

## The nature of capital punishment

Capital punishment is execution – where the life of a condemned prisoner is taken away. It has been abolished completely in the UK, although some countries, as well as some states in the USA, still have the death penalty.

EN AMÉRIQUE – EXECUTION D'UNE FEMME AUX ÉTATS-UNIS

Death by hanging of a woman convicted of murder in the USA, 1906.

## The purpose of capital punishment

1. To offer a punishment for the most severe crimes committed.

2. To act as a deterrent for other criminals.

3. To make victims feel as though punishment has been given and to offer closure for the victim's family.

4. To make sure that the offender cannot commit the same crime again.

5. To give a chance for the offender to repent by facing up to what they have done.

## Muslim attitudes to the use of capital punishment

| In support of capital punishment | Against capital punishment |
| --- | --- |
| • The Qur'an says the death penalty can be used for certain crimes. <br> • Shari'ah law agrees with the Qur'an. <br> • Muhammad made statements suggesting he agreed with the death penalty. <br> • When Muhammad was the ruler of Medinah, he sentenced people to death for committing murder. | • The scholars of Shari'ah law do not agree when or how the death penalty should be applied, showing there are differences in opinion. <br> • The Qur'an states that capital punishment is one option – but it is not the only option. <br> • Strict conditions given by the Qur'an about capital punishment are often not met. <br> • Some Muslims may use the argument that life is special and sacred and it is not the place of humans to take it away in any circumstances. <br> • If there is no capital punishment in the country they live in, then they accept this law. |

## Muslim teachings on capital punishment

In Hadith (Sahih Muslim 16:4152), it suggests that the death penalty can be used for the crimes of murder and for Muslims who refuse to do their Islamic duty. The Qur'an also indicates that the death penalty can be for crimes of rape, homosexual acts and apostasy (when someone works against Islam).

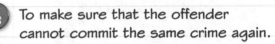

## Non-religious attitudes

Humanists and atheists generally oppose the use of the death penalty, as they believe premeditated killing is wrong – even when carried out by the state. There is also the possibility of error. When situation ethics are applied, some may believe that in certain circumstances capital punishment might be the better option.

## Now try this

Explain **two** reasons why some Muslims might support the use of the death penalty.    **(4 marks)**

# Peace

'Islam' is derived from the root of the word 'salaam' which is often understood to mean 'peace'. The Qur'an teaches about peace and that peace is not easy to achieve. Muslims accept that sometimes war may be necessary in certain circumstances in order to bring about peace.

## Nature of peace

For Muslims, peace is understood to be the absence of oppression, tyranny, injustice and corruption. They believe it is directly linked to the attaining of justice within the world.

Muslims at a rally in the USA promoting peace

## Islam as a religion of peace

1. Islam is a religion that has been misrepresented and associated with terrorism where, in reality, it is a religion of peace.

2. Muslims believe Allah created and wants a peaceful world.

3. There are many examples of peace being shown within Islam, demonstrating its importance. For example, Muslims greet each other with the words 'As-salamu alaykum' (peace be with you).

4. The Qur'an is seen to promote messages of peace and Muslims promote peace and unity through being part of the ummah.

## The Qur'an and peace

> And the servants of the Most Merciful are those who walk upon the earth easily, and when the ignorant address them [harshly], they say [words of] peace. (Surah 25:63)

The Qur'an teaches that peace is an important idea for Muslims, even when they may face criticism or hate towards them.

## Muslim teachings about peace

1. Allah created the world with the intention that peace would be part of his creation.

2. Muslims believe in the personal struggle for peace or the greater jihad.

3. All Muslims belong to the ummah, which demonstrates ideas of living together peacefully.

4. Standing up for justice in the world is one way of achieving peace.

5. In some cases, it may be necessary to go to war to secure peace.

## Worked example

Explain **two** ways in which peace may be understood in the life of a Muslim. In your answer you should make reference to a source of wisdom or authority. **(5 marks)**

One way is how Muslims should behave towards others in a peaceful way. The ummah unites all Muslims in peace, as they are all equal and should help and care for each other. A quote that supports this is: 'And the servants of the Most Merciful are those who walk upon the earth easily, and when the ignorant address them [harshly], they say [words of] peace' (Surah 25:63).

Another way is how Muslims may greet each other with a message of peace. They may say 'As-salamu alaykum', which means 'peace be with you'. This shows they are giving them their good wishes.

The reason given is stated and then developed. This student then gives a quote from a source of authority to support the point they have made.

## Now try this

Outline **three** reasons why peace is important to Muslims. **(3 marks)**

106

# Peacemaking

Peace is important to Muslims and there are examples of organisations who promote ideas of peace, such as Islamic Relief and Muslim Peace Fellowship.

## Importance of justice, forgiveness and reconciliation

### Justice

Muslims believe there is a direct link between the ideas of **justice** and peace. If justice and fairness can be attained, peace will follow. The ummah demonstrates ideas of equality and justice, as all Muslims are of equal worth and value and support each other.

> And not equal are the good deed and the bad. Repel [evil] by that [deed] which is better; and thereupon the one whom between you and him is enmity [will become] as though he was a devoted friend. (Surah 41:34)

Surah 41:34 reinforces the view that good deeds and evil deeds are not equal and that justice, forgiveness and reconciliation are important in overcoming conflict and bringing peace.

### Forgiveness

Muslims believe that **forgiveness** is important in achieving peace. They recognise that everyone makes mistakes and deserves to be given a second chance. Muslims believe Allah is merciful and they should follow his example and try to forgive others when they do wrong.

### Reconciliation

**Reconciliation** is the idea of making up after conflict. According to Muslims, this is needed in order to live in an ordered and peaceful world as Allah intends.

## Muslim organisations working for peace

Islamic Relief:

- Founded in 1984 to help victims of war.
- Inspired by Islam to promote ideas of caring for others and achieving peace.
- Works in countries such as Somalia, Iraq and Bosnia.
- Raises awareness of children living in extreme poverty.
- Provides teachers and school materials for children living in poverty.
- Supports refugees with medical care and food in war-torn countries.
- Provides emergency aid and relief.

Muslim Peace Fellowship:

- Founded in 1994 and works to promote world peace.
- Works against injustice – reaches out to people of all faiths.
- Develops understanding and mutual respect.
- Promotes the Islamic ideas of peace and non-violence through conferences, publications, talks and prayer.

Remember that you need to relate one of your reasons in your answer to a quote from a source of authority or wisdom.

### Why do Muslims work for peace?

- ✓ To follow the teachings of Islam, which promote peace and working together rather than conflict.
- ✓ The Qur'an contains many quotes relating to ideas of peace. Muslims believe they should apply these through supporting charity and helping others.
- ✓ To live as Allah intended and to work to try to bring justice to the world.
- ✓ To help care for others in the world, which is a duty outlined by Muhammad to humans.
- ✓ To support and strengthen the ummah.

**Now try this**

'Peace is the most important thing in today's world for Muslims.'
Evaluate this statement considering arguments for and against. In your response you should:
- refer to Muslim teachings
- reach a justified conclusion.

**(12 marks)**

# Conflict

Conflict, where an argument or disagreement has led to a breakdown in a relationship, can cause problems within society such as a lack of communication and trust. Muslims believe everything possible should be done to try to resolve conflicts within the world.

## Causes of conflict

There can be many causes of conflict, including politics, resources, history, culture and religion. Many conflicts that emerge do so because of differing beliefs or a greed for wanting something someone else may have, such as land, power and resources.

## The Qur'an on conflict

Fight in the way of Allah those who fight you but do not transgress. Indeed. Allah does not like transgressors. (Surah 2:190)

## Muslim teachings and responses to the nature and cause of conflict

1. Every Muslim is part of the ummah and deserves equality and respect. When conflict happens, Muslims should work to resolve it.

2. Muslims may try to reconcile groups who are in conflict in order to achieve peace.

3. Muslims believe that Allah is merciful and forgiving and they should try to follow this principle in their own lives.

4. Muslims can be seen to adopt a situation ethics standpoint on issues of conflict, and the action taken may differ from one situation to another.

5. Despite Islam being a religion that supports the idea of peace, it does recognise that war and fighting may be needed in some circumstances as a last resort when all else has been tried and failed.

6. Muslims believe that they should not forgive those who work against Islam.

Muslims believe that Allah commands that they should fight back when necessary but remain just. This is a form of situation ethics where sometimes conflict is needed to bring peace.

## Worked example

Outline **three** Muslim responses to the problems conflict causes within society. **(3 marks)**

1. Muslims may respond by working to resolve conflict.

2. Muslims may respond by working to resolve conflict through getting people to talk. They could educate others about peace and reconciliation. They could also look to teachings of the Qur'an to help people understand the importance of working together to overcome conflict.

This student has given one response – to improve this answer, two more responses must be included, as in answer 2.

## Muslim response to non-religious views on conflict

Religion is a cause of conflict, as different beliefs between religious groups can cause problems in society.

Non-religious view

Allah wishes for a peaceful world without conflict and all Muslims should work to achieve this.

Muslim view

## Now try this

Explain **two** reasons why Muslims believe they should work to bring an end to conflict. **(4 marks)**

# Pacifism

Muslims believe it is important to promote ideas of peace, forgiveness and reconciliation. Islam is not a **pacifist** religion as it is accepted that sometimes war and fighting is necessary, but it can sometimes be seen to promote ideas that are in line with pacifism.

## Nature of pacifism

Pacifism is a belief held that war and violence are wrong under all circumstances. This is the logo for CND (Campaign for Nuclear Disarmament) – an organisation that campaigns non-violently to rid the world of nuclear weapons.

## History of pacifism in Islam

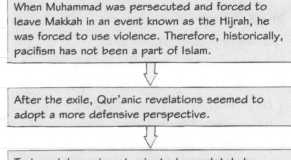

When Muhammad was persecuted and forced to leave Makkah in an event known as the Hijrah, he was forced to use violence. Therefore, historically, pacifism has not been a part of Islam.

After the exile, Qur'anic revelations seemed to adopt a more defensive perspective.

Today, violence is not rejected completely by Islam, but ideas of peace are promoted within a minority movement.

If you should raise your hand against me to kill me – I shall not raise my hand against you to kill you. Indeed, I fear Allah, Lord of the worlds. (Surah 5:28)

This quote suggests ideas in line with pacifism or passive resistance. Namely, that a person should not face violence with violence. Some Muslims may interpret it this way, while others may argue that it is not suggesting the use of non-violence, but rather that a Muslim should not be the first person to attack another.

## Muslim teachings about passive resistance

 Islam teachings in the Qur'an and Hadith strive for justice and to resist oppression.

 Muslims believe it is important to resist zulm cruelty and injustice).

 Islam teaches the importance of reconciliation and working together to achieve peace using non-violent protest.

4 'Islam' is often taken to mean 'submission to Allah' and 'peace'.

## Passive resistance in Islam

Muhammad and his followers continued to preach the message of Allah and confronted non-believers even when faced with violence.

Not all Muslims are pacifists however, and warfare has been part of the religion since the time of Muhammad, both for the defence and spread of the religion. Muhammad fought in the Battle of Badr to protect Muslims, and the idea of jihad has been used to justify fighting since.

The Arab Spring was a democratic uprising that spread across much of the Arab world in 2011. It contained elements of protest using passive resistance.

## Now try this

Explain **two** reasons why Muslims may accept ideas of passive resistance. **(4 marks)**

# The Just War theory

A just war is one that is fought for the right reasons, in the right way and is, therefore, seen as being justified. The **Just War theory** is a set of principles that is used to decide whether a war is fair and just and meets the criteria to be justified.

## The nature and importance of the Just War theory

The theory suggests that:

- it is wrong to take human life
- countries may need to protect their people and war may be necessary to do this
- protecting moral values may require force.

The Just War theory is important because it:

- provides a set of rules as to the best way to act at times of conflict
- offers a framework to decide whether war is the best option
- aims to prevent war.

## Just War theory in Islam

Has the support of the community and not one person

Is declared by a religious leader

Is an act of defence

**Conditions of a Just War – the lesser jihad**

Will not harm the environment

Does not aim to win new land or power

Will not threaten lives

Is a last resort

Is not an act to convert people to Islam

> And what is [the matter] with you that you fight not in the cause of Allah and [for] the oppressed among men, women, and children who say, 'Our Lord, take us out of this city of oppressive people and appoint for us from Yourself a protector and appoint for us from Yourself a helper?' (Surah 4:75)

## Divergent responses to the Just War theory

Some Muslims believe that war is permitted in self-defence. Other Muslims believe war is never justified and should never happen.

Tanks at war

- Some Muslims recognise that war is necessary and sometimes required as a last resort – the Just War theory permits this.
- Sunni and Shi'a Muslims may conflict over the exact interpretation of the Just War theory. Shi'a Muslims recognise jihad as one of the Ten Obligatory Acts, whereas Sunni Muslims do not place the same emphasis on it.
- Some may traditionally accept that Islam allows war in self-defence and to protect the innocent and oppressed, for example, as seen in the Hijrah when Muhammad and his followers were persecuted or the Battle of Badr.
- Other Muslims may believe that war is never the right choice, believing that peace and reconciliation are at the heart of Islam.

## Is a just war possible?

| Yes | No |
|---|---|
| Depending on the circumstances (situation ethics), it might be reasonable | No circumstances would necessitate war |
| Fighting might be the only way to achieve peace | Other ways can achieve better results |
| Weapons programmed to damage set targets rather than affect innocent lives | There's always the risk of causing suffering |
| Qur'an suggests fighting to defend Islam is acceptable | Should a religious leader declare a just war, it may be too influenced by their faith |

This quote refers to the people of Makkah, who were persecuted for embracing Islam. This illustrates one reason why it may be justified to fight – to protect the religion of Islam.

## Now try this

1 Outline **three** Muslim conditions of the Just War theory.     **(3 marks)**

2 Explain **two** conditions of the Just War theory.     **(4 marks)**

# Holy war

Holy war, or Harb al-Maqadis, is the name for war fought because of religious differences.

## The nature of Harb al-Maqadis in Islam

Harb al-Maqadis is only justifiable in cases where the intention is to defend the religion of Islam. This can involve:

- protecting the freedom of Muslims to practise their faith

- strengthening the religion of Islam if it is being threatened

- protecting Muslims against an attack.

Muhammad and his followers were involved in holy wars, such as the Battle of Badr and the Conquest of Makkah.

Then when the Sacred Months (the Ist, 7th, 11th, and 12th months of the Islamic calendar) have passed, then kill the Mushrikun (see V. 2:105) wherever you find them, and capture them and besiege them, and prepare for them each and every ambush. But if they repent and perform As-Salat (Iqamat-as-Salat), and give Zakat, then leave their way free. Verily, Allah is Oft-Forgiving, Most Merciful. (Surah 9:5)

But if the enemy incline towards peace, do thou (also) incline towards peace, and trust in Allah; for He is One that heareth and knoweth (all things). (Surah 8:61)

The first quote suggests the agreement of using violence when necessary, but gives allowance if the opposition repents. This suggests peace and forgiveness are important. The second quote supports ideas of working towards peace. These quotes may appear to be in conflict and this can also be applied to lesser jihad, with diversity over its understanding and justification for war.

## Teachings about holy war

The conditions for holy war to happen must:

- be for reasons of defence
- be declared by a religious leader
- be a last resort
- avoid harming innocent civilians
- not be fought to gain land
- be fought to bring about end goal
- not harm innocent people
- not cause women to be abused or raped
- treat enemies fairly, including enemy soldiers
- be stopped as soon as enemy ask for it
- not target property

## Worked example

'War is always wrong.'
Evaluate this statement considering arguments for and against. In your response you should:
- refer to Muslim teaching
- refer to different Muslim points of view
- reach a justified conclusion.    **(12 marks)**

Some Muslims would agree with this statement, arguing that Islam is a religion of peace and it is always wrong to use violence. They may use arguments such as teachings from the Qur'an that show ideas of peace, or use the example of Muhammad, who appeared to sometimes use examples of passive resistance and not violence. This would help them to support the idea that life is sacred as it was created by Allah and innocent people should not be threatened through war.

This student has made a good start, offering one Muslim viewpoint. To continue, the student needs to give an alternative view and include sources of wisdom, along with a conclusion.

## Now try this

Explain **two** reasons why some Muslims may support war.    **(4 marks)**

Paper 2

# Weapons of mass destruction

Weapons of mass destruction (WMD) include nuclear, biological or chemical weapons that are able to cause widespread devastation and destruction of resources and loss of life.

## Why some people might think there are perceived benefits to WMD

Minimal losses are incurred by the attackers

Nuclear warheads

Weapons of mass destruction can be used as a deterrent to other nations

They provide the ability to end a war quickly, preventing further casualties

## Why some people might think there are problems with WMD

Moral issues of the amount of destruction and devastation caused

The attack is indiscriminate and can kill innocent victims

Can make war unfair

The destruction caused by the dropping of a nuclear bomb on Hiroshima, Japan, in 1945 by US aircraft.

Problems of stockpiling dangerous weapons

The conditions of the Just War theory would not be met using this type of weapon

## Muslim teachings and responses on WMD

The Qur'an was recorded long before WMD came into existence, but lessons from the Qur'an can still be applied.

> That if any one slew a person – unless it be for murder or for spreading mischief in the land – it would be as if he slew the whole people; and if any one saved a life, it would be as if he saved the life of the whole people …
> (Surah 5:32)

**1** Use of WMD not supported because of the extensive damage they would cause.

**2** Innocent life should not be threatened.

**3** Impossible to regulate WMD under Islamic conditions of war because of the damage that could be caused.

## Non-religious attitudes and utilitarianism

It is difficult to find any justification for the use of weapons that cause so much damage and threaten innocent life to such as great extent.

Non-religious view

WMD may be justified if peace is achieved in the long term and if they act as a deterrent.

Utilitarian view

WMD are too great a threat to life and the creation of Allah.

Muslim view

Remember that this question asks you to refer to a quote from a source of authority for Muslims. You could use the Qur'anic quote on this page in your explanation.

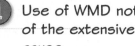 Now try this

Explain **two** reasons why many Muslims would not support the use of weapons of mass destruction. In your answer you must refer to a source of wisdom and authority. **(5 marks)**

# Issues surrounding conflict

Conflict has always existed, but today's world contains new forms of war, violence and terrorism.

## Nature of conflict

 **1 Violence**

Violent acts are constantly being reported, with people seeming to be less afraid of laws and consequences, creating a sense of fear within society. Examples: increase in knife and gun crime or attacks on religious or racial grounds.

 **2 War**

War has taken on a new role with the development of new, stronger and more damaging weapons in, for example, Afghanistan, Iraq and Syria.

**3 Terrorism**

This is a violent form of protest that has occurred all over the world. It often has religious links, with some religious groups claiming to commit acts of terrorism in the name of God. For example, 9/11 and the attacks in Paris, Brussels and Tunisia.

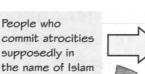
A fighter

## Divergent Muslim views on conflict

⬅ Islam as a religion of peace

In support of war if defending Islam ➡

⬅ Speak out against those who commit atrocities

People who commit atrocities supposedly in the name of Islam ➡

There are many examples of Muslim leaders speaking out against terrorism, including Iranian president Hassan Rouhani and Qatari foreign minister Khalid al-Attiyah, who both spoke out after the Paris attacks in November 2015.

## Non-religious views on conflict

Non-religious people may be concerned about the growing number of conflicts in society, as well as the increasing use of violence. Even though they hold no religious beliefs, they would value human life and believe in principles of justice and equality.

Some non-religious people may even hold religion at fault for the conflict within the world, seeing the rise in examples of terrorism and violence as centrally connected to religion.

## How Muslims have worked to overcome these issues

- The Muslim Council of Britain runs education programmes to inform and break down barriers.
- Peaceful rallies and marches are held to promote peace.
- Interfaith groups work together across religions to promote peace.
- Police and community groups work together.
- Organisations such as Mosaic work to bring people within communities together.

I advise you ten things: Do not kill women or children or an aged, infirm person. Do not cut down fruit-bearing trees. Do not destroy an inhabited place. Do not slaughter sheep or camels except for food. Do not burn bees and do not scatter them. Do not steal from the booty, and do not be cowardly. (Malik's Muwatta)

This quote states the things that Muslims should not do in terms of causing conflict, using violence or starting war.

### Now try this

'The biggest threat facing Muslims in the world today is conflict.'
Evaluate this statement considering arguments for and against. In your response you must:
- refer to Muslim teachings
- refer to different Muslim points of view
- reach a justified conclusion.
(12 marks)

# Revelation

Many people claim to have experienced God, either directly or indirectly. These types of experiences allow Muslims to 'know' Allah, understand better what he is like and have confirmation or proof of his existence.

## Direct and indirect revelation

**Revelation** is the way in which God reveals his presence.

 Direct revelation is revelation that comes directly from God.

 Indirect revelation is through a messenger, such as a prophet.

Muslims believe Allah must exist because, if he did not, he wouldn't choose to reveal himself in these ways.

## The Qur'an as revelation

If I should err, I would only err against myself. But if I am guided, it is by what my Lord reveals to me. Indeed, He is Hearing and near. (Surah 34:50)

This demonstrates that Allah chooses to reveal himself directly. The Qur'an itself is revelation – Muslims can know Allah better through reading his words as they believe he is the author. Muslims can understand what Allah is like – for example, **omnipotent** or **benevolent** – as well as his teachings about how he wants Muslims to live their lives and behave.

## Revelation through messengers

Muslims believe that Allah chose to reveal himself through prophets – messengers who were specially chosen. These include Adam, Ibrahim, Isma'il, Musa, Dawud, Isa and Muhammad, who is the 'Seal of the Prophets' as the final messenger. Some of these messengers brought messages from Allah, while others, such as Muhammad, brought holy books as well. Muslims believe that the messengers reveal aspects of Allah as they share his teachings with the world. Muslims can look to sources of authority such as the Qur'an for support and understanding of what Allah is like.

## Divergent understandings of what revelation shows about the nature of Allah

The Qur'an demonstrates that Allah is omnipotent, **omniscient** and benevolent and cares about his creation.

But he also takes on the role of judge, especially after death in the afterlife.

Allah communicates with us so shows he exists and is close.

But he is also transcendent and remains beyond full human understanding.

## Worked example

Outline **three** ways revelation proves the existence of Allah. **(3 marks)**

Revelation proves the existence of Allah in that the Qur'an is believed to be the words of Allah showing he exists. Through messengers such as Musa, Ibrahim and Muhammad, Allah is shown to exist. Revelation helps Muslims to understand what Allah is like and also proves he exists.

In this answer the student has given three different ideas in three separate sentences.

## Now try this

Explain **two** ways in which Allah reveals himself for Muslims. **(4 marks)**

# Visions

A **vision** is something that a person sees, possibly in a dream, which may connect to a supernatural being or God. Often a revelation is made in the vision.

## Nature of visions in Islam

Many people associated with Islam, including prophets and **imams**, have undergone religious experiences where they have received a vision. Often angels or messengers appear and pass on messages from Allah, proving to Muslims that Allah is real.

## Importance of visions in Islam

Visions are an important form of religious experience. People often only believe things that they can see, so experiencing a vision may be considered to be more reliable than other types of experiences. Visions provide evidence and help to strengthen faith for believers or lead people to believe in the existence of Allah because they believe:

- ✓ Allah is contacting them
- ✓ they can get closer to Allah
- ✓ they can understand Allah better.

## Examples of visions

**1** Musa's vision of Allah

And when Moses arrived at Our appointed time and his Lord spoke to him, he said, 'My Lord, show me (Yourself) that I may look at You.' (God) said, 'You will not see Me, but look at the mountain; if it should remain in place, then you will see Me.' But when his Lord appeared to the mountain, He rendered it level, and Moses fell unconscious. And when he awoke, he said, 'Exalted are You! I have repented to You, and I am the first of the believers.'(Surah 7:143)

These two visions are not direct visions of Allah, but Muslims believe that Allah is transcendent and, therefore, too great to be seen directly.

**2** The vision of Mary

And mention, [O Muhammad], in the Book [the story of] Mary, when she withdrew from her family to a place toward the east. And she took, in seclusion from them, a screen. Then We sent to her Our Angel, and he represented himself to her as a well-proportioned man. She said, 'Indeed, I seek refuge in the Most Merciful from you, [so leave me], if you should be fearing of Allah.' He said, 'I am only the messenger of your Lord to give you [news of] a pure boy.' She said, 'How can I have a boy while no man has touched me and I have not been unchaste?' (Surah 19:16–20)

## Divergent understandings of visions

Different Muslims may place a different level of emphasis on visions as proof of the existence of Allah.

Some Sunni Muslims may accept visions and use them as proof of the existence of Allah to strengthen faith. However, other Muslims, including some Shi'a Muslims, believe that visions are not needed, as faith means to put trust in Allah and therefore proof is not required. Some Muslims, such as those in the **Sufi** tradition, are more spiritual and accept ideas of mysticism, meaning they may place more emphasis on visions within their faith.

## Muslim responses to non-religious arguments

Visions are not real. They are hallucinations or dreams. I would only believe in them if they were verified scientifically.

Non-religious view

Visions do happen and they are evidence of the existence of Allah.

Muslim view

## Now try this

1 Outline **three** reasons why visions do not prove the existence of Allah. **(3 marks)**

2 Explain **two** reasons why visions are important as evidence of Allah for some Muslims. **(4 marks)**

# Miracles

**Miracles** are amazing events that can't be explained by the laws of nature or science. They are believed to show the power and presence of Allah in the world.

## Importance of miracles for Muslims

Miracles are important because:

- they suggest a greater being, such as Allah, who is involved and acting within the world
- the Qur'an makes it clear Allah can perform miracles if he wishes
- people often question the existence of Allah when people seem to suffer. Therefore, when miracles happen that can be attributed to him, it gives comfort and belief in a loving Allah.

## Why miracles might lead to belief in the existence of Allah

**1** Amazement by what has happened – there is no other way to explain it except through Allah.

**2** Evidence that Allah is active within the world – they show Allah cares for creation and wants humanity to know he is there.

**3** Proof of the existence of Allah because they show his love for the world.

**4** Demonstrate the power of Allah in that he can act within the world.

## Examples of miracles

| The miracle of Nuh surviving the floods | The Qur'an as a miracle | The miracle of Al-Mi'raj when Muhammad was taken to meet Allah in the heavens |
| --- | --- | --- |
|  | Say, 'If mankind and the jinn gathered in order to produce the like of this Qur'an, they could not produce the like of it, even if they were to each other assistants.' (Surah 17:88) | This event occurred in the year 621 and is explained in the Qur'an and Hadith  |

This event is considered miraculous because it would seem impossible.

You will need to be familiar with the whole Qur'anic passage 17:84–89. The Qur'an itself is seen as a living miracle due to the way it was passed down to Muhammad. Many Muslims believe that the Qur'an contains information that could not have been known at the time, which adds to its miraculous nature.

## Non-religious arguments against miracles

Miracles can be explained scientifically. They are everyday events interpreted as miracles.

Different interpretations of events cause doubt as to their truth. They don't provide proof that Allah exists.

## Muslim arguments for miracles

Miracles are real and they prove the existence of Allah.

Miracles strengthen and confirm my faith in Allah. I trust Allah.

Some Muslims place less importance on miracles. They find reading the teachings in the Qur'an, or learning through Muhammad, a better way of getting to know Allah.

## Now try this

Explain **two** reasons why miracles may lead a Muslim to believe in Allah. **(4 marks)**

# Religious experiences

A **religious experience** is an experience that people claim is caused by or related to God. This could include a miracle, vision, dream or simply a connection to God. Although many Muslims claim religious experiences confirm their beliefs about Allah, many people do not accept religious experiences are real.

## Islam and religious experiences

> Those who do not know say, 'Why does Allah not speak to us or there come to us a sign?' Thus spoke those before them like their words. Their hearts resemble each other. We have shown clearly the signs to a people who are certain [in faith]. (Surah 2:118)

Muslims believe that Allah clearly reveals himself to his followers. One way of doing this is through religious experiences, as Muslims can gain a personal connection and understanding of Allah.

## The varying importance of religious experiences to Sunni, Shi'a and Sufis

- All Muslims recognise religious experience to some extent, as they believe the Qur'an was revealed to Muhammad through religious experience.
- Some Muslims, however, place slightly less importance on religious experience within the religion. Sunni and Shi'a Muslims believe that sources of authority, such as the prophets and the Qur'an, are better sources of evidence.
- Sufism is a smaller branch of Islam and is often considered to be more mystical. Sufis place great importance on personal experiences of Allah and their significance to following Islam and connecting with Allah.

## Muslim responses to religious experiences

There are the experiences of Muhammad and modern-day Muslims to prove that religious experience is real.

> As a Muslim, I would argue that religious experiences do happen and there is evidence in the Qur'an.

> As a Muslim, I believe Allah reveals himself to us in order to confirm belief and provide understanding of who he is.

> As a Muslim, I believe that if Allah wants to communicate with us, he is able to do so through religious experiences.

## Non-religious arguments questioning religious experiences

- There is a lack of evidence
- People might have been under the influence of drink or drugs
- People may have been ill and hallucinating
- People may be looking intentionally for experiences – looking for meaning to their lives.

## Now try this

Explain **two** ways in which Muslims may respond to arguments against religious experience offered by non-religious people.    **(4 marks)**

# The design argument

The **design argument** tries to prove the existence of Allah by arguing that the universe was designed.

## Overview of the design argument

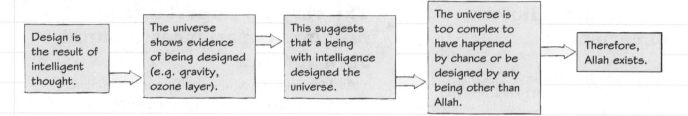

Design is the result of intelligent thought. → The universe shows evidence of being designed (e.g. gravity, ozone layer). → This suggests that a being with intelligence designed the universe. → The universe is too complex to have happened by chance or be designed by any being other than Allah. → Therefore, Allah exists.

## Existence and nature of Allah

Muslims believe that the design argument shows that Allah is omnipotent – all powerful. The fact that he was able to design the universe shows his power. Muslims also believe that Allah took time and care to plan and design the world to suit humans. This shows that he cares for his creation and is benevolent and omniscient.

Muslims believe that the Qur'an offers good **philosophical proof** to suggest that Allah exists, and evidence that he designed the world can be seen all around.

## The Qur'an and the design argument

Indeed, in the creation of the heavens and earth, and the alternation of the night and the day, and the [great] ships which sail through the sea with that which benefits people, and what Allah has sent down from the heavens of rain, giving life thereby to the earth after its lifelessness and dispersing therein every [kind of] moving creature, and [His] directing of the winds and the clouds controlled between the heaven and the earth are signs for a people who use reason. (Surah 2:164)

Muslims would respond to non-religious views by arguing that there is no other explanation other than Allah for the amazing world in which we live. How much emphasis Muslims place on the design argument may vary:
- Some will believe it is true, but unnecessary in confirming their belief.
- Others will say it is essential in confirming their belief.

## Non-religious views against design as proof of the existence of Allah

**1** Design might actually be the result of evolution (the idea that species developed gradually over millions of years) and Allah might not be needed to explain the evidence of design in the world.

**2** Evidence of 'design' in the universe only suggests Allah is the designer – it is impossible to 'prove' this idea.

**3** The universe may not be planned and show evidence of design – the argument that it happened by chance is equally strong.

**4** There is evidence of 'bad design' in the world (e.g. volcanoes, earthquakes), which may lead some people to question why a god would design these things. This suggests that Allah did not and, therefore, does not exist.

### Now try this

1 Explain **two** reasons why Muslims believe the design argument is important. **(4 marks)**

2 'The design argument is proof of the existence of Allah.'
Evaluate this statement considering arguments for and against. In your response you should:
- refer to Muslim teachings
- refer to non-religious views
- reach a justified conclusion. **(12 marks)**

# The cosmological argument

The **cosmological argument** tries to prove the existence of Allah by showing that everything happens for a reason. Islam has used this philosophical proof to support the view that Allah exists.

## Overview of the cosmological argument

Nothing happens by itself.

↓

Everything that happens must be **caused** by something else.

↓

The universe cannot have caused itself.

↓

A **powerful** cause was necessary to cause the universe.

↓

This cause has to be Allah.

↓

Therefore, Allah exists.

## The cosmological argument and its use in Islam

The cosmological argument was first put forward in the 12th century in 'the kalam', written by Al-Ghazali in his book 'Kitab al-Iqtisad fil'Itiqad'. Al-Ghazali argued:

| Whatever begins to exist has a cause. | → | The universe began to exist. | → | Therefore, the universe has a cause. |

The Qur'an (Surah 79:27–33) reinforces the idea that Allah created the universe.

### The cosmological argument:

✓ Shows Allah's omnipotence in being able to create the universe.

✓ Shows Allah's omniscience in being able to see everything he created.

✓ Shows Allah caused the universe to exist.

✓ Shows Allah is benevolent and cares for his creation.

✓ Reinforces the teachings in the Qur'an about the creation of the universe.

✓ Supports the beliefs held about what Allah is like.

## Strengths and challenges of the cosmological argument

| Strengths | Challenges |
|---|---|
| Cause and effect can be seen within everything in the universe | Cannot prove that Allah caused the universe |
| Supports the Islamic story of creation in the Qur'an | If we accept everything within the universe has a cause, it doesn't mean that the universe itself has a cause |
| Compatible with scientific theories: if the Big Bang caused the universe, it could itself have been caused by Allah | If everything has a cause, what caused Allah? |
| There must be a first cause of the universe | |

## Non-religious arguments against the cosmological argument and the Muslim response

I believe the scientific explanations of how the universe came about and do not believe in the cosmological argument.

As a Muslim, I agree that science can help us to understand creation. I also accept the existence of a first cause and that cause would be Allah.

### Now try this

'The cosmological argument does not prove the existence of Allah.'

Evaluate this statement considering arguments for and against. In your response you should:

- refer to Muslim teachings
- refer to non-religious points of view
- reach a justified conclusion. **(12 marks)**

Paper 3

# The existence of suffering

**Evil** and **suffering** may create problems for Muslims who believe in Allah as compassionate. It may lead some to question their faith in Allah or even reject his existence altogether.

## Surah 1 and the nature of Allah as compassionate

> In the name of Allah, the Entirely Merciful, the Especially Merciful. [All] praise is [due] to Allah, Lord of the worlds – The Entirely Merciful, the Especially Merciful, Sovereign of the Day of Recompense. It is You we worship and You we ask for help. Guide us to the straight path – The path of those upon whom You have bestowed favour, not of those who have evoked [Your] anger or of those who are astray. (Surah 1:1–7)

This quote from the Qur'an suggests Allah is merciful and forgiving. It also suggests that Allah guides Muslims and helps them. Yet, this view of Allah seems to be in conflict with the fact that there is evil and suffering in the world. It can lead some to question their faith, while others may reject religion altogether.

## Types of evil in the world

**Natural evil**, for example disasters like earthquakes, which may cause multiple deaths and much suffering

**Moral evil**, for example wars that cause death, destruction and suffering

## Suffering and the nature of Allah

If there is suffering and evil in the world, then this raises questions for Muslims as to the compassionate nature of Allah.

If Allah is **all-good**, he would want to remove evil and suffering as he cares for his creation

omnibenevolent

If Allah is **all-knowing**, he would know how to remove evil and suffering

omniscient

**Allah**

If Allah is **all-powerful**, he would be able to remove evil and suffering

omnipotent

## Does Allah exist at all?

Some Muslims may find that evil questions their faith in Allah existing at all.

If he exists, why doesn't he stop the evil?

If Allah existed, there would be no evil.

In your answer you must refer to a source of authority, such as the Qur'an.

## Now try this

Explain **two** reasons why evil and suffering cause a problem for Muslims and their understanding of Allah as compassionate. In your answer you must refer to a source of wisdom and authority. **(5 marks)**

# Solutions to the problem of suffering

The problem of evil and suffering is a challenge for Muslims. They may respond to it in different ways, perhaps by looking to sources of authority such as the Qur'an or offering practical solutions.

## What the Qur'an says about coping with suffering

O you who have believed, seek help through patience and prayer. Indeed, Allah is with the patient. (Surah 2:153)

Muslims believe that the Qur'an commands them to use prayer to cope with challenges in the world – they believe this develops characteristics such as patience.

Surely we shall test you with something of fear and hunger, and loss of wealth and loves and crops … but give glad tidings to the steadfast who say when misfortune strikes: we are Allah's and to Him we are returning. (Surah 2:155–156)

Muslim's believe evil is a test of humanity's freewill – a test of their faith in Allah when things seem difficult. They also believe that they should accept suffering and not question it, as they are taught that Allah is compassionate and they will be reunited with him. (See also Surah 2:177.)

### Life is a test

Muslims live their lives always aware that their actions will determine their afterlife. Most Muslims would recognise that there is a purpose to suffering and it is not their place to question it.

### Prayer

Muslims believe regular prayer is essential and Salah is a requirement to pray five times a day. Prayer would help them to deal with the pain they may be suffering and it will offer comfort from Allah. Some may question whether more practical options have more success in helping others.

**Muslim responses to the problem of evil and suffering**

A person praying.

### Charity

Muslims would believe that charity work is a practical way of helping those who are suffering cope with what they are going through. Many Muslims may feel this has the most impact, as it will directly benefit those who are suffering.

A Zakah box where charity money is collected.

Think about three things that Muslims can do to help relieve suffering.

## Now try this

Outline **three** ways in which Muslims may respond to suffering in the world.     **(3 marks)**

# Human rights

**Human rights** are the basic rights and freedoms to which all human beings are entitled.

## Nature and purpose of human rights

In the UK today, human rights are protected by law. The **Universal Declaration of Human Rights**, adopted by the UN General assembly in 1948, says all humans are born free and equal in dignity and rights. The purpose of human rights is to ensure equality and fairness to humans. Muslims would support human rights being upheld.

Human rights entitles every citizen of the UK to these basic rights.

## Muslim teachings on human rights

 It is our duty in life.

 All humans were created equal by Allah – all Muslims should have the same entitlements.

**3** We stand up against injustice in the world where human rights are being denied.

**4** Muhammad tried to demonstrate the fair treatment of all people and we want to follow his example.

**5** The Qur'an has teachings in it that support human rights.

## Problems of human rights for Muslims

- When there is conflict between a human right and a law within Islam, or where individual conscience seems in conflict.

- When a Muslim sees a conflict between a human right and a law of the country they live in.

- When one human right being applied against another

- When countries have different laws and rules, resulting in inequality.

O you who have believed, be persistently standing firm for Allah, witnesses in justice, and do not let the hatred of a people prevent you from being just. Be just; that is nearer to righteousness. And fear Allah; indeed, Allah is Acquainted with what you do. (Surah 5:8)

This demonstrates that Allah wants his people to be fair and why. Muslims believe they should support human rights.

## Divergent Muslim responses to human rights

☑ The majority of Muslims agree that human rights are important and need to be upheld

☑ It is fair to say that no two situations will ever be the same, yet, when rules and laws are applied, they may be dealt with in the same way, which may seem unfair to some.

☑ Some Muslims may wish for people to be treated differently depending on their circumstances – as in situation ethics.

☑ Some human rights (for example same-sex marriage) may conflict with Islamic teachings, which can cause problems.

## Non-religious views about human rights

I am an atheist and I believe that every person has the right to be treated fairly.

I am a humanist and believe that human rights are at the centre of the beliefs of being a humanist – it is important that people's basic rights are recognised, established and upheld.

**Muslim response:** As a Muslim, I believe in human rights and equality and fairness for all, but I refer to Muslim teachings to justify why.

## Now try this

1 Outline **three** Muslim teachings about human rights.    **(3 marks)**

2 Explain **two** reasons why Muslims may support human rights.    **(4 marks)**

# Equality

Equality is a key idea in Islam. The religion of Islam has many followers across the world in many different countries. They believe all Muslims are part of the ummah and are equal. However, there are many causes of inequality in the world – ignorance, selfishness and greed are some of them.

## Problems caused by inequality and Muslim teachings

The Hadith demonstrates that equality is needed in order for society to be fair. Sometimes the behaviour and attitudes of people can cause inequality, and problems arise as a result, impacting on people's well being. The Hadith shows that whoever commits the crime the same punishment should be given.

Breakdown in communication between people can lead to inequality

> The people of Quraish worried about the lady from Bani Makhzum who had committed theft. They asked, 'Who will intercede for her with Allah's Apostle?' Some said, 'No one dare to do so except Usama bin Zaid the beloved one to Allah's Apostle.' When Usama spoke about that to Allah's Apostle, Allah's Apostle said, (to him), 'Do you try to intercede for somebody in a case connected with Allah's Prescribed Punishments?' Then he got up and delivered a sermon saying, 'What destroyed the nations preceding you, was that if a noble amongst them stole, they would forgive him, and if a poor person amongst them stole, they would inflict Allah's Legal punishment on him. By Allah, if Fatima, the daughter of Muhammad stole, I would cut off her hand. (Sahih al-Bukhari 56:681)

Lack of respect for sources of authority and those in power as people bend the rules when they want to suit themselves leads to inequality

Refusal to follow laws as they do not see them being applied fairly can lead to inequality

## Different Muslim teachings and practices that reflect equality

Islam teaches that all people were created by Allah and created equally, although not the same. This can be interpreted to mean men and women are equal but also unequal.

The Qur'an teaches: 'And among His signs is the creation of the heavens and the earth, and the difference of your languages and colours' (Surah 30:22). This shows that differences between people are not important.

Muslims are united as they are all part of the ummah, regardless of colour and nationality. They have a duty to help others and treat everyone equally.

There are many practices in Islam that show equality: completion of Hajj, all wearing white garments, praying at the same time every day, etc.

Muhammad's final sermon before his death spoke of equality and tolerance.

## Islamic solutions to inequality

Zakah    Muslim Aid    Work of mosques    Prayer

Charity

Islamic Relief

**Solutions to inequality**

Imams speaking out against inequality

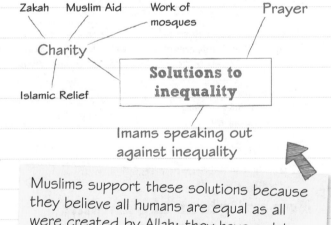

Muslims support these solutions because they believe all humans are equal as all were created by Allah; they have a duty to care for others and they should follow the example of Muhammad.

### Now try this

Explain **two** ways that Muslims work to reduce inequality in the world.  **(4 marks)**

123

# Religious freedom

Muslims believe that having the freedom to be able to choose your religion is important.

## Nature of religious freedom

Religious freedom is when a person is free to choose their religion, change their religion, or choose to not have any religion at all.

Symbols of different religions.

> And Allah is Hearing and Knowing. Allah is the ally of those who believe. He brings them out from darknesses into the light. And those who disbelieve – their allies are Taghut. They take them out of the light into darknesses. Those are the companions of the Fire; they will abide eternally therein. (Surah 2:256–57)

This quote shows that Muslims believe religious freedom is important.

## Living in a multifaith society

### Benefits

| | |
|---|---|
| Greater tolerance and understanding of the beliefs of others | Varied and rich cultural life from experiencing the religions and traditions of others |
| Better understanding of different viewpoints | New ways of living and enjoying life |

### Challenges

| | |
|---|---|
| It is not always easy to be open and understanding towards the views of others | There have been examples of religious persecution and hatred |
| Religious tension exists between different faith groups | Beliefs and values of some groups may be ignored |

Most Muslims in the UK live side by side in harmony with other religious groups.

## Non-religious arguments against religious freedom

Some people with non-religious views may be against religious freedom because of the impact it might have on the lives of others. For example, people might find the methods of killing animals for halal food inhumane and object to Muslims having the right to use these methods. Other examples may include the celebration of religious festivals or allowing Muslims to participate in religious holidays and prayer on a Friday.

## Importance of religious freedom

Religious freedom is a fundamental human right and is part of the Universal Declaration of Human Rights. If this right is upheld, it creates the conditions for peace, and peace is an important idea within Islam. Muslims believe that community is important – demonstrated by the ummah.

## Divergent responses of Muslims to a multifaith society

**Limited religious freedom**

Some believe that Islam is the only true faith and the only religion exclusively correct

Some hold that Islam has the whole truth but other religions have parts of the truth

Some believe they have a mission to lead non-Muslims to Allah

Some accept that all righteous people will be favoured by Allah and, therefore, it does not matter which religion a person belongs to.

**Maximum religious freedom**

### Now try this

'It is difficult for Muslims to live in a multifaith society.'

Evaluate this statement considering arguments for and against. In your response you should:

- refer to Muslim teachings
- refer to different Muslim points of view
- reach a justified conclusion. **(12 marks)**

Use divergent responses of Muslims to a multifaith society to help you.

Muslims would say that religious freedom as part of human rights covers all aspects of their religion.

# Prejudice and discrimination Paper 3

You need to know what the terms **'prejudice'** and **'discrimination'** mean – be careful to make sure you understand each one and don't get them confused!

## Prejudice

Prejudice is pre-judging a person or making a judgement about someone before you actually know them.

Prejudice and discrimination can lead to problems in society. People may find they are in conflict with others and it could lead to physical violence.

## Discrimination

Discrimination is an action – it is when a person is actually treated differently as a result of a prejudice. It can take the form of positive or negative discrimination – when a person is treated positively against others or when a person is treated negatively and unfairly.

O mankind, indeed We have created you from male and female and made you peoples and tribes that you may know one another. Indeed, the most noble of you in the sight of Allah is the most righteous of you. Indeed, Allah is Knowing and Acquainted. (Surah 49:13)

This quote shows the importance of the belief that all humans were created equally by Allah. This is a key teaching when considering why Muslims believe prejudice and discrimination is wrong.

## Muslim teachings on the nature of prejudice and discrimination

1. Muslims believe Allah created all humans – they are equal although not the same – and all deserve equal respect and treatment. This includes people of different religions.

2. Muhammad taught about the importance of treating everyone equally in his final sermon. Therefore, Muslims believe they should treat a person of any faith in the same way.

3. Muslims believe it is important to educate others about religion rather than to treat people differently because they are of a different religion.

## Situation ethics

This ethical theory states that the action that should be taken in moral situations is the one that is considered to be the most loving to the individual in the given situation. However, if humans are equal, they should all be treated the same. This could lead to problems when considering issues of prejudice and discrimination because situation ethics determines that each situation should be taken separately and, therefore, universal, absolute rules cannot be applied. This could result in people being treated differently, which seems to go against teachings such as the Qur'anic one above.

### Now try this

Make sure you state three separate teachings.

Outline **three** Muslim teachings on prejudice and discrimination.    **(3 marks)**

Had a look ☐    Nearly there ☐    Nailed it! ☐

# Racial harmony

Islam teaches that all people are equal and, therefore, racial harmony is essential. All Muslims are part of the ummah – the worldwide Islamic community. Muslims encourage racial harmony with non-Muslim communities as well.

## Muslims and racial harmony

Muslims from all around the world pray together in Arabic – a shared language of all Muslims.

Muhammad declared in his last sermon that 'there is no difference between Arabs and non-Arabs', which means that racism is wrong and people from all races are equal.

Muslims from all around the world face Makkah when praying, attend Hajj and fast during the month of Ramadan.

The Qur'an teaches that no race is better than any other.

There are Muslim organisations who campaign non-violently against racism, e.g. MuslimARC.

| **How Muslims work towards racial harmony** | **Why Muslims work towards racial harmony** |

Muslims believe Allah created all humans equally and, therefore, all humans should be treated the same, regardless of race.

There are examples of individual Muslims who campaigned/ campaign for racial equality, such as Muhammad Ali and Malcolm X.

All Muslims are part of the worldwide ummah and come from every race in the world.

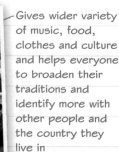

Muhammad Ali and Malcolm X in 1964.

For more on Malcolm X, see page 129.

## Muslim teachings on racial harmony

All mankind is descended from Adam and Eve, an Arab is not better than a non-Arab and a non-Arab is not better than an Arab; a white person is not better than a black person, nor is a black person better than a white person except by piety and good actions. Learn that every Muslim is the brother of every other Muslim and that Muslims form one brotherhood. (From the Final Sermon of Muhammad)

This teaching suggests that racial harmony is important in Islam.

## The benefits of living in a multi-ethnic society

Encourages racial harmony – helps people of different cultures, races and religions to understand each other

Helps to reduce discrimination and race attacks

Brings together people with fresh new ideas – people can learn from those who have different faiths and ethnic backgrounds, as well as sharing their faith and individual ethnic backgrounds

Gives wider variety of music, food, clothes and culture and helps everyone to broaden their traditions and identify more with other people and the country they live in

Community centre, Keighley, West Yorkshire

## Now try this

Make sure you give three different beliefs for this question.

Make sure you explain one benefit and then add a second sentence to develop it fully – this could be more explanation, an example or a quote.

1  Outline **three** reasons why Muslims work for racial harmony.                                    **(3 marks)**

2  Explain **two** benefits for Muslims of living in a multi-ethnic society.                         **(4 marks)**

# Racial discrimination

Discrimination on racial grounds is illegal in the UK. Muslim teachings support these laws to protect people from **racial discrimination**.

## Racial discrimination and our society

Racial discrimination occurs when a person is treated differently, often negatively, because of their race, colour, descent, national or ethnic origin or immigrant status. This could include both positive and negative discrimination.

REST ROOMS
WHITE ←    COLORED →
L&N

A march in Glasgow in 2015 in support of the International Day for the Elimination of Racial Discrimination

In the USA, signs such as these were legal until the Civil Rights Act of 1964 outlawed segregation. Use of the signs persisted illegally for some years after.

## Muslim teachings about racial discrimination

**1** Muslims believe everyone was made equal by Allah.

**2** The Qur'an teaches: 'And of His signs is the creation of the heavens and the earth and the diversity of your languages and your colors. Indeed in that are signs for those of knowledge' (Surah 30:22). This suggests that Islam recognises there is diversity between people in terms of race, but they are all equal.

**3** Muslims recognise that diversity between people can cause problems in society and lead to conflict.

O mankind, indeed We have created you from male and female and made you peoples and tribes that you may know one another. Indeed, the most noble of you in the sight of Allah is the most righteous of you. Indeed, Allah is Knowing and Acquainted. (Surah 49:13)

This quote promotes ideas of equality as it shows all humans were created as equal by Allah. Racial discrimination is wrong for Muslims as Islam recognises that one race is no different from another.

## Malcolm X and divergent Muslim responses to racial discrimination

 Malcolm X was an African-American Muslim who campaigned for racial equality after his family.

✓ He became a minister for the radical Nation of Islam organisation to try to spread the message for a 'Black people only state'.

✓ In his speeches, Malcolm X said that his followers should not start violence but should defend themselves if attacked. Some Muslims today may share his view.

✓ Some Muslims today believe that equality should be achieved by entirely peaceful methods.

For more on Malcolm X, see page 128.

### Now try this

1 Explain **two** Muslim beliefs on racial discrimination. **(4 marks)**

2 'We should all stand up to racial discrimination.'
Evaluate this statement considering arguments for and against. In your response you should:
• refer to Muslim teachings
• reach a justified conclusion.
**(12 marks)**

You are required to consider this statement from different points of view. Make sure you give a Muslim view and refer to their teachings. You could use Malcolm X as an example of a Muslim who was willing to use violence in certain circumstances.

# Social justice

Justice in society is the equal distribution of wealth, opportunities and privileges.

## Wealth and opportunity in the UK and world

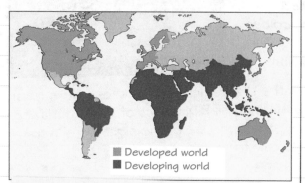

■ Developed world
■ Developing world

Wealth and opportunity are not distributed equally among people in the UK, nor in the rest of the world. Small numbers of people hold very large amounts of wealth, resulting in many people living in poverty. Wealth gives these people far greater opportunities in life than the majority of people worldwide.

## Muslim teachings about social justice

Muslims believe:

✓ they have a duty to work for social justice

✓ Allah is always watching and they will be judged after death by Allah on their actions

✓ all humans are equal as they were made equal by Allah

✓ everyone is human and is entitled to human rights

✓ the Qur'an teaches Muslims they should work for social justice

✓ in Shari'ah law, which promotes social justice

✓ in the Five Pillars, which promote social justice – Zakah (charity) and Sawm (fasting) is done to sympathise with the poor in society

✓ that each situation should be taken individually and appropriate help given – this could be seen to be applying the ethical theory of situation ethics, which means the action taken in each individual situation is what is most loving.

## The Qur'an and social justice

Those who follow the Messenger, the unlettered prophet, whom they find written in what they have of the Torah and the Gospel, who enjoins upon them what is right and forbids them what is wrong and makes lawful for them the good things and prohibits for them the evil and relieves them of their burden and the shackles which were upon them. So they who have believed in him, honored him, supported him and followed the light which was sent down with him – it is those who will be the successful. (Surah 7:157)

This quote talks of the importance of helping others through social justice in order to relieve the inequality within the world.

## Worked example

Outline **three** ways in which Muslims work for social justice. **(3 marks)**

Muslims give Zakah (2.5%) to charity every year. Islamic charities such as Islamic Relief work for social justice. Muslims will try to educate others about social justice.

Other points you could include are the giving of sadaqah (voluntary charitable donations); helping others; and giving other examples of charities, such as Muslim Aid.

## Now try this

Make sure you include a source of wisdom, such as a quote from the Qur'an or Hadith, within at least one of the reasons you explain.

Explain **two** reasons why Muslims work for social justice in the world. In your answer you must refer to a source of wisdom and authority. **(5 marks)**

# Wealth and poverty

Poverty causes great suffering for many people in many countries around the world. The cause of poverty and its effects are of great concern for Muslims. Muslims believe wealth is a gift from Allah that should not be wasted but shared.

## Nature of poverty

Poverty is the state of being extremely poor or lacking in basics. This could lead to a lack of food, safe drinking water, sanitation facilities, health, shelter, education or information.

## Causes of poverty in the UK and world

Poverty is often caused by a number of combined factors. Some of the common causes of poverty are:

1 inequality in wages

2 lack of provision of benefits

3 population growth

4 war

5 unemployment

6 being made homeless

7 illness or injury.

## Muslim teachings about wealth and poverty

Disapproval of greed and waste – all possessions belong to Allah

Expected to act responsibly and help those in need

Paying Zakah

> And be steadfast in prayer and regular in charity: and whatever good ye send forth for your souls before you, ye shall find it with Allah: for Allah sees well all that ye do. (Surah 2:110)

Choosing to give sadaqah

Disagreeing with gambling or lending money for profit

> Righteousness is not that you turn your faces toward the east or the west, but [true] righteousness is [in] one who believes in Allah, the Last Day, the angels, the Book, and the prophets and gives wealth, in spite of love for it, to relatives, orphans, the needy, the traveler, those who ask [for help], and for freeing slaves; [and who] establishes prayer and gives zakah; [those who] fulfill their promise when they promise; and [those who] are patient in poverty and hardship and during battle. Those are the ones who have been true, and it is those who are the righteous. (Surah 2:177)

Believing that every person needs to be treated as an individual and helped according to their needs

Giving to charities such as Muslim Aid and Islamic Relief

Explain each idea fully using evidence and examples to support what you write.

## Now try this

Explain **two** reasons why Muslims believe it is important to share wealth with others. **(4 marks)**

# The paper and (a) type questions

You take two exam papers from a choice of three areas of study. Each area of study must be on a different religion, e.g. Islam and Christianity.

- Paper 1 area of study 1: Religion and Ethics
- Paper 2 area of study 2: Religion, Peace and Conflict
- Paper 3 area of study 3: Religion, Philosophy and Social Justice

Each exam paper is separated into four sections (questions 1, 2, 3 and 4) and each question has four parts: (a), (b), (c) and (d). There are 102 marks available for each paper and you have 1 hour and 45 minutes to complete the paper, giving you 25 minutes to complete each section or 1 minute per mark.

## (a) type questions

(a) type questions are worth 3 marks and ask you to outline or state three things. Aim to spend approximately 3 minutes answering each (a) type question. These may be beliefs, teachings, features, reasons or something else.

For example:

> (a) Outline **three** Muslim beliefs about the nature of Allah.    **(3 marks)**

In this question you are asked to outline three separate beliefs. You must give three beliefs about what Muslims hold to be true about Allah. To be successful, you must give three accurate and factual ideas. Write a brief statement about the three things. You do not need to explain them, give examples (unless asked) or give extra quotes.

### Worked example

> (a) Outline **three** Muslim beliefs about jihad.    **(3 marks)**

One belief is that jihad is a striving every Muslim should make for Allah.

Another belief is that greater jihad (personal struggle) is more important than lesser jihad (outer struggle).

A third Muslim belief is that lesser jihad is understood as being a holy war.

This answer is concise and offers three correct statements.

### Worked example

> (a) Outline **three** Muslim beliefs about Akhirah.
>
>    **(3 marks)**

One Muslim belief is that after death they will be judged by Allah.

Also, they believe that if they are a good Muslim, they will be rewarded in paradise.

This answer makes a good start and offers relevant and accurate information, but it is only a partial answer as it gives two beliefs instead of three.

### Improved sample answer

Muslims believe that after death they are judged by Allah.

They believe good Muslims will go to paradise.

They believe that people who have not been good will go to hell.

**Remember:**
- ✓ Make sure you state three things as required by this type of question.
- ✓ Write each idea in a separate sentence.
- ✓ Keep your answers short and to the point – you are **not** asked to explain the ideas, only state them.

This answer is an improvement as it gives three separate beliefs, which is a requirement of the question.

# (b) type questions

(b) type questions are worth 4 marks and require you to **describe** or **explain** two key areas within the Christian or Islamic faith. Aim to spend approximately 4 minutes answering each (b) type question. This could include beliefs, teachings, ideas, features, events or ways, to name a few.

## Applying your skills

To do well on a (b) type question, you should:

- state **two** points, e.g. two beliefs, teachings or reasons for a Christian or Muslim view
- **develop** each point you give by adding a second sentence that explains the point you have given, adds new information that answers the question or offers an example to demonstrate your understanding. You can also include a quote that is relevant to an example.

### Worked example

(b) Describe **two** ways in which prayer is different for Muslims and Christians. **(4 marks)**

One way that prayer is different for Muslims compared to Christians is that Muslims have set prayers (Salah). Although Christians are expected to pray every day to God, there is no set time.

Another way that prayer is different for Muslims is that they have a set of prayer positions, whereas Christians may sit, stand or kneel during prayer.

> Be aware that you could be asked to compare and contrast how ideas, beliefs or practices are different between one religion and another, as shown in this question.

> The two differences have been described, showing that the student clearly understands the practice of prayer and how it differs between Muslims and Christians. There is no need for development or explanation.

### Worked example

(b) Explain **two** reasons why Muslims believe racial harmony is important. **(4 marks)**

The ummah shows that racial harmony is important. Muhammad spoke about it in his final sermon.

### Improved sample answer

One Muslim belief is that the ummah shows racial harmony is important. The ummah includes all Muslims from every country and every race, showing that Islam teaches all Muslims are equal.

Also, Muhammad spoke about racial harmony in his final sermon. He spoke about there being no difference between Arabs or non-Arabs, showing that he taught all people of every race were equal.

> Although the student has offered **two** reasons, these are briefly stated and not developed. Neither one is fully explained, which is required by this type of question.

> This improved answer gives two different reasons and each one is developed by adding an explanation to show the student fully understands the reasons offered.

### Remember:

- ✓ Make sure that the two reasons you give and develop in your answer are different from each other. You cannot include repetition in your reasons or development.
- ✓ Also make sure that the development you offer relates directly to both the question and the reason you have given.

# (c) type questions

(c) type questions are worth 5 marks and require you to **explain** key areas within the Christian or Islamic faith. Aim to spend approximately 4 minutes answering each (c) type question. This could include beliefs, teachings, ideas, features, events or ways of worship.

## Applying your skills

To do well on a (c) type question, you should:

- state **two** points, e.g. two beliefs, teachings or reasons for a Christian or Muslim view

- **develop** each point you give by adding a second sentence that explains the point you have given, adds new information which answers the question or offers an example to demonstrate your understanding

- add in a relevant **source of authority** for one of the two points given in your answer – this could be ,for example, a quotation from a relevant holy text, or writings and sayings of relevant leaders. This part is only worth 1 mark and can be a paraphrase, so do not worry if you can't remember the exact wording of the source.

## Worked example

(c) Explain **two** reasons why some Muslims will not accept the use of contraception. In your answer you must refer to a source of wisdom and authority.    **(5 marks)**

Some Muslims believe that some forms of contraception actually cause an early abortion, which is considered murder.

Permanent contraception is used to intentionally lead a child-free life, which is against Muslim teachings about the importance of family and that only Allah, not people, should make decisions about life; as the Hadith states: 'No soul which Allah has destined to exist, but will surely come into existence'.

> The two different ideas explained in this answer are both developed, adding further information to the first point made. The second reason has also been linked to a source of wisdom and authority. Remember that this can be from the Hadith, as this example shows.

## Worked example

(c) Explain **two** reasons why forgiveness is important to Muslims. In your answer you must refer to a source of wisdom and authority.    **(5 marks)**

One belief is that Allah is forgiving: 'Allah is Forgiving and Merciful' (Surah 64:14).

Another is that they must follow the example of Muhammad who forgave others.

> This student has offered two reasons but they are not developed, although one quote from a source of authority has been given to support the answer.

## Improved sample answer

Muslims believe that Allah is forgiving, and so it is important for them to be forgiving in their own lives. As the Qur'an says: 'Allah is Forgiving and Merciful.' (Surah 64:14)

Muslims also believe that they must follow the example of Muhammad by forgiving others. If they don't, they cannot expect forgiveness from Allah.

> This improved answer gives two different reasons and each one has been developed by adding new information. The first reason has also been successfully linked to a relevant source of wisdom and authority.

## Remember:

The main difference between type (b) and type (c) questions is that (c) type questions have the added requirement of a reference to a source of wisdom and authority.

# (d) type questions

(d) type questions are worth 12 marks and require you to **evaluate** a stimulus and consider different viewpoints about the significance of a particular aspect of belief. Aim to spend approximately 15 minutes answering each (d) type question.

## Remember:

Questions 1 and 3 of the (d) type questions have 3 extra marks available for your use of **spelling, punctuation and grammar (SPaG)**, as well as your use of **specialist terminology**, making them worth 15 marks. Always go back to check your answers!

## Applying your skills

To do well on a (d) type question, you should:

- consider a **range of viewpoints** on a given statement
- present **justified reasons** for those views within your answer
- try to **use examples** to illustrate the ideas you include
- **include teachings** – where possible, you could quote these within your answer
- **structure your answer** – make your point, develop it and give a source to support it
- use the arguments and reasons offered to create a **justified conclusion**.

## Worked example

(d) 'Everyone should pay Zakah.'
Evaluate this statement considering arguments for and against.
In your response you should:
- refer to Muslim teachings
- refer to different Muslim points of view
- reach a justified conclusion.

**(15 marks)**

Read the question carefully – you could be asked to refer to Muslim teachings, different Muslim points of view, non-religious points of view or even ethical theories. Make sure you check that you have met all the required elements.

Sunni Muslims would agree as they believe Zakah is a religious duty for every Muslim as it is one of the Five Pillars. The money is used to help the poor and needy, which the Qur'an includes when it lists the people – it is 'an obligation [imposed] by Allah' to help.

Caring for others and supporting the ummah (Muslim community) is seen as another duty. Zakah can be used to help all Muslims; therefore, everyone should pay it. As the Qur'an states: '[true] righteousness is [in] one who believes in Allah, the Last Day, the angels, the Book, and the prophets and gives wealth.'

Giving Zakah promotes social justice and equality. These are also important as this is how Muslims believe Allah wants them to live their lives.

This answer offers a coherent argument of agreement, offering a number of reasons that are supported using appropriate quotes from a source of authority.

Some Shi'a Muslims may disagree, believing that Zakah is voluntary and a private decision. They place greater importance on khums as it is one of the Ten Obligatory Acts – Zakah is not the only way to help others. They may also point out that some Muslims are not expected to give Zakah and are exempt, e.g. due to poverty, so it is impossible for everyone to be expected to pay.

Finally, Zakah is a Muslim idea so non-Muslims would not be expected to give this money.

Here, an alternative view is offered. The student has successfully referred to different Muslim points of view through offering the view of Shi'a Islam. A number of reasons have been given to disagree – each with developed evidence and ideas.

Overall, I think most Muslims would agree with this statement as they view Zakah as compulsory and a way of helping others. Even khums is used to help others, showing that Shi'a Muslims believe this idea is important. By paying Zakah, Muslims are showing submission to Allah – the central belief in Islam.

Here, the student has made reasoned judgements that are supported by the evidence and the argument is brought together through the conclusion.

# Answers

*Where an example answer is given, this is not necessarily the only valid response. In most cases there is a range of responses that can gain full marks.*

## Unit 1 Catholic beliefs

### 1 The Trinity

Award 1 mark for each point identified, up to a maximum of 3 marks.
- The Trinity is the way Catholic Christians understand God (1).
- The Trinity is God as Father, Son and Holy Spirit (1).
- Catholics believe in One God understood in three different ways (1).
- The beliefs of the Trinity form the basis of Catholic Christians' relationship with God (1).

Accept any other valid response.

### 2 God as a Trinity of persons

Award 1 mark for each point identified, up to a maximum of 3 marks.
- 2nd-century Theophilus of Antioch was the first person to officially use the term 'Trinity' (1).
- The First Council of Nicaea looked at how the Trinity was first to be understood (1).
- The idea of God as Father and Son was established first; later in CE 381 the Holy Spirit was formally added by the First Council of Constantinople (1).
- The understanding of the Trinity as the Father, Son and Holy Spirit continues to this day (1).

Accept any other valid response.

### 3 Creation

Award 1 mark for each point identified, up to a maximum of 2 marks.
- The literalists' view (1): they accept that only the Bible account is correct and anything that conflicts (e.g. science) is wrong (1).
- The non-literalists' view (1): they accept that religion and science together can explain how the world was created (1).
- Pope Francis as a scientist and leader of the Catholic Church is an important supporter of the non-literalist interpretation of the Creation story (1).

Accept any other valid response.

### 4 The significance of the Creation account

Candidates must underpin their analysis and evaluation with knowledge and understanding. Candidates will be required to demonstrate thorough knowledge and understanding, as well as accuracy of religion and belief when responding to the question and in meeting AO2 descriptors.
Arguments for the statement:
- Humans were given dominion from God. This means they have been given the power to do what they want with the world and can use the world as they like.
- The Bible says humans can rule over the fish, birds and creatures. If this is the case, it suggests that humans are superior and can do as they wish with other living creatures.
- Humans were made 'in the image of God', showing they are special and different to all other creations. This means they can make decisions about what they do to the world.

Arguments against the statement:
- Catholics believe God gave humans stewardship, which is a responsibility to care for the world and his Creation.
- Catholics believe they have responsibilities and duties from God, which means they cannot just use the world as they like.
- Catholics believe they have a purpose in the world and, although they were given dominion, they understand this to be a duty to care for others through stewardship and not to abuse God's Creation.

Accept any other valid response.

### 5 The Incarnation

Award 1 mark for each point identified, up to a maximum of 3 marks.
- Jesus is omnipotent and omniscient (1).
- Jesus forgives sins (1).
- Jesus performed miracles (1).
- People worshipped and prayed to Jesus who is God in human form (1).
- Jesus was resurrected after death (1).

Accept any other valid response.

### 6 Events of the Paschal Mystery

Award 1 mark for each point identified, up to a maximum of 3 marks.
- Catholics believe in the events of the Paschal Mystery – Jesus' passion, his death on the cross, then subsequent resurrection and ascension into heaven (1).
- The Paschal Mystery is linked to the central Catholic belief in mankind's redemption and salvation through Jesus' life and death (1).
- Catholics believe the Paschal Mystery provides proof of an afterlife in heaven (1).

Accept any other valid response.

### 7 Jesus' life, death and resurrection

Candidates must underpin their analysis and evaluation with knowledge and understanding. Candidates will be required to demonstrate thorough knowledge and understanding, as well as accuracy of religion and belief when responding to the question and in meeting AO2 descriptors.

Arguments for the statement:
- These events are crucial to Catholicism, shown by their reference and use in services such as Mass. They symbolise Jesus' sacrifice and the possibility of redemption for all people.
- The events provide hope of an afterlife, which Catholics can follow and achieve where the relationship between God and humanity is restored. Salvation through God's grace becomes possible through Jesus' sacrifice.
- They confirm belief in God and his attributes and characteristics. Through greater knowledge of what God is like, people can become closer to him.

Arguments against the statement:
- Some Christians may argue that, although these beliefs are important, others such as helping other people and caring for the world (stewardship) are just as important. As there are many beliefs within Christianity, it is possible to argue that many are equally important.
- Some Christians may argue that we are now facing new challenges in life that need to be addressed. These challenges were not present in the time when Christianity began, showing that some beliefs may now be out of date.

- Different Christians may place different emphasis on these events today. This means that their interpretation can vary from one person to another and may not always have the same importance.

Accept any other valid response.

## 8 Eschatology

Award 1 mark for each point identified, up to a maximum of 3 marks.

- Catholics believe in heaven, hell and purgatory (1).
- Catholics believe death is not the end (1).
- Some Catholics believe in the resurrection of the body after death, as indicated in the Catechism, while others believe that only the soul is judged by God (1).

Accept any other valid response.

# Unit 2 Marriage and the family

## 9 Marriage

1  Award 1 mark for each point identified, up to a maximum of 3 marks.
   - Marriage is intended to be a lifelong union between a man and a woman (1).
   - Marriage is a sacrament (1).
   - Marriage is the correct context in which to have children (1).
   - Marriage is a promise made before God (1).

   Accept any other valid response.

## 10 Sexual relationships

Award 1 mark for each reason. Award further marks for each development of the reason, up to a maximum of 4 marks. Award 1 further mark for any relevant source of wisdom or authority.

- Sex within marriage is what God intended (1). The purpose of sex is to procreate and the family unit is the best place for this (1): 'God blessed them and said to them, "Be fruitful and increase in number; fill the earth and subdue it"' (Genesis 1:28) (1).
- Adultery is wrong (1). It is forbidden in the Ten Commandments (1): 'You shall not commit adultery' (Exodus 20:14) (1).
- The Catholic Church teaches that fidelity in marriage is important (1). It is part of the Catholic Catechism teaching (1): 'The Sacrament of Matrimony enables man and woman to enter into Christ's fidelity for his Church. Through conjugal chastity, they bear witness to this mystery before the world' (CCC 2365) (1).

Accept any other valid response.

## 11 Families

Award 1 mark for each point identified, up to a maximum of 3 marks.

- The family is the right place for a married couple to have children (1).
- The family is believed to provide stability and security for society (1).
- The family is where children can be educated (1).

Accept any other valid response.

- Family is regarded as the foundation of society (1). The Bible has many references to the importance of family, citing that it provides stability (1).
- It is where children are raised and educated (1). They can be taught the difference between right and wrong (1).
- It is where children are raised as Catholic Christians (1). It is where they can be introduced to rites of passage, worship and Catholic Christian morals (1).

Accept any other valid response.

## 12 Support for the family in the Catholic parish

1  Award 1 mark for each reason. Award further marks for each development of the reason, up to a maximum of 4 marks.
   - Classes for parents and children (1). Classes to help new parents gain experience and Catechism classes for children to be raised in the Catholic faith (1).
   - Shorter Masses and special children's liturgies (1). These will introduce children to services and help them understand the key teaching being promoted (1).
   - Support to bind members of the family together (1). The Family Group Movement is an example of a group providing support, including opportunities for families to talk and discuss (1).

   Accept any other valid response.

2  Candidates must underpin their analysis and evaluation with knowledge and understanding. Candidates will be required to demonstrate thorough knowledge and understanding, as well as accuracy of religion and belief when responding to the question and in meeting AO2 descriptors.

   Arguments for the statement:
   - Catholics believe they have a duty or responsibility to support the family as this is what God intended. The Bible talks about the importance of family and how the Christian community should support this ideal.
   - Many forms of support such as classes can be practical or events that have a social nature can help the family. These can help to bring family members together and share things they have in common.
   - The family is at the centre of Catholic beliefs; it is where faith is instilled and education can happen so the parish has an important role in this. Children can be raised as good Christians and introduced to the Catholic faith.

   Arguments against the statement:
   - Many people may want to have support outside their religious community.
   - Sometimes a family might not want to share their problems.
   - Some people are not religious and do not want support from a religious community.

   Accept any other valid response.

## 13 Family planning

Award 1 mark for each reason. Award further marks for each development of the reason, up to a maximum of 4 marks.

- The use of artificial forms of contraception intentionally avoids the conception of a child (1). Catholics believe this goes against God's teaching to procreate (1).
- Artificial methods of contraception put a barrier between husband and wife (1). A sexual relationship is supposed to be natural, so artificial forms of contraception are wrong (1).
- The *Humanae Vitae* by Pope Paul VI does not accept the use of artificial contraception (1). He argued its use is a sin against God because God's wish is for people to procreate (1).

Accept any other valid response.

## 14 Divorce

1  Award 1 mark for each point identified, up to a maximum of 3 marks.
   - Catholics do not accept divorce (1).
   - Catholics believe marriage is intended to be for life (1).
   - Catholics will accept an annulment in certain circumstances (1).
   - Catholics view divorce and remarriage as adultery (1).

   Accept any other valid response.

## 15 Men and women in the family

1 Award 1 mark for each point identified, up to a maximum of 3 marks.
- Men are traditionally seen as being providers in the family (1).
- Women are traditionally seen as having the role of caring for the home and children in the family (1).
- Catholics view men and women in the family as equal, as this is what the Bible says (1).
- Catholics believe men and women are suited to different family roles, although both are of equal value (1).

Accept any other valid response.

## 16 Gender prejudice and discrimination

Candidates must underpin their analysis and evaluation with knowledge and understanding. Candidates will be required to demonstrate thorough knowledge and understanding, as well as accuracy of religion and belief when responding to the question and in meeting AO2 descriptors.

Arguments for the statement:
- Some Christians believe God created all humans equally; they should therefore be treated the same in all areas of life – including in their religious life.
- Some Christians believe Jesus showed that all people should be treated with the same respect. He associated with the poor, sick and needy, as well as women in society who may not have been regarded as important as men.
- Many Christians believe that God intended for all humans – men and women – to be treated as having the same value. There are many Bible quotes that support this.

Arguments against the statement:
- Catholics believe that men and women are equal but may be suited to different roles. For example, in jobs where physical strength is needed, men may be better suited. Current teaching does not accept that women can be priests, as this represents the role of Jesus who was male.

Accept any other valid response.

# Unit 3 Living the Catholic life

## 17 Sacramental nature of reality

Award 1 mark for each point identified, up to a maximum of 3 marks.
- Baptism usually takes place at the font (1).
- Godparents make promises to raise the child as a Catholic Christian (1).
- A lit candle is used (1).
- Water is poured over the head of the person (1).
- Baptism welcomes the child into the Catholic community (1).

Accept any other valid response.

## 18 Liturgical worship

Award 1 mark for each point identified, up to a maximum of 3 marks.
- Liturgical worship has a set structure (1).
- It includes services such as the Eucharist (1).
- The sign of the cross may be made (1).
- Set prayers will be spoken (1).
- Hymns may be sung (1).

Accept any other valid response.

## 19 Liturgy of the funeral rite

1 Award 1 mark for each point identified, up to a maximum of 3 marks.
- There may be a vigil with prayers (1).
- The coffin is carried into church while the Office of the Dead is recited/sung (1).
- The body in the coffin is covered with a pall (1).
- A Paschal candle is lit (1).
- A requiem Mass may be spoken or sung (1).
- The coffin is sprinkled with holy water (1).
- The coffin is buried while prayers are said (1).

Accept any other valid response.

2 Candidates must underpin their analysis and evaluation with knowledge and understanding. Candidates will be required to demonstrate thorough knowledge and understanding, as well as accuracy of religion and belief when responding to the question and in meeting AO2 descriptors.

Arguments for the statement:
- Some non-religious people may favour a more personal or individual way of saying goodbye. Some people are not religious and may not want religious rituals performed.
- Some Christians may not want the set structure of the Catholic funeral service and may want an individual ceremony. Different Christian denominations place different importance on elements of the service being formal or informal.
- Some people today may feel that it is hypocritical for a person to have a religious ceremony, especially if they do not believe in God or have not spent their life being religious. They may not want religious readings during the ceremony.

Arguments against the statement:
- A funeral ceremony of some kind brings closure and acceptance that a person has died. It allows people time to remember, grieve for the person and move on with their lives.
- It is a way of saying goodbye to the person and celebrating their life. It helps bring closure to family and friends left behind.
- It is a method of remembering Jesus' sacrifice and his overcoming death. It provides hope of eternal life with God for the deceased and the Catholic community especially.

Accept any other valid response.

## 20 Prayer

Award 1 mark for each reason. Award further marks for each development of the reason, up to a maximum of 4 marks. Award 1 further mark for any relevant source of wisdom or authority.
- Prayer is a way of communicating with God (1). Through prayer, Catholics are able to develop a personal relationship with God and affirm their belief about his nature (1): 'In the name of the Father, and of the Son, and of the Holy Spirit. Amen' (1).
- Jesus commands people to pray in the Bible (1); it is considered to be an important part of being a Christian (1): 'Pray without ceasing. In all circumstances give thanks, for this is the will of God for you in Christ Jesus' (1 Thes 5:17–18) (1).
- Prayer helps to deepen a person's faith (1). Catholics can understand God and their religion better through the reflection of prayer (1): St Paul says 'Prayer is the raising of one's mind and heart to God or the requesting of good things from God' (CCC 2590) (1).

Accept any other valid response.

## 21 Popular piety

Award 1 mark for each reason. Award further marks for each development of the reason, up to a maximum of 4 marks.
- The Catholic Catechism emphasises that it is acceptable to have different forms of worship (1). Demonstrating devotion to the Catholic faith through a variety of forms of piety is seen as important for developing a stronger relationship with God (1).
- Catholics believe popular piety can strengthen faith (1). Key teachings, beliefs and ideas are included in the Rosary, giving time to reflect on the meaning of the Catholic faith (1).
- Popular piety can help Catholics celebrate key events in the Christian calendar (1). For example, the Stations of the Cross are a powerful reminder of Jesus' suffering and sacrifice during Lent and on Good Friday (1).

Accept any other valid response.

## 22 Pilgrimage

Award 1 mark for each reason. Award further marks for each development of the reason, up to a maximum of 4 marks. Award 1 further mark for any relevant source of wisdom or authority.
- Some places such as Rome have religious significance for Catholics (1). They believe they have been instructed to visit places of religious significance (1): 'Pilgrimages evoke our earthly journey toward heaven and are traditionally very special occasions for renewal in prayer. For pilgrims seeking living water, shrines are special places for living the forms of Christian prayer "in Church"' (CCC 2691) (1).
- Pilgrimage helps Catholics get closer to God (1). Many Catholics believe they can strengthen their faith and help renew their faith and worship (1): 'Pilgrimages evoke our earthly journey toward heaven and are traditionally very special occasions for renewal in prayer. For pilgrims seeking living water, shrines are special places for living the forms of Christian prayer "in Church"' (CCC 2691) (1).
- Catholics may visit places of importance (1). The Virgin Mary has been seen at many sites Catholics visit and she is venerated in Catholicism (1): 'The most appropriate places for prayer are… places of pilgrimage' (CCC 2696) (1).

Accept any other valid response.

## 23 Catholic social teaching

Award 1 mark for each reason. Award further marks for each development of the reason, up to a maximum of 4 marks. Award 1 further mark for any relevant source of wisdom or authority.
- The Bible talks of helping others (1). The Parable of the Sheep and the Goats suggests rewards for those who show kindness towards others (1): 'For I was hungry and you gave me something to eat, I was thirsty and you gave me something to drink, I was a stranger and you invited me in, I needed clothes and you clothed me, I was sick and you looked after me, I was in prison and you came to visit me' (Matthew 25:35–36) (1).
  Students do not have to reproduce the whole quote here – any relevant part will be credited.
- The Bible teaching to 'love thy neighbour' is important (1). It suggests we should help others and is reiterated in the Catholic Church Catechism (1): '"You shall love your neighbour as yourself." There is no other commandment greater' (CCC 2196) (1).
- Pope Francis has taught about the importance of helping others in society (1). In *Evangelii Gaudium* he argued for including the poor in society (1): 'The earth is our common home and all of us are brothers and sisters' (*Evangeli Gaudium* 183) (1).

Accept any other valid response.

## 24 Mission and evangelism

Award 1 mark for each point identified, up to a maximum of 3 marks.
- Evangelism work is commanded in the Bible (1).
- Pope Francis raised awareness about helping others (1).
- Teachings such as the Parable of the Sheep and the Goats teach this (1).
- It is following the example of Jesus (1).
- Helping others is a duty for Catholics (1).

Accept any other valid response.

# Unit 4 Matters of life and death

## 25 Origins of the universe

Award 1 mark for each point identified, up to a maximum of 3 marks.
- God created it (1).
- God made it for humans (1).
- They should thank God for his Creation (1).
- God gave humans stewardship (1).
- The universe is a gift (1).

Accept any other valid response.

## 26 Sanctity of life

1 Award 1 mark for each reason. Award further marks for each development of the reason, up to a maximum of 4 marks. Award 1 further mark for any relevant source of wisdom or authority.
   - It was created by God (1). Humans were made to be special and different to all of God's other creations (1): 'So God created mankind in his own image, in the image of God he created them; male and female he created them' (Genesis 1:27) (1).
   - Life belongs to God (1). He created it and the Bible teaches that humans should value it (1): 'You shall not commit murder' (Exodus 20) (1).
   - The Bible refers to the body as a 'temple' (1). This suggests respect should be shown towards something God created and made to be special and holy (1): 'Your body is a temple of the Holy Spirit' (1 Corinthians 6:19) (1).

   Accept any other valid response.

2 Candidates must underpin their analysis and evaluation with knowledge and understanding. Candidates will be required to demonstrate thorough knowledge and understanding, as well as accuracy of religion and belief when responding to the question and in meeting AO2 descriptors.

   Arguments for the statement:
   - Many passages in the Bible teach that life is special and are still relevant today; life was created by God and should be valued.
   - Catholics believe God made man 'in his image' and this teaching does not change; it does not mean humans look like God, but that they have the ability to develop like God.
   - Teachings about the sanctity of life argument can be used to inform actions in cases of abortion and euthanasia; they give guidance on what is the right action and why.

   Arguments against the statement:
   - Some people may believe these teachings are out of date; the Bible was written so long ago that it is not relevant to life today.

- Some people may want variety and choice rather than absolute rules in ethical situations; this means that teachings on the sanctity of life may not be relevant today.
- Some people today may not be religious; these teachings may not be relevant to all.

Accept any other valid response.

## 27 Origins of human life

Award 1 mark for each point identified, up to a maximum of 3 marks.

- Catholics accept that science and religion can work together to explain the origins of human life.
- Pope Francis made a statement about how evolution was part of God's plan and, as Head of the Church, his teaching is accepted by Catholics.
- Catholics believe that God's involvement in all creation is still necessary to explain humans coming into existence and their continuation.

Accept any other valid response.

## 28 Abortion

Candidates must underpin their analysis and evaluation with knowledge and understanding. Candidates will be required to demonstrate thorough knowledge and understanding, as well as accuracy of religion and belief when responding to the question and in meeting AO2 descriptors.

Arguments for the statement:

- Catholics believe in the sanctity of life; life is special and sacred as it was created by God. They therefore would always view abortion as wrong.
- Catholics follow Bible teachings about abortion being wrong. Teachings such as the Ten Commandments say murder is wrong and influence Catholics against abortion.
- Catholics follow the *Humanae Vitae* by Pope John Paul II, which states that abortion is wrong. Following this means they believe it is an absolute and unchangeable rule.

Arguments against the statement:

- Some Christians do not like abortion, but accept that it may sometimes be a necessary option. They would therefore argue that sometimes abortion is not wrong.
- Non-religious people may believe life is special, but may also think that in issues such as abortion it is up to the mother to make the correct decision for herself.
- Ethical theories such as situation ethics teach that the correct action is what is best in the given situation; abortion may sometimes therefore be acceptable.

Accept any other valid response.

## 29 Life after death

Award 1 mark for each reason. Award further marks for each development of the reason, up to a maximum of 4 marks.

- They accept the resurrection of Jesus (1). They believe that Jesus coming back to life after death demonstrates there is an afterlife (1).
- The Bible contains many teachings about the afterlife (1). It says that God has prepared a place for people in heaven (1).
- It makes sense to accept there is reward and punishment after death (1). Catholics believe that if people try to act as God wants, they will be rewarded (1).

Accept any other valid response.

## 30 Non-religious arguments against life after death

Award 1 mark for each reason. Award further marks for each development of the reason, up to a maximum of 4 marks.

- Catholics believe that Bible teachings provide evidence of life after death, which disproves non-religious arguments of no evidence (1). The Bible teaches of an afterlife with God as a reward for a good life on Earth and Catholics accept this without question (1).
- They use Jesus' resurrection as evidence against non-religious arguments that there is no proof of life after death (1). It shows that if they follow Jesus' example, they too can achieve salvation in heaven (1).
- They believe that having faith means trusting in God's love for his Creation, and that such belief is not false comfort (1). The Bible has promised an afterlife, so they accept that having faith means trusting in this and believing God will provide for them after death (1).

Accept any other valid response.

## 31 Euthanasia

Award 1 mark for each reason. Award further marks for each development of the reason, up to a maximum of 4 marks. Award 1 further mark for any relevant source of wisdom or authority.

- Catholics believe euthanasia is always wrong (1). Life is special as it is a gift from God and humans were made in his image (1): 'So God created man in his own image...' (Genesis 1:27) (1).
- Catholics regard euthanasia as murder (1). The Ten Commandments, which are rules from God, state murder is always wrong (1): 'You shall not commit murder' (1).
- The Catholic Church Catechism teaches that euthanasia is wrong (1). Catholics value all life as a gift from God (1): 'Those whose lives are diminished or weakened deserve special respect. Sick or handicapped persons should be helped to lead lives as normal as possible. Whatever its motives and means, direct euthanasia consists in putting an end to the lives of handicapped, sick, or dying persons. It is morally unacceptable' (CCC 2276–2277) (1).

Accept any other valid response.

## 32 Issues in the natural world

Award 1 mark for each point identified, up to a maximum of 3 marks.

- They have a duty of stewardship (1).
- They should care for the world because it is God's Creation (1).
- Catholics believe they will be judged on how they care for the world (1).
- They should not waste the Earth's resources (1).
- They should care for the world for future generations (1).

Accept any other valid response.

# Unit 5 Crime and punishment

## 33 Justice

Award 1 mark for each point identified, up to a maximum of 3 marks.

- The Bible states that justice is important (1).
- Catholics believe all humans deserve equal treatment (1).
- They follow the teachings of Jesus (1).
- God is understood to be just (1).
- God expects humans to act justly (1).

Accept any other valid response.

## 34 Crime

Award 1 mark for each reason. Award further marks for each development of the reason, up to a maximum of 4 marks. Award 1 further mark for any relevant source of wisdom or authority.

- Christians believe everyone has the potential to sin (1). This Bible teaching suggests no human is perfect (1): 'Everyone sins and falls short of God's standards' (Romans 3:22) (1).
- Catholics believe the causes of crime are not always the fault of an individual (1). People's upbringing, situation in terms of money or ability to better themselves may make them give in to the temptation of a life of crime (1): 'People sin when they give in to the temptations of their own evil desires' (James 1:14) (1).
- Catholics believe they have a responsibility from God to help others (1). This duty, known as stewardship, includes caring for all humans as they were created by God; anyone not doing this is sinning against God (1): 'Anyone, then, who knows the good he ought to do but does not do it, sins' (James 4:17) (1).

Accept any other valid response.

## 35 Good, evil and suffering

Award 1 mark for each reason. Award further marks for each development of the reason, up to a maximum of 4 marks.

- Some people choose to exercise free will and turn away from God, which results in evil and suffering (1). This is in Jesus' Parable of the Sheep and the Goats (1).
- Suffering is a test of faith (1). Catholics follow the teachings of the Bible and Jesus to understand that a caring God can exist despite human suffering (1).
- Everyone suffers (1). Suffering can make a person stronger (1).

Accept any other valid response.

## 36 Punishment

1 Award 1 mark for each reason. Award further marks for each development of the reason, up to a maximum of 4 marks.

- There are Bible teachings on punishment for wrongdoing (1). They suggest that when a crime has been committed, a person deserves to be punished (1).
- Punishment helps people learn that their behaviour is wrong (1). It gives them an opportunity to change and become better citizens in society (1).
- Some Catholic teachings suggest God will judge people for their actions for the afterlife (1). God is presented in the Bible as a God of justice, suggesting that crimes should be punished (1).

Accept any other valid response.

2 Award 1 mark for each reason. Award further marks for each development of the reason, up to a maximum of 4 marks. Award 1 further mark for any relevant source of wisdom or authority.

- Catholics are taught to treat others the way they would want to be treated – fairly and with justice (1). Punishments need to be applied when necessary (1): 'If, however, non-lethal means are sufficient to defend and protect people's safety from the aggressor, authority should limit itself to such means, as these are more in keeping with the concrete conditions of the common good and more in conformity with the dignity of the human person' (CCC 2267).

- When punishment is required, Catholics are taught it is important to be merciful as God was merciful (1). Fairness is important and God teaches us to forgive so we can move on with our lives (1): 'Be merciful, just as your Father is merciful… Do not judge and you will not be judged. Do not condemn, and you will not be condemned. Forgive and you will be forgiven' (Luke 6:36–37).
- Catholics follow Jesus' teaching – he used parables to teach about punishment (1). Fairness and justice are seen as important in cases where punishment is required (1): 'The servant who knows the master's will and does not get ready or does not do what the master wants will be beaten with many blows. But the one who does not know and does things deserving punishment will be beaten with few blows. From everyone who has been given much, much will be demanded; and from the one who has been entrusted with much, much more will be asked' (Luke 12:47–48) (1).

Accept any other valid response.

## 37 Aims of punishment

Award 1 mark for each reason. Award further marks for each development of the reason, up to a maximum of 4 marks.

- Catholics do not agree with revenge as an aim of punishment (1). The only way Catholics would see a purpose in retribution is through making a criminal realise and accept that what they have done is wrong (1).
- Catholics believe the main aim of punishment is to allow criminals time to reform and change their behaviour (1). If this condition is not met, Catholics might not always accept that a punishment is necessary (1).
- Catholics believe the aims of punishment are to help society and protect people from potentially harmful criminals (1). If these conditions are not met, Catholics might not always accept that a punishment is necessary (1).

Accept any other valid response.

## 38 Forgiveness

Award 1 mark for each point identified, up to a maximum of 3 marks.

- Jesus taught about forgiveness (1).
- Catholics are taught they should try to forgive when others wrong them (1).
- Forgiveness is taught in the Lord's Prayer (1).
- Catholics believe it is important to repent and ask for forgiveness when they do wrong (1).
- Catholics believe in the power of the sacrament of reconciliation to achieve forgiveness (1).

Accept any other valid response.

## 39 Treatment of criminals

Award 1 mark for each point identified, up to a maximum of 3 marks.

- Criminals are also humans and were created by God (1).
- All human life deserves respect and dignity, including criminals (1).
- All humans, including criminals, are entitled to basic human rights (1).
- Justice and fair punishment for wrongdoing is a key Catholic teaching (1).
- The Bible teaches that all should be treated justly according to what they deserve, including criminals (1).

Accept any other valid response.

## 40 Capital punishment

Candidates must underpin their analysis and evaluation with knowledge and understanding. Candidates will be required to demonstrate thorough knowledge and understanding, as well as accuracy of religion and belief when responding to the question and in meeting AO2 descriptors.

Arguments for the statement:
- Some Catholics would agree, as some Bible teachings suggest that capital punishment is acceptable. The Old Testament implies that for serious crimes, the death penalty should be used and it therefore should be brought back: 'Anyone who strikes a person with a fatal blow is to be put to death' (Exodus 21:12).
- Some Bible teachings can be used to support its return – such as 'Whoever sheds the blood of man, by man shall his blood be shed' (Genesis 9:6). If a source of authority supports it, it would be acceptable to bring it back.
- The death penalty has been used as a form of punishment and deterrence in the past. If it was a successful deterrent, there is an argument that it should be brought back.

Arguments against the statement:
- In cases of miscarriages of justice, innocent people could be put to death. This is not a risk worth taking.
- Although the death penalty was used in the past, this doesn't mean that it should be brought back, and there is no real proof that it acted as a deterrent.
- There are many biblical teachings that suggest the death penalty is wrong. The Ten Commandments contain God's teaching that it is wrong to take life, which would make capital punishment wrong under any circumstances.
- Many non-religious people, as well as many religious believers, may claim that it is not justice for someone to have their life taken away, as this is too easy a punishment; instead, they should be made to 'pay' for their crime, especially if it is serious, by a life of imprisonment with the possibility of repentance.

Accept any other valid response.

# Unit 6 Peace and conflict

## 41 Peace

Award 1 mark for each point identified, up to a maximum of 3 marks.
- Jesus is called the 'Prince of peace' (1).
- Jesus taught about the importance of peace between people (1).
- Peace is what God intended for the world (1).
- The Bible states peace is what God wants for people (1).
- Jesus is seen as a peacemaker by Catholics (1).

Accept any other valid response.

## 42 Peacemaking

Award 1 mark for each point identified, up to a maximum of 3 marks.
- Pax Christi campaigns against military spending on weapons (1).
- Pax Christi tries to educate people about the work they do in the world (1).
- Pax Christi works to try and bring peace in places in the world, such as Israel (1).
- Pax Christi encourages peace talks between nations (1).
- Pax Christi holds peace vigils (1).

Accept any other valid response.

## 43 Conflict

Award 1 mark for each point identified, up to a maximum of 3 marks.

- Catholics may work to reconcile people (1).
- They may adopt a position of pacifism (1).
- They may refer to examples of conflict resolution in the Bible (1).
- They may refer to Jesus' teaching that people should work together in peace (1).

Accept any other valid response.

## 44 Pacifism

Candidates must underpin their analysis and evaluation with knowledge and understanding. Candidates will be required to demonstrate thorough knowledge and understanding, as well as accuracy of religion and belief when responding to the question and in meeting AO2 descriptors.

Arguments for the statement:
- Some Catholics may agree, believing that peace is always the answer, not violence. There are many Bible teachings such as 'do to others as you would have them do to you' (Luke 6:31) that support the idea of peace; if everyone followed these, peace could be achieved.
- Quakers would agree as they are pacifists and do not accept any form of violence. They believe they should always act justly and peacefully, and if everyone behaved this way more could be achieved.
- Some Catholics may agree, as they may support ideas of pacifism and passive resistance, believing the only way to bring about change is not to use violence. They may refer to examples of Jesus' avoidance of conflict, such as when the disciples wanted to use violence when he was arrested in the Garden of Gethsemane.

Arguments against the statement:
- People such as Martin Luther King achieved a lot by peaceful means, but he was assassinated so paid for his principles with his life, which for some might represent too great a sacrifice.
- The Bible suggests that sometimes violent means have to be used in cases where attempts at all peaceful solutions have been exhausted.
- Non-religious people may believe that in today's modern warfare the only way to bring about peace and work together is to use violence initially.

Accept any other valid response.

## 45 The Just War theory

Award 1 mark for each reason. Award further marks for each development of the reason, up to a maximum of 4 marks.
- The Bible recognises that sometimes war is necessary (1). It suggests that war may be acceptable if all peaceful methods to reach a solution have been tried and have failed (1).
- The Catholic Church Catechism has teachings that are similar to the Just War theory (1). This is a source of authority for Catholics and suggests that sometimes war is acceptable (1).
- Jesus and St Paul taught about obedience to the government of the country where you live (1). If a valid source of authority has made the decision that war is correct, the Bible teaches that this should be followed (1).

Accept any other valid response.

## 46 Holy war

Award 1 mark for each reason. Award further marks for each development of the reason, up to a maximum of 4 marks.
- Catholics believe that Bible teachings suggest any war is wrong, which would also include holy war (1). Jesus taught about peace and showed this was the way forward rather than using violence (1).

- Catholics believe all human life is sacred and should not be taken away (1). It was created by God and therefore is special, so Catholics believe war – which causes people's deaths – is wrong (1).
- Catholics support ideas of justice and reconciliation between people rather than war (1). They believe God created a world where people should get on with each other, despite any religious differences between them (1).

Accept any other valid response.

## 47 Weapons of mass destruction

Candidates must underpin their analysis and evaluation with knowledge and understanding. Candidates will be required to demonstrate thorough knowledge and understanding, as well as accuracy of religion and belief when responding to the question and in meeting AO2 descriptors

Arguments for the statement:
- Catholic teachings show peaceful methods should be found rather than using violence. Jesus taught that peace was the solution, not violence, so WMD should not be used.
- One major problem with WMD is that they do not distinguish between soldiers fighting and innocent civilians. As human life is sacred because it was created by God, the use of WMD cannot be justified.
- WMD damage the environment, which was created by God. Humans were given stewardship, which is a responsibility to care for the world, not damage it, so WMD should not be used.

Arguments against the statement:
- Some people may believe that the benefits of WMD outweigh the problems. Maintaining the weapons as a threat may prevent having to use violence.
- Some non-religious people may not have a problem with using WMD, believing that some circumstances call for the most extreme possible use of violence in order to bring peace.
- Some people may believe that WMD are a necessity in today's world to face threats such as terrorism, and that there is no other way to bring peace, therefore their use is justified.

Accept any other valid response.

## 48 Issues surrounding conflict

Award 1 mark for each reason. Award further marks for each development of the reason, up to a maximum of 4 marks.
- Some Catholics have spoken out against injustice (1). Dorothy Day used her newspaper *Catholic Worker* to highlight injustices such as the denial of women's rights (1).
- Some people have given their lives to a just cause of conflict (1). Oscar Romero was assassinated for speaking up against injustices, such as the army killing innocent people (1).
- Some people have used Bible teachings to show that conflict and violence is wrong (1). They have spoken out and shared Jesus' teaching of non-violence, such as in the Garden of Gethsemane, to demonstrate that violence does not bring peace (1).

Accept any other valid response.

# Unit 7 Philosophy of religion

## 49 Revelation

1  Award 1 mark for each point identified, up to a maximum of 3 marks.
- God is omnipotent and omnipresent (1).
- He is benevolent (1).
- He wants to communicate with humanity (1).
- He is transcendent (1).
- He is immanent (1).

Accept any other valid response.

2  Award 1 mark for each reason. Award further marks for each development of the reason, up to a maximum of 4 marks.
- Jesus is understood to be the 'culmination' of God's plan (1). He is the final and best part of God's Creation, as he was sent to save the sins of the whole world and demonstrate to Catholics how they should live their lives (1).
- Catholics believe Jesus was sent to Earth to save the sins of the whole world (1). His purpose was to repair the broken relationship between God and humanity so all humans could go to heaven and be with God (1).
- Jesus is God incarnate (1). Through Jesus, Catholics can understand God's nature (1).

Accept any other valid response.

## 50 Visions (1)

Award 1 mark for each point identified, up to a maximum of 3 marks.
- Transfiguration of Jesus (1).
- Covenant made with Abraham (1).
- Joan of Arc (1).
- St Bernadette of Lourdes (1).
- Dreams of Joseph (1).

Accept any other valid response.

## 51 Visions (2)

Award 1 mark for each reason. Award further marks for each development of the reason, up to a maximum of 4 marks. Award 1 further mark for any relevant source of wisdom or authority.
- Visions reveal the omnipotence (power) of God (1). This can be seen in the vision of the transfiguration of Jesus, where the prophets Moses and Elijah are seen (1): 'There he was transfigured before them. His face shone like the sun, and his clothes became as white as the light. Just then there appeared before them Moses and Elijah, talking with Jesus' (Matthew 17:2–3) (1).
- Visions reveal the benevolence that God feels towards the world (1). This can be seen in the covenant he makes with Abraham for him to have descendants and land (1): 'After this, the word of the Lord came to Abram in a vision: "Do not be afraid, Abram. I am your shield, your very great reward"' (Genesis 15:1) (1).
- Visions reveal the all-knowing nature of God and his wish to communicate with humanity (1). This can be seen in the visions received by prophets who passed important messages on to humanity (1): 'After this, the word of the Lord came to Abram in a vision: "Do not be afraid, Abram. I am your shield, your very great reward"' (Genesis 15:1) (1).

Accept any other valid response.

## 52 Miracles

Award 1 mark for each reason. Award further marks for each development of the reason, up to a maximum of 4 marks.
- People are amazed by miraculous happenings because they are not usual occurrences (1). They cannot be explained any other way – e.g. by science – except through God (1).
- Catholics believe that miracles are evidence of God's existence and help them understand what he is like (1). It shows God intervening in individual lives and caring for his Creation (1).
- Catholics believe that miracles confirm their faith in God (1). Examples in the Bible and non-biblical examples strengthen everything their faith teaches them (1).

Accept any other valid response.

## 53 Religious experiences

Candidates must underpin their analysis and evaluation with knowledge and understanding. Candidates will be required to demonstrate thorough knowledge and understanding, as well as accuracy of religion and belief when responding to the question and in meeting AO2 descriptors.

Arguments for the statement:

- Non-religious people claim that it could be wish fulfilment, that people want to experience God or a higher being and so interpret normal everyday events as 'religious'. If this is what proof of God's existence is based on, the 'evidence' does not provide proof.
- Some people claim that the use of stimulants such as drugs or alcohol could make people think they have had a religious experience when they are just under the influence of what they have taken. This does not provide proof that God exists.
- Some people have been known to claim to have had religious experiences of God when in reality they have mental health issues. This is not good proof of God's existence.

Arguments against the statement:

- Catholics would argue that religious experience helps them to understand God. The Catholic Church recognises (CCC 66) that religious experience alone is not evidence of God as it needs to be interpreted and understood fully, but it helps to confirm faith in God's existence.
- Catholics would argue that the Bible and Jesus' stories are proof of God's existence. The Bible contains the Word of God and his teachings about how he wants people to live their lives. This is sufficient proof of God's existence.
- Catholics may argue that faith is about trusting God and you cannot necessarily have 'proof' of that. Having faith is subjective and individual proof is actually not required.

Accept any other valid response.

## 54 The design argument

Award 1 mark for each reason. Award further marks for each development of the reason, up to a maximum of 4 marks.

- The design argument shows God's power (1). His power is shown in the way he designed the universe to suit human life, e.g. green plants to provide oxygen (1).
- The design argument shows the benevolence God feels towards his Creation (1). In wanting to create a world that suits humans, God planned it the way it is (1).
- The design argument shows God's unknowable nature – his transcendence (1). God is so great that humans cannot grasp him fully even through all he designed and created (1).

Accept any other valid response.

## 55 The cosmological argument

Candidates must underpin their analysis and evaluation with knowledge and understanding. Candidates will be required to demonstrate thorough knowledge and understanding, as well as accuracy of religion and belief when responding to the question and in meeting AO2 descriptors.

Arguments for the statement:

- Catholics believe the cosmological argument reinforces Bible teachings that God created the world. It can be used as evidence to respond to scientific claims that the Big Bang caused the world.
- It helps to prove God's existence by arguing that he cannot *not* exist. It offers logical proof that there is a first cause of the universe who is God.
- It offers explanations about God's nature as well as proving his existence. The argument can be used to respond to criticisms and helps to confirm Catholics' faith.

Arguments against the statement:

- The scientific theory of the Big Bang is an alternative view of how the world was created. The Big Bang could be the explanation of the cause of the universe and therefore God is not needed. If this is the case, the theory does not prove God's existence.
- It takes a leap of faith to accept that God is the cause of the universe. If this is challenged, the argument fails to prove God's existence.
- An important criticism is that the argument contradicts itself, saying everything has a cause but that God is uncaused. The argument cannot respond to this problem and therefore does not succeed in proving God's existence.

Accept any other valid response.

## 56 The existence of suffering

Award 1 mark for each reason. Award further marks for each development of the reason, up to a maximum of 4 marks.

- If something bad happens, Catholics may believe that God does not exist (1). Catholics believe God is all-powerful and all-knowing, so it is difficult to understand why he does not help when they are suffering if he is aware of it and has the power to stop it (1).
- Catholics may question their understanding of God's nature (1). They may not believe God is all-loving, as an all-loving God would not allow his Creation to suffer (1).
- They may question their understanding of God's power (1). Teachings suggest he is all-powerful and can do anything, yet he doesn't intervene when bad things happen (1).

Accept any other valid response.

## 57 Solutions to the problem of suffering

Award 1 mark for each point identified, up to a maximum of 3 marks.

- Catholics may respond to the problem of evil and suffering by referring to Bible teachings (1).
- Catholics may look to examples such as that of Job (1).
- Catholics may pray more regularly in response to evil and suffering (1).
- They may help out with charity work or give donations to charity (1).
- They may look to Church teachings for an explanation as to why humans suffer (1).

Accept any other valid response.

# Unit 8 Equality

## 58 Human rights

Award 1 mark for each reason. Award further marks for each development of the reason, up to a maximum of 4 marks. Award 1 further mark for any relevant source of wisdom or authority.

- Human rights seem to be in line with key Catholic principles (1). For example, Catholics believe life is special as it was created by God and upholding human rights recognises this (1): 'So God created mankind in his own image, in the image of God he created them; male and female he created them' (Genesis 1:27) (1).
- Human rights seem to be in line with key Catholic Church teachings (1). Catholics promote ideas of equality and respect, which can be seen in their social teachings (1): 'Catholic moral theology tells us that it is the destiny and duty of each human being to become more fully human. A society that observes human rights will be a society in which this true human growth is encouraged' (The Common Good and the Catholic Church's Social Teaching 37) (1).

- Human rights seem to agree with Jesus' teachings (1). Jesus taught that we should treat people with kindness and love, and human rights seem to demonstrate this (1): '...do unto others what you would have done unto you' (Matthew 7:12) (1).

Accept any other valid response.

## 59 Equality

Award 1 mark for each point identified, up to a maximum of 3 marks.
- All humans are created by God and are of equal value for him (1).
- Jesus' teachings say all humans should be treated with fairness and justice (1).
- Catholics believe they should stand up to inequality in the world (1).
- The Catholic Church teaches that social injustice is wrong (1).
- Stories such as the Good Samaritan show people should be treated with equal respect (1).

Accept any other valid response.

## 60 Religious freedom

Award 1 mark for each reason. Award further marks for each development of the reason, up to a maximum of 4 marks.
- Catholics living in a multi-faith society can interact with people from different faiths (1). This can lead to greater tolerance and understanding of other beliefs and provide opportunities for different faith groups to work together towards common aims (1).
- They have opportunities to experience enriching events from other faiths (1). They have access to different services, religious observances and celebrations they can learn from (1).
- Living in a multi-faith society could lead to improved communication and reduced tensions between different groups (1). In the past, there have been clashes between different faith groups, so access to better understanding may reduce mistrust, prejudice and discrimination in society as people understand each other better (1).

Accept any other valid response.

## 61 Religious prejudice and discrimination

Award 1 mark for each point identified, up to a maximum of 3 marks.
- They follow Jesus' example, who taught that religious discrimination is wrong and treated all religions the same (1).
- The Catholic Church Catechism says all people are of equal value, and so their choice of religion deserves equal respect (1).
- God created all humans to be of equal value, and so should be free to follow whichever religion they choose (1).
- Catholics believe they should treat people from all faith backgrounds with agape love, which means it is wrong to discriminate negatively, including on the grounds of faith (1).

Accept any other valid response.

## 62 Racial harmony

Award 1 mark for each reason. Award further marks for each development of the reason, up to a maximum of 4 marks.
- Catholic leaders promote racial harmony (1). They themselves demonstrate diversity, so they use this to educate on racial equality and promote unity between all races (1).
- The Catholic Church offers help and support for those who may be facing persecution due to their race (1). They may pray for them as well as offer them support in their communities by trying to educate others (1).

- There are various Catholic organisations that work to promote racial harmony (1). One example is CARJ, which works with local parishes and schools to organise meetings and seminars to share their message (1).

Accept any other valid response.

## 63 Racial discrimination

Award 1 mark for each reason. Award further marks for each development of the reason, up to a maximum of 4 marks.
- They may feel that some minority groups are isolated (1). They may not be catered for or involved in society, so this may lead to further problems such as illness or worry (1).
- It could lead to ill-feeling between different groups (1). Catholicism teaches the importance of working together and living in peace, which is against racial discrimination (1).
- It could lead to a lack of access to resources and facilities (1). Some people may not be able to access what they need such as support groups or help (1).

Accept any other valid response.

## 64 Social justice

Award 1 mark for each point identified, up to a maximum of 3 marks.
- The Catholic Church raises money to help work towards social justice (1).
- It works for social justice through charity work (1).
- The Church educates others about injustices (1).
- It promotes cohesion and social justice (1).
- The Church refers to Bible teachings on social justice (1).

Accept any other valid response.

## 65 Wealth and poverty

Award 1 mark for each reason. Award further marks for each development of the reason, up to a maximum of 4 marks.
- Bible teachings tell Catholics that all humans are made in God's image and so are all special (1). Putting these teachings into practice means working to reduce the effects of poverty and showing respect for all humans (1).
- Jesus helped others less fortunate than himself, especially those who were poor (1). Catholics want to follow his example and put his teachings into practice (1).
- Catholics are taught that they will be judged on their actions in order to be rewarded in the afterlife (1). Helping others who are less fortunate than themselves, e.g. those in poverty, is one aspect of how they can achieve eternal life in heaven.

Accept any other valid response.

## Unit 1 Muslim beliefs

## 66 The Six Beliefs of Islam

Award 1 mark for each point identified, up to a maximum of 3 marks.
- During prayers – Salah or du'a (1).
- Through reading the Qu'ran (1).
- Through their actions and behaviour (1).
- Through the way they help others (1).
- Through the way they live their lives – e.g. following the Five Pillars, going to the mosque, etc. (1).

Accept any other valid response.

## 67 The five roots of 'Usul ad-Din in Shi'a Islam

Candidates must underpin their analysis and evaluation with knowledge and understanding. Candidates will be required to demonstrate thorough knowledge and understanding, as well as accuracy, of religion and belief when responding to the question and in meeting AO2 descriptors.

Augments for the statement:

- Tawhid (the belief in the oneness of Allah) is at the heart of the Islamic faith. Awareness of Allah affects every action a Muslim performs and their prayers are directed towards him.
- Many Muslims (Sunni and Shi'a) view Tawhid as underpinning all other beliefs, such as those found in the six Beliefs for Sunni Muslims and those found in the five roots of 'Usul ad-Din.
- When Muslims pray, perform the Five Pillars or go to the mosque, everything they do is directed towards Allah and they want to please him within their lives.

Arguments against the statement:

- There are many other beliefs in Islam that are equally important – Akhirah, risalah, etc.
- Islam is a religion of beliefs and practices. How a Muslim behaves and acts is just as important as what they believe.
- Muslims would argue that, although Allah is central to the faith, other beliefs have equally as much influence on their lives.

Accept any other valid response.

### 68 The nature of Allah

1 Award 1 mark for each way. Award a second mark for development of the way, up to a maximum of 4 marks.
- Tawhid (1): Allah is one and has no start or end (1).
- Transcendent (1): Allah is beyond human understanding (1).
- Omnipotent (1): Allah is all-powerful and created the world (1).

Accept any other valid response.

2 Award 1 mark for each reason. Award further marks for each development of the reason, up to a maximum of 4 marks.
- To help Muslims understand Allah better (1). They can relate to him and develop a more personal relationship (1).
- To follow Allah (1). By using the characteristics Muslims can understand how he wants them to live their lives (1): 'And We certainly sent into every nation a messenger, [saying], "Worship Allah and avoid Taghut".' (Surah 16:36) (1).
- They are given in the Qur'an (1). This is an important source of authority that Muslims follow (1): 'The most beautiful names belong to Allah: so call on him by them.' (Surah 7:180) (1).

Accept any other valid response.

### 69 Risalah

1 Award 1 mark for each point identified, up to a maximum of 3 marks.
- They are messengers of Allah (1).
- They are the channel of communication between Allah and humanity (1).
- Some are rasuls, who are messengers who have had their message written down (1).
- They have revealed truths to humanity (1).

Accept any other valid response.

2 Candidates must underpin their analysis and evaluation with knowledge and understanding. Candidates will be required to demonstrate thorough knowledge and understanding, as well as accuracy, of religion and belief when responding to the question and in meeting AO2 descriptors.

Arguments for the statement:

- Without the prophets, Allah couldn't have communicated to humanity.
- Without prophets such as Muhammad, holy books such as the Qur'an would not have been received.

- Risalah is an important belief within the central teachings of Islam – Six Beliefs and five roots of 'Usul al-Din.

Arguments against the statement:

- Tawhid is perhaps more important, as this is belief in one God – Allah.
- Tawhid is seen to underpin all other beliefs including risalah, demonstrating its importance.
- Actions may be more important than beliefs in Islam, as this is what Muslims believe they will be judged on after death.

Accept any other valid response.

### 70 Muslim holy books

1 Award 1 mark for each point identified, up to a maximum of 3 marks.
- Revealed by Muhammad (1).
- Main holy book for Muslims (1).
- Contains teachings of Allah (1).
- Muslims look to it for guidance in their lives (1).
- Used within Muslim prayer (1).

Accept any other valid response.

2 Award 1 mark for providing a reason. Award a second mark for development of the reason, up to a maximum of 4 marks.
- Other holy books are mentioned in the Qur'an (1), for example Tawrat, Zabur, etc. (1).
- Muslims believe there were prophets who were messengers before Muhammad (1). They recognise messengers such as Ibrahim and Isa, who brought messages and holy books (1).
- Muslims believe they are commanded to recognise other holy books (1) such as the Tawrah, as this was also revealed by Allah (1).

Accept any other valid response.

### 71 Malaikah

1 Award 1 mark for each point identified, up to a maximum of 3 marks.
- Angels are called malaikah (1).
- They are believed to be messengers from Allah (1).
- They are not considered to have free will or physical bodies (1).
- Some of the angels are Jibril, Mika'il and Izra'il (1).
- They have been revealed to prophets (1).

Accept any other valid response.

2 Award 1 mark for each reason. Award further marks for each development of the reason, up to a maximum of 4 marks. Award 1 further mark for any relevant source of wisdom or authority.
- They have brought messages to humanity (1), for example Jibril gave the Qur'an to Muhammad (1): ' ... then We sent her our angel, and he appeared before her as a man in all respects.' (Surah, 19 (Maryam):17)
- They are mentioned in the Qur'an (1). Jibril, Mika'il and Izra'il are all mentioned as angels of significance (1): 'Whoever is an enemy to Gabriel – for he brings down the (revelation) to thy heart by Allah's will, a confirmation of what went before, and guidance and glad tidings for those who believe, – Whoever is an enemy to Allah and His angels and messengers, to Gabriel and Michael, – Lo! Allah is an enemy to those who reject Faith.' (Surah 2 (Al-Baqara):97–98)
- Angels are given roles within Islam (1), for example Izra'il is the angel of death (1): 'The angel of death will take you who has been entrusted with you. Then to your Lord you will be returned.' (Surah 32:11)

Accept any other valid response.

## 72 Al-Qadr

Award 1 mark for each way. Award a second mark for development of the way, up to a maximum of 4 marks.
- It affects their beliefs about the afterlife (1), so will have an impact on making them aware of how they act and behave in their lives (1).
- Muslims will want to help others (1). Behaving in this way will gain them favour with Allah (1).
- Muslims may read the Qur'an more often (1) to help them understand what Allah wants them to do (1).

Accept any other valid response.

## 73 Akhirah

Award 1 mark for each point identified, up to a maximum of 3 marks.
- Akhirah is the word for life after death in Islam (1).
- Muslims believe in the idea of reward and punishment (1).
- Muslims believe actions on Earth will determine their afterlife (1).
- Muslims believe Allah will judge them after death (1).
- The good will go to paradise and the bad to hell (1).

Accept any other valid response.

## Unit 2 Marriage and the family

### 74 Marriage

Award 1 mark for each point identified, up to a maximum of 3 marks.
- To bring a man and woman together to have children (1).
- To share love and companionship (1).
- To follow what Allah wants (1).
- To create a family (1).
- To bring stability to society (1).

Accept any other valid response.

### 75 Sexual relationships

Candidates must underpin their analysis and evaluation with knowledge and understanding. Candidates will be required to demonstrate thorough knowledge and understanding, as well as accuracy, of religion and belief when responding to the question and in meeting AO2 descriptors.

Arguments for the statement:
- Muslims believe sex is a gift and it is what Allah intended for a married couple.
- Islam teaches that sex fulfils physical, emotional and spiritual needs.
- Islam teaches that sex is an act of worship.

Arguments against the statement:
- Society today is changing and some people may believe that the idea of sex being a gift from Allah is outdated.
- Many atheists and humanists may challenge this, believing that sex is a gift for procreation but has no religious basis.
- Some may disagree, arguing that sex is a way of deepening a relationship rather than being a gift from God just for children.

Accept any other valid response.

### 76 Families

Candidates must underpin their analysis and evaluation with knowledge and understanding. Candidates will be required to demonstrate thorough knowledge and understanding, as well as accuracy, of religion and belief when responding to the question and in meeting AO2 descriptors.

Arguments for the statement:
- A non-religious individual may agree if they have an unsupportive family or have had bad experiences of family.
- Some people may have different types of family in society today, which may impact on their opinion.
- Some people may prefer friends to family.

Arguments against the statement:
- Muslims would argue that family provides stability and structure to society – some non-religious individuals may agree.
- Family helps to strengthen the ummah in Islam.
- Family is where children are taught right and wrong and raised as good Muslims.

Accept any other valid response.

### 77 The family in the ummah

1  Award 1 mark for each point identified, up to a maximum of 3 marks.
- Worship (1).
- Rites of passage (1).
- Classes for parents (1).
- Groups for children (1).
- Counselling (1).

Accept any other valid response.

2  Award 1 mark for providing a reason. Award a second mark for development of the reason, up to a maximum of 4 marks.
- Children can be raised correctly (1) as good Muslims (1).
- Support can be given when facing personal problems (1), difficulties in the marriage or with raising the children (1).
- Strengthening the ummah (1) so all Muslims are united (1).

Accept any other valid response.

### 78 Contraception

Award 1 mark for providing a reason. Award a second mark for development of the reason, up to a maximum of 4 marks.
- Muslim authorities allow its use to preserve the life of the mother (1). If she could die through having another child, this would be a threat to her life and other children in the family (1).
- Some believe Muhammad supported the withdrawal method (1). This seems to be suggested in some Hadith (1).
- Some accept non-permanent methods for use by married couples (1). They can then plan when to have their family.

Accept any other valid response.

### 79 Divorce

Award 1 mark for each reason. Award further marks for each development of the reason, up to a maximum of 4 marks.
- Muhammad did not divorce (1). Muslims want to follow his example (1).
- Divorce is seen to threaten and damage the family unit (1). It can lead to problems in the family, which is not desirable as Muslims consider the family to bring stability to society (1).
- Muslims believe divorce is detestable (1). It is hated by Allah as it is disrespectful to him and the gift of marriage between the couple (1).

Accept any other valid response.

### 80 Men and women in the family

1  Award 1 mark for each way. Award a second mark for development of the way, up to a maximum of 4 marks.
- Men and women are seen to have contrasting roles (1). Men are the providers and women are the home keepers in charge of raising children (1).
- Men and women are seen to have equal responsibilities (1). They are both to raise their children as good Muslims (1).
- Men and women are completely equal (1). Both can go out and work and have a career (1).

Accept any other valid response.

2 Candidates must underpin their analysis and evaluation with knowledge and understanding. Candidates will be required to demonstrate thorough knowledge and understanding, as well as accuracy, of religion and belief when responding to the question and in meeting AO2 descriptors.

Arguments for the statement:
- Most Muslims believe men and women are equal in their roles within the family.
- Sources of authority suggest men and women are equal.
- Muslims believe men and women were created to be equal by Allah.

Arguments against the statement:
- Men and women are seen to have different roles in the family, suggesting inequality.
- Men and women are suited to different tasks, so should be treated this way.
- There are sources of authority that suggest inequality within Islam in terms of men and women and their roles.

Accept any other valid response.

## 81 Gender prejudice and discrimination

1 Award 1 mark for each point identified, up to a maximum of 3 marks.
- Gender prejudice and discrimination are wrong (1).
- Allah created all humans – men and women – as equal (1).
- Men and women were created from the same soul (1).
- Muslims believe they should fight against gender prejudice and discrimination (1).
- The Qur'an contains many teachings suggesting men and women are equal (1).

Accept any other valid response.

2 Award 1 mark for each way. Award a second mark for development of the way, up to a maximum of 4 marks.
- Malala Yousafzai (1) stood up for girls' education against the Taliban (1).
- Nadiya Hussain (1) inspired others through her own individual achievements in winning 'The Great British Bake Off competition' (1).
- Organisations such as Sisters in Islam (1) work to challenge gender inequality (1).

Accept any other valid response.

## Unit 3 Living the Muslim life

### 82 The Ten Obligatory Acts of Shi'a Islam

Award 1 mark for providing a reason. Award a second mark for development of the reason, up to a maximum of 4 marks.
- They help them to worship Allah in their daily lives (1). By performing actions such as giving money to charity, fasting or praying Shi'a Muslims get closer to Allah (1).
- They provide guidance (1). The practices are seen to be commanded by Allah, which show Muslims how to act and behave (1).
- They help to identify key beliefs and practices (1). As they are mentioned in the Qur'an, it helps Shi'a Muslims to know what Allah wants them to do in their lives (1).

Accept any other valid response.

### 83 The Shahadah

Candidates must underpin their analysis and evaluation with knowledge and understanding. Candidates will be required to demonstrate thorough knowledge and understanding, as well as accuracy, of religion and belief when responding to the question and in meeting AO2 descriptors.

Arguments for the statement:

- The Shahadah is considered to underpin all other pillars, therefore, showing its importance as containing the central belief in Allah.
- The Shahadah is spoken daily, makes up part of the adhan (call to prayer), is whispered into the ears of newborn babies and should be spoken, if possible, before death, demonstrating the role it plays within the life of every Muslim and showing its central importance.
- The Shahadah is the first of the Five Pillars, which suggests it is the most important as it comes before all others.

Arguments against the statement:
- The pillars are all equally important as they are all considered to be duties and practices performed for Allah that all Muslims should perform within their lives.
- Salah (prayer) could be seen as more important as the Shahadah as this happens five times daily and is regular communication with Allah. Therefore, it is a practical way of developing a closer relationship with him.
- Zakah and Sawm are seen to be when Muslims can help others who are poor and needy and sympathise with their situation, so could be considered to have more of an impact in the world than the Shahadah, which is a personal proclamation of faith.

Accept any other valid response.

### 84 Salah

1 Award 1 mark for each point identified, up to a maximum of 3 marks.
- Regular communication with Allah (1).
- Commanded by Muhammad (1).
- One of the Five Pillars (1).
- Considered a duty to pray five times a day (1).
- Demonstrates equality between all members of the ummah (1).

Accept any other valid response.

2 Award 1 mark for each reason/belief. Award further marks for each development of the reason/belief, up to a maximum of 4 marks. Award 1 further mark for any relevant source of wisdom or authority.
- It is one of the Five Pillars (1). It is therefore considered compulsory, as it is a duty given to Muslims by Allah (1): 'So exalt [Allah] with praise of your Lord and be of those who prostrate [to Him]. And worship your Lord until there comes to you the certainty (death)'. (Surah 15:98–99) (1).
- It is communication with Allah (1). This is commanded in the Qur'an and demonstrates the key belief of Tawhid, which is at the centre of the Islamic faith (1): 'So exalt [Allah] with praise of your Lord and be of those who prostrate [to Him]. And worship your Lord until there comes to you the certainty (death)'. (Surah 15:98–99) (1).
- Salah was prescribed by Muhammad (1). Muhammad prayed to Allah regularly and taught his followers to do the same. It is in sources of authority (1): 'He said: "O Muhammad, they are five prayers each day and night, for every prayer there will be a tenfold (reward), and that is fifty prayers."' (Hadith Al-Bukhaari (349)) (1).

Accept any other valid response.

### 85 Sawm

Award 1 mark for providing a reason. Award a second mark for development of the reason, up to a maximum of 4 marks.
- If they are sick (1). It may affect their recovery and long-term health (1).
- If they are pregnant (1). They need to stay healthy so their unborn child gains nutrients to grow and develop (1).
- If they are travelling on long journeys (1). It may affect their ability to complete their journey or make them sick (1).

Accept any other valid response.

### 86 Zakah and khums

Award 1 mark for each benefit. Award a second mark for development of the benefit, up to a maximum of 4 marks.

- It can help the poorest and neediest in society (1). It is used to try to improve the conditions for many and make their lives more bearable (1).
- It reminds Muslims of the importance of all humans to Allah (1). Muslims believe Allah created all humans equally and this is a way of demonstrating equality.
- It shares and distributes wealth in the world (1). This is what Allah intended for his creation (1).

Accept any other valid response.

### 87 Hajj

1 Award 1 mark for each point identified, up to a maximum of 3 marks.
- Tawaf – circling of the Ka'bah seven times (1).
- Sa'y – running between the hills of Marwa and Safa (1).
- Mount Arafat – standing and praying or reading the Qur'an (1).
- Stoning of the devil at Mina – throwing stones at the pillars (1).
- Sacrifice of an animal (1).

Accept any other valid response.

2 Award 1 mark for each benefit. Award a second mark for development of the benefit, up to a maximum of 4 marks.
- It shows commitment to Allah (1) it is one of the Five Pillars of Islam and a duty all Muslims complete for Allah
- Completing Hajj strengthens the ummah (1) it unites all Muslims in their shared faith and belief in Allah as they all complete the same actions at the same time (1)
- It gives individual Muslims an opportunity to reflect on their belief and faith in Allah (1) they ask Allah for forgiveness and get closer to him (1)

Accept any other valid response.

### 88 Jihad

1 Award 1 mark for each point identified, up to a maximum of 3 marks.
- Fought for a just cause – to defend Islam or injustice (1).
- A last resort (1).
- Authorised by an accepted Muslim authority (1).
- Minimum amount of suffering is caused (1).
- Innocent civilians are not attacked (1).

Accept any other valid response.

2 Award 1 mark for providing a reason. Award a second mark for development of the reason, up to a maximum of 4 marks.
- Sources of authority have emphasised this (1). The Qur'an and Muhammad both stated this (1).
- It is viewed as an act of sacrifice to Allah (1). It is more important to overcome daily challenges rather than just go to war (1).

Accept any other valid response.

### 89 Celebrations and commemorations

Award 1 mark for each point identified, up to a maximum of 3 marks.
- Sacrifice of an animal (1).
- Sending of Id cards (1).
- Attending the mosque (1).
- Sharing a meal with friends and family (1).

Accept any other valid response.

## Unit 4 Matters of life and death

### 90 Origins of the universe

Candidates must underpin their analysis and evaluation with knowledge and understanding. Candidates will be required to demonstrate thorough knowledge and understanding, as well as accuracy, of religion and belief when responding to the question and in meeting AO2 descriptors.

Arguments for the statement:
- The Qur'an says Allah created the universe – science says it was the Big Bang. These are different theories.
- Science seems to suggest the universe was created by chance, while the Qur'an suggests Allah planned and designed it.
- The Qur'an suggests a loving God, while science suggests no planning or designing from a loving God.

Arguments against the statement:
- Many Muslims believe that science helps to further explain teachings about creation in the Qur'an – it fills in the gaps.
- Several passages are seen by some Muslims to refer to the event known as the Big Bang.
- Many Muslims believe that science helps them to understand Allah better.

Accept any other valid response.

### 91 Sanctity of life

Award 1 mark for providing a reason. Award a second mark for development of the reason, up to a maximum of 4 marks.
- Life was created by Allah (1). Muslims believe that he created life to be holy and special, which is taught in the Qur'an (1).
- Muslims believe it is wrong to take life (1). All human life should be respected as a gift from Allah as he created it (1).
- Islam has many teachings about life being preserved (1). Muslims accept that abortion and euthanasia is wrong, as it means ending life created by Allah (1).

Accept any other valid response.

### 92 The origins of human life

Candidates must underpin their analysis and evaluation with knowledge and understanding. Candidates will be required to demonstrate thorough knowledge and understanding, as well as accuracy, of religion and belief when responding to the question and in meeting AO2 descriptors.

Arguments for the statement:
- Evolution does conflict with the Qur'an. Evolution suggests that life happened by chance as organisms adapted to their environments, whereas Qur'anic teachings suggest life was planned and intended by Allah.
- Evolution rests on the assumption that humans were created by the strongest characteristics surviving and the weakest ones dying out, making human life evolve from animals, whereas Muslim teachings reinforce the view that Allah loved his creation so much that he designed the world for human life to exist.
- There seems to be no common ground between Muslim teachings and scientific theories such as evolution, which leads some Muslims to reject modern theories offered by science and only accept the traditional teachings offered by the religion of Islam.

Arguments against the statement:
- Some Muslims believe that science can help to explain teachings that the Qur'an is not clear about. Although the Qur'an explains the origin of human life (Allah), evolution helps to explain his plan for how it was created within the world.

- Many Muslims believe that science and Islam can be brought together as they view evolution as part of Allah's plan, meaning that these teachings and ideas can work alongside each other rather than in conflict.
- Many Muslims believe that in today's modern, technological world you cannot deny scientific theories such as evolution, so you need to look for ways of making them work alongside traditional teachings. Muslims accept that evolution can help them to understand Allah and his ways better.

Accept any other valid response.

### 93 Muslim attitudes to abortion

Award 1 mark for each point identified, up to a maximum of 3 marks.

- The sanctity of life teaches that Allah created life and is holy, so abortion is wrong (1).
- Ensoulment means the soul is not believed to enter the body until 40 or even 120 days, so abortion could be seen as acceptable before this time as it is not killing life (1).
- The Qur'an contains teachings on the sanctity of life showing abortion is wrong as life is holy (1).
- Accepted reasons for abortion include the life of the mother being in danger (1).
- Islam teaches through the Qur'an that reasons not justified for abortion include a lack of money or a child born as the result of adultery (1).

Accept any other valid response.

### 94 Death and the afterlife (1)

Award 1 mark for providing a reason. Award a second mark for development of the reason, up to a maximum of 4 marks.

- Teachings from the Qur'an highlight the importance of life after death (1). They teach that life is a test in order that a person can be rewarded or punished after death (1).
- Islamic teachings reflect the importance of living life as Allah intended (1). This is connected to the afterlife as Muslims believe they will be judged by Allah after death on how they have lived their lives (1).
- Muslims teach that there is a connection between life and life after death (1). Living a good life will ensure a person is rewarded and not punished (1).

Accept any other valid response.

### 95 Death and the afterlife (2)

Award 1 mark for each reason/belief. Award further marks for each development of the reason/belief, up to a maximum of 4 marks. Award 1 further mark for any relevant source of wisdom or authority.

- Muslims reject humanist beliefs that there is no life after death by pointing to teachings in the Qur'an (1). They believe that the Qur'an teaches of an afterlife where people will be judged and rewarded or punished, therefore, it must exist (1). They say, "'There is not but our worldly life; we die and live, and nothing destroys us except time." And they have of that no knowledge; they are only assuming. And when Our verses are recited to them as clear evidences, their argument is only that they say, "Bring [back] our forefathers, if you should be truthful."' (Surah 45:24–25)
- Muslims reject arguments of social control as they believe there is a direct link between life and death (1). Islam teaches that how a person lives their life will determine how they are judged by Allah after death. This is taught in the Qur'an (1).

### 96 Euthanasia

1  Award 1 mark for each point identified, up to a maximum of 3 marks.
   - Euthanasia is always wrong as it goes against the sanctity of life (1).

- Only Allah can give and take away life, so euthanasia is wrong (1).
- Muslims believe that human life has been given a purpose by Allah. To end it through euthanasia is wrong as this purpose is special and holy (1).
- Euthanasia is suicide, which is not allowed in Islam (1).
- The Qur'an teaches that no one dies 'unless Allah permits' (Surah 3:145), so euthanasia is wrong (1).

Accept any other valid response.

2  Award 1 mark for providing a reason. Award a second mark for development of the reason, up to a maximum of 4 marks.
   - Muslims believe in the sanctity of life (1). As Allah gave life only he can take it away, meaning that euthanasia goes against this (1).
   - Muslims believe that suffering in life has a purpose and euthanasia should not be used to take this away (1). They believe that Allah has a plan for every human life which should not be interfered with. People will be judged after death on how they acted in life, which may mean that someone who has had euthanasia may be punished (1).
   - The Qur'an teaches that euthanasia is wrong (1). Muslims believe the Qur'an is the word of God and guides them on issues such as euthanasia. As it says that euthanasia is wrong, it should not happen (1).

Accept any other valid response.

### 97 Issues in the natural world

Candidates must underpin their analysis and evaluation with knowledge and understanding. Candidates will be required to demonstrate thorough knowledge and understanding, as well as accuracy, of religion and belief when responding to the question and in meeting AO2 descriptors.

Arguments for the statement:
- Muslims believe they have a duty of stewardship (khalifah) given to them by Allah, which means they should take care of the world.
- Muslims believe the world was created by Allah and given to humans as a gift, so they have a responsibility to look after it and take care of it.
- Islam teaches in the Qur'an that Muslims should not damage the world as it should be preserved for future generations.

Arguments against the statement:
- Some people without religious beliefs may claim that they do not have a responsibility to care for the world and, if they have not damaged it, they have no duty to help.
- Some people may believe that the people who did the damage should be the ones to work to save the world.
- Some people may believe that they are only one person and cannot make that big a difference to the world. They may believe that those in authority and with power should be the ones working to help the world.

Accept any other valid response.

## Unit 5 Crime and punishment

### 98 Justice

Award 1 mark for each point identified, up to a maximum of 3 marks.

- Justice is what Allah intended for his creation (1).
- The Five Pillars of Islam demonstrate ideas of justice (1).
- Shari'ah law reinforces ideas of justice (1).
- Muslims believe that they will be judged in the afterlife on how just they have been in their lives (1).
- The Qur'an contains many teachings that reference ideas of justice (1).

Accept any other valid response.

## 99 Crime

1 Award 1 mark for each point identified, up to a maximum of 3 marks.
  - Muslim individuals and organisations may work to try to reduce the impact, causes and effects of crime (1).
  - They may teach about the importance of avoiding crime (1).
  - They may reinforce the belief that Allah will judge Muslims after death on the way they have behaved in life (1).
  - They may try to set an example of how a Muslim should live their life (1).
  - They may refer to Qur'anic teachings to show that crime is wrong (1).

  Accept any other valid response.

2 Award 1 mark for providing a reason. Award a second mark for development of the reason, up to a maximum of 4 marks.
  - They believe they have a duty from Allah to care for others in society (1). Muslims believe Allah created all humans to be equal and this means they should support each other and try to make society just and fair (1).
  - The ummah is important in Islam (1). One part of belonging to the ummah is supporting all Muslims all over the world, so working to reduce crime can benefit others (1).
  - Muslims believe they should try to follow the example of Muhammad (1). Muslims believe Muhammad helped others and tried to improve their lives, so they should do the same for Allah (1).

  Accept any other valid response.

## 100 Good, evil and suffering

Award 1 mark for each teaching. Award further marks for each development of the teaching, up to a maximum of 4 marks.
- Muslims believe that there is a reason why they suffer (1). It is part of Allah's plan, although Muslims do not know what this is (1).
- Muslims believe that suffering is a test of faith and character (1). Allah gave humans free will and they need to choose right or wrong actions in order to deserve reward in the afterlife (1).
- Muslims believe that some suffering is due to humans (1). For example, famine or war is the result of humans using free will, given to them by Allah, and choosing to hurt others (1).

Accept any other valid response.

## 101 Punishment

1 Award 1 mark for providing a reason. Award a second mark for development of the reason, up to a maximum of 4 marks.
  - The Qur'an teaches the importance of punishment (1). Muslims believe a just society is what Allah intended and they should try to put this into action (1).
  - Punishment is important in teaching people that some actions are wrong (1). Islam teaches that after death people will be rewarded if they have been good and punished if they have been evil, so punishment for any wrongdoing seems fair (1).
  - Punishment creates a fair and just society (1). The Qur'an and the example of Muhammad shows that this is important in society (1).

  Accept any other valid response.

2 Award 1 mark for each reason. Award further marks for each development of the reason, up to a maximum of 4 marks. Award 1 further mark for any relevant source of wisdom or authority.
  - The Qur'an teaches the importance of justice and punishment is part of this (1). It teaches that Allah intended for a just and fair society, so punishment for a crime works to achieve this (1): 'And We ordained for them therein a life for a life, an eye for an eye, a nose for a nose, an ear for an ear, a tooth for a tooth, and for wounds is legal retribution.' (Surah 5:45) (1).
  - Punishment maintains order and stability in society (1). Shari'ah law is based on the principles of justice, equality and order, and generates suitable punishments (1).
  - Muslims believe the laws of the country should be followed (1). The Qur'an teaches this (1).

  Accept any other valid response.

## 102 Aims of punishment

1 Award 1 mark for each point identified, up to a maximum of 3 marks.
  - To protect society (1).
  - To offer opportunity for the offender to reform (1).
  - To deter other offenders from committing the same crime (1).
  - To give retribution (1).

  Accept any other valid response.

2 Candidates must underpin their analysis and evaluation with knowledge and understanding. Candidates will be required to demonstrate thorough knowledge and understanding, as well as accuracy, of religion and belief when responding to the question and in meeting AO2 descriptors.

  Arguments for the statement:
  - Muslims are taught that forgiveness and repentance are important. Following these teaching would mean giving the offender the opportunity to change their behaviour and become a better person.
  - Muslims believe they have a responsibility from Allah to help people – an idea that is shown through the ummah. Helping offenders means giving them a second chance and an opportunity to reform.
  - Criminals need time to be shown why their behaviour is wrong and this will have the biggest impact on society in bringing justice and fairness.

  Arguments against the statement:
  - The victim of the crime and their loves ones could be seen as more important than the offender. If their needs are put first, it would seem that perhaps retribution or protection is more important. The Qur'an has many teachings about justice being attained for the victim.
  - Protection for others in society is more important as life is special and sacred. If others are not protected, they could be harmed.
  - Muslims believe that justice is the most important aim of punishment as this is what Allah wants for society. In order to achieve this, everyone's needs must be taken into account – offender's and victim's.

  Accept any other valid response.

## 103 Forgiveness

Award 1 mark for providing a reason. Award a second mark for development of the reason, up to a maximum of 4 marks.
- Forgiveness is a key teaching in Islam (1). The Qur'an teaches Muslims to forgive and they follow the example of Muhammad who was forgiving (1).
- Forgiving means everyone can move forward in their lives (1). It stops hatred and bad feeling between the offenders, which can have a negative impact on their lives (1).

- Islam teaches that Allah is compassionate and merciful and wants humans to be the same (1). By forgiving the offender, Muslims are demonstrating how Allah wants them to live and following his will (1).

Accept any other valid response.

### 104 Treatment of criminals

Award 1 mark for providing a reason. Award a second mark for development of the reason, up to a maximum of 4 marks.

- Allah is seen by Muslims as just and merciful and Muslims want to apply these characteristics to their lives (1). They believe that they will be judged after death by Allah on their actions, so acting fairly and in a just way towards others will help them to be rewarded.
- The Qur'an teaches that everyone should be treated equally and with fairness (1). Teachings such as this come from Allah and Muslims believe they should follow them in their lives (1).
- Muslims believe that all humans were created by Allah and deserve equal respect and dignity (1). They accept that all life is sacred and holy and, therefore, even if a person has done wrong, they deserve a level of respect in their treatment (1).

Accept any other valid response.

### 105 The death penalty

Award 1 mark for providing a reason. Award a second mark for development of the reason, up to a maximum of 4 marks.

- The Qur'an states that capital punishment is an option that can be considered in cases of punishment (1). For the most severe crimes, some Muslims may feel that this teaching should be applied (1).
- Shari'ah law agrees with the Qur'an about the use of capital punishment for the most serious crimes (1). This code of behaviour is referred to in law courts when considering what punishments to give, so capital punishment can be considered (1).
- Muhammad is sometimes seen to have supported the idea of capital punishment (1). There is some evidence that he sentenced people to death for committing murder (1).

Accept any other valid response.

## Unit 6 Peace and conflict

### 106 Peace

Award 1 mark for each point identified, up to a maximum of 3 marks.

- It is what Allah wants (1).
- It is what the Qur'an teaches (1).
- The ummah demonstrates ideas of peace (1).
- Peace is important for justice in the world (1).
- Getting on with others and helping those around the world is a teaching in Islam (1).

Accept any other valid response.

### 107 Peacemaking

Candidates must underpin their analysis and evaluation with knowledge and understanding. Candidates will be required to demonstrate thorough knowledge and understanding, as well as accuracy, of religion and belief when responding to the question and in meeting AO2 descriptors.

Arguments for the statement:

- Islam teaches that Allah created the world to be a peaceful society. As Muslims believe this is what Allah wants and they will be judged on how they have behaved in this life for the afterlife, it is an important idea.

- The ummah demonstrates ideas of peace showing its importance. As the ummah is how Allah intended people to live their lives in harmony with others and caring for them, it is an important teaching.
- Muslims would argue that without peace in the world justice cannot be achieved. Justice is another key idea promoted in Islam through teachings in the Qur'an and taught by Muhammad.

Arguments against the statement:

- Although peace is important, other beliefs and teachings may be equally or more important. For example, belief in Allah and Muhammad as the prophet is central to the Islamic faith.
- Some practices within Islam might have more impact and achieve peace indirectly. Some of the Five Pillars, such as Zakah or Sawm, may help more people and work to achieve peace and justice within the world.
- Muslims believe that they have duties that they must perform and, through doing so, they work for peace.

Accept any other valid response.

### 108 Conflict

Award 1 mark for providing a reason. Award a second mark for development of the reason, up to a maximum of 4 marks.

- Islam teaches that all Muslims are part of the ummah and are equal, so should work to bring justice (1). Through educating others or resolving differences, they believe they can achieve peace and an end to conflict.
- Muslims believe Allah is merciful and compassionate and they should follow his example in bringing an end to conflict (1). They believe that Allah intended the world to be peaceful where people live in harmony, so they should work to achieve this (1).
- There are many examples of sayings from Muhammad on the importance of overcoming conflict (1). Muslims believe that they should follow the example of Muhammad in their lives in order that they may go to al-Jannah in the afterlife (1).

Accept any other valid response.

### 109 Pacifism

Award 1 mark for each condition. Award further marks for each development of the condition, up to a maximum of 4 marks.

- Muslims strive for justice and to resist oppression (1). It is a good thing if this can be achieved in a non-violent way, as this is putting the teachings into practice (1).
- Islam teaches the importance of peace and reconciliation, which could be achieved in a non-violent way (1). Working together to achieve peace through marching peacefully or writing letters can have an impact (1).
- Islam is often understood as 'submission to Allah', which suggests non-violence (1). These methods would be preferred by Muslims.

Accept any other valid response.

### 110 The Just War theory

1 Award 1 mark for each point identified, up to a maximum of 3 marks.

- Declared by a religious leader (1).
- Is a last resort (1).
- Will not threaten life (1).
- Is an act of defence (1).
- Will not harm the environment (1).

Accept any other valid response.

2 Award 1 mark for providing a reason. Award a second mark for development of the reason, up to a maximum of 4 marks.

- It must be a last resort (1). All peaceful methods of achieving peace should have been tried first before war is declared (1).
- It must not threaten human life (1). The war must be fought in such a way that innocent civilians are neither targeted nor accidently injured as a result of warfare (1).
- It should be an act of defence (1). It should be to defend Islam when the religion is attacked or to help people who are persecuted to escape their situation (1).

Accept any other valid response.

## 111 Holy war

Award 1 mark for providing a reason. Award a second mark for development of the reason, up to a maximum of 4 marks.

- The Qur'an seems to suggest that, in some situations war is acceptable (1). If it is to defend Islam, protect the freedom of Muslims or to strengthen the religion, holy war can be justified (1).
- There are examples that Muhammad was involved in fighting (1). Examples include the Battle of Badr, where he and his followers fought to defend Islam (1).
- Sometimes Muslims recognise that in order to achieve the end goal of peace, war is needed (1). This is a view reinforced in the Qu'ran and Hadith (1).

Accept any other valid response.

## 112 Weapons of mass destruction

Award 1 mark for each reason. Award further marks for each development of the reason, up to a maximum of 4 marks. Award 1 further mark for any relevant source of wisdom or authority.

- Muslims do not support the use of WMD as Islam has a set of rules that must be followed when considering war (1). One of the rules is that innocent life should not be threatened, which cannot be met if WMD are used (1): 'That if any one slew a person – unless it be for murder or for spreading mischief in the land – it would be as if he slew the whole people; and if any one saved a life, it would be as if he saved the life of the whole people …' (Surah 5:32) (1).
- Muslims would believe that the conditions of Just War theory wouldn't be met with the use of WMD (1). They indiscriminately affect innocent lives, which is not what Allah intended (1): 'That if any one slew a person – unless it be for murder or for spreading mischief in the land – it would be as if he slew the whole people; and if any one saved a life, it would be as if he saved the life of the whole people …' (Surah 5:32) (1).

Accept any other valid response.

## 113 Issues surrounding conflict

Candidates must underpin their analysis and evaluation with knowledge and understanding. Candidates will be required to demonstrate thorough knowledge and understanding, as well as accuracy, of religion and belief when responding to the question and in meeting AO2 descriptors.

Arguments for the statement:

- Conflict is a growing issue in the world and Islam's association with acts of terrorism has led to there being misconceptions about the religion. Better understanding of Islam is needed in order to be able to overcome the challenges of conflict.
- There have been many occurrences recently of a rise in the use of violence; both by Muslims and towards Muslims. This has led to a breakdown in relationships with Muslims, which is a big threat to all followers of the religion.

- From a non-religious point of view, the growing threat of conflict and violence in the world is due to religion; this has led to distrust and examples of aggression towards Muslims and those of other faiths.

Arguments against the statement:

- Although conflict is an issue facing Muslims, there are other issues such as the damage being caused to the universe, which Muslims believe is wrong because it is the creation of Allah; this could be the biggest threat as it could threaten human life and future generations.
- Conflict is not the biggest threat as the violence that Muslims are experiencing today through hate crimes is the worst challenge. There have been examples of damage to property, verbal abuse and even physical attacks; this is the greatest challenge Muslims are facing.
- Poverty and injustice in the world is considered to be an issue facing Muslims today – greater than the conflict they may face. Muslims feel they have a duty to help others as this is taught in the Qur'an and led in example through Muhammad. Facing this is the biggest threat in the world for Muslims.

Accept any other valid response.

# Unit 7 Philosophy of religion

## 114 Revelation

Award 1 mark for each way. Award a second mark for development of the way, up to a maximum of 4 marks.

- Through direct revelation (1); this is where Allah communicates directly with humanity, for example through giving the world the Qur'an (1).
- Through messengers (1). Prophets such as Ibrahim, Musa and the 'Seal of the Prophets', Muhammad, brought messages from Allah, which is another way he reveals himself (1).
- Sources of authority such as the Qur'an demonstrate to Muslims what Allah is like (1). The Qur'an shows that he is benevolent and cares for his creation (1).

Accept any other valid response.

## 115 Visions

1 Award 1 mark for each point identified, up to a maximum of 3 marks.
- They could be hallucinations (1).
- They cannot always be verified scientifically (1).
- Some people believe they are not real (1).
- They may be illusions (1).
- People could be mistaken (1).

Accept any other valid response.

2 Award 1 mark for providing a reason. Award a second mark for development of the reason, up to a maximum of 4 marks.
- Visions can help to strengthen belief in Allah (1). They confirm that he is real and examples such as Muhammad's vision prove that he is real (1).
- Visions can provide evidence of the teachings of Islam and the nature of Allah (1). Allah revealing himself through a vision such as to Mary shows his power and benevolence he has for the world (1).
- Visions can help Muslims to understand what Allah is like (1). It is a way of Allah communicating with humanity either directly or through prophets, which helps Muslims to understand him better (1).

Accept any other valid response.

## 116 Miracles

Award 1 mark for providing a reason. Award a second mark for development of the reason, up to a maximum of 4 marks.

- There is no other explanation (1). Miracles such as the Night Journey, which Muhammad experienced, cannot be explained scientifically or in any other way other than Allah (1).
- Miracles are amazing events that prove the existence of Allah (1). They demonstrate what Allah is like and the characteristics he is believed to have, such as his power (1).
- They demonstrate that Allah is active within the world (1). They show that he loves his creation and wants to be close and involved with the world he created (1).

Accept any other valid response.

### 117 Religious experiences

Award 1 mark for each way. Award a second mark for development of the way, up to a maximum of 4 marks.

- Muslims may respond by arguing that religious experiences are real (1). Although some Muslims do not place great emphasis on them, they accept that Allah has the power to be able to communicate with humanity in this way (1).
- Muslims may respond by arguing that religious experience is a good way of Allah revealing himself (1). They believe that it is a way of Allah connecting with his creation and showing what he is like (for example, having power, being benevolent) (1).
- Muslims may respond by arguing that sources of authority such as the Qur'an give evidence of the truth of religious experience (1). There are examples such as the Night Journey of Muhammad, which shows that religious experience is real (1).

Accept any other valid response.

### 118 The design argument

1 Award 1 mark for providing a reason. Award a second mark for development of the reason, up to a maximum of 4 marks.
   - It seems to confirm and agree with teachings in the Qur'an (1). Surah 2:164 seems to mention the evidence of design in the world, so it strengthens previously held beliefs.
   - It seems to confirm the nature of Allah (1). The design argument suggest Allah is loving, cares for his creation and is all-powerful, which are ideas upheld by acceptance of the argument.
   - It uses evidence from within the world to prove its conclusion that Allah exists (1). This is evidence that can be seen, which supports previously held beliefs about Allah and strengthens belief in him (1).

   Accept any other valid response.

2 Candidates must underpin their analysis and evaluation with knowledge and understanding. Candidates will be required to demonstrate thorough knowledge and understanding, as well as accuracy, of religion and belief when responding to the question and in meeting AO2 descriptors.

   Arguments for the statement:
   - It confirms beliefs about the nature of Allah. It suggests that Allah cares for his creation and took time to plan and design it, as well as showing he has the power; therefore, it is good in reinforcing beliefs held by Muslims.
   - It offers an explanation for how the universe came to exist. It is important for Muslims to understand where the world came from and it confirms the beliefs and teachings within the Qur'an, showing that it is important.
   - Evidence from the world around us is used, which means it can be seen by Muslims. This means that it is good evidence of the existence of Allah as it is using his creation to prove that he exists.

   Arguments against the statement:

- Non-religious people may claim that the existence of the universe can be explained today by science and reference to Allah is not needed. The theory of evolution explains the apparent design in the world, which means that people do not need the explanations offered by Islam and the argument is not good evidence of the existence of Allah.
- The argument cannot be 'proved' and, therefore, it means the existence of Allah also cannot be proved. This means it is not good evidence.
- Many people argue that it is equally as valid to suggest that the universe came about by chance, which challenges belief in Allah. If this is the case, it is not sufficient evidence to confirm the existence of Allah.

Accept any other valid response.

### 119 The cosmological argument

Candidates must underpin their analysis and evaluation with knowledge and understanding. Candidates will be required to demonstrate thorough knowledge and understanding, as well as accuracy, of religion and belief when responding to the question and in meeting AO2 descriptors.

Arguments for the statement:
- Non-religious individuals would agree. They offer criticisms such as the Big Bang theory being a more viable option to explain where the universe came from and, therefore, the argument cannot be used to prove the existence of Allah.
- Some Muslims do not use this argument as they prefer to use religious sources of authority such as the Qur'an on which to base their beliefs and teachings. Although they may recognise the argument, they would not use it to try to prove the existence of Allah.
- Some may argue that the cosmological argument only suggests that Allah exists and is not proof of this. As there are some criticisms, they may choose to not use this argument as proof of the existence of Allah.

Argument against the statement:
- Some Muslims believe that the cosmological argument reinforces their beliefs held in the Qur'an. As it appears to agree with their source of authority, many Muslims would uphold the argument as good evidence for belief in the existence of Allah.
- Al-Ghazali in the 12th century formulated his own Islamic version of this argument. As Islam has a proponent of the argument, many Muslims would point to this in showing its success at proving the existence of Allah.
- Many Muslims believe the argument can respond to challenges such as that offered by the Big Bang by incorporating both into the explanation for the creation of the universe. If this is accepted, it could be seen as good evidence for belief in Allah.

Accept any other valid response.

### 120 The existence of suffering

Award 1 mark for each reason. Award further marks for each development of the reason, up to a maximum of 4 marks. Award 1 further mark for any relevant source of wisdom or authority.
- It challenges the omnipotence of Allah (1). If he is forgiving and all-powerful, Muslims may question why he does not stop evil such as murder and killing (1): 'In the name of Allah, the Entirely Merciful, the Especially Merciful. [All] praise is [due] to Allah, Lord of the worlds – The Entirely Merciful, the Especially Merciful, Sovereign of the Day of Recompense. It is You we worship and You we ask for help. Guide us to the straight path – The path of those upon whom You have bestowed favour, not of those who have evoked [Your] anger or of those who are astray.' (Surah 1) (1).

- It challenges whether he is all-loving, as the Qur'an suggests (1). Wouldn't a God who sees his creation suffering want to stop it? (1): 'In the name of Allah, the Entirely Merciful, the Especially Merciful. [All] praise is [due] to Allah, Lord of the worlds – The Entirely Merciful, the Especially Merciful, Sovereign of the Day of Recompense. It is You we worship and You we ask for help. Guide us to the straight path – The path of those upon whom You have bestowed favour, not of those who have evoked [Your] anger or of those who are astray.' (Surah 1) (1).
- It challenges the very existence of Allah (1). If he is what the Qur'an claims he is, why doesn't he step in and prevent suffering in the world? (1): 'In the name of Allah, the Entirely Merciful, the Especially Merciful. [All] praise is [due] to Allah, Lord of the worlds – The Entirely Merciful, the Especially Merciful, Sovereign of the Day of Recompense. It is You we worship and You we ask for help. Guide us to the straight path – The path of those upon whom You have bestowed favour, not of those who have evoked [Your] anger or of those who are astray.' (Surah 1) (1).

Accept any other valid response.

### 121 Solutions to the problem of suffering

Award 1 mark for each point identified, up to a maximum of 3 marks.
- Pray for Allah to help them (1).
- Give money to charity (1).
- Volunteer or give time to help others through charity work (1).
- Share Islamic teachings with others about why they suffer (1).
- Remind people of the need to accept this life in order to achieve a good afterlife (1).

Accept any other valid response.

## Unit 8 Equality

### 122 Human rights

1 Award 1 mark for each point identified up to a maximum of 3 marks.
- Islam teaches the importance of helping others (1).
- Islam teaches all humans were created as equal by Allah (1).
- Islam teaches that Muslims have a duty to stand up against injustice in the world (1).
- Muslims follow the example of Muhammad, who treated all people equally (1).
- The Qur'an supports all humans having human rights (1).

Accept any other valid response.

2 Award 1 mark for providing a reason. Award a second mark for development of the reason, up to a maximum of 4 marks.
- Islam teaches that all Muslims have a duty to help others (1). When human rights have been ignored, Muslims believe that they should stand up against these injustices (1).
- Muslims believe all humans were created as equal by Allah (1). This means that everyone is the same and deserves fair treatment. When this doesn't happen, others should stand up and help (1).
- Islam teaches Muslims to follow the example of Muhammad, who stood up for the human rights of others (1). He fought for equality for women and took care of the most vulnerable in society (1).

Accept any other valid response.

### 123 Equality

Award 1 mark for each way. Award a second mark for development of the way, up to a maximum of 4 marks.
- Through charity work (1). They can support charities such as Islamic Relief or Muslim Aid to help others all around the world facing inequality. For example, providing relief in emergency situations (1).
- They can educate others (1). This will help others to accept that all humans are equal as created by Allah and try to improve the quality and situation of the lives of others (1).
- They can give money in Zakah (1). This is one of the Five Pillars and money is given every year to support the most needy in society (1).

Accept any other valid response.

### 124 Religious freedom

Candidates must underpin their analysis and evaluation with knowledge and understanding. Candidates will be required to demonstrate thorough knowledge and understanding, as well as accuracy, of religion and belief when responding to the question and in meeting AO2 descriptors.

Arguments for the statement:
- Other people do not understand the Muslim faith and Muslims may face negativity and discrimination. It can be difficult for them to integrate and educate others making it problematic to live in a multifaith society.
- It may be difficult for Muslims to practise their faith and follow all aspects. This could be seen on a Friday which, traditionally, is a day of work in the UK, but which is the holy day for Muslims.
- Muslims may feel intimidated or excluded within society. After world events linking Islam to atrocities such as terrorism, all Muslims may feel they are stereotyped and treated differently.

Arguments against the statement:
- Many people today want to find out more about all religions in the UK. Muslims may value being open and honest about their faith, as well as learning about other faiths.
- There are many benefits from living in a multifaith society, including access to new cultures, foods, music and diversity.
- Muslims can help to bridge the gaps in understanding between different religions. There has been lots of work done between different religious groups in order to show the things they share in common, rather than their differences which could divide.

Accept any other valid response.

### 125 Religious prejudice and discrimination

Award 1 mark for each point identified, up to a maximum of 3 marks.
- Prejudice and discrimination is always wrong (1).
- Allah created all humans equally (1).
- Muhammad taught that all humans are equal (1).
- People should not be discriminated for their religion (1).
- Muslims should always work to help those facing discrimination (1).

Accept any other valid response.

### 126 Racial harmony

1 Award 1 mark for each point identified, up to a maximum of 3 marks.
- It is taught in the Qur'an (1).
- Muhammad preached about it (1).
- Muslims believe all humans were created equally by Allah (1).
- All races are believed to be equal (1).

- All Muslims believe they are part of the ummah, which demonstrates equality (1).

Accept any other valid response.

2 Award 1 mark for each benefit. Award a second mark for the development of the benefit, up to a maximum of 4 marks.
- Encourages racial harmony (1). All humans are recognised as being equal and should have fair treatment.
- Gives wider variety of cultural differences and influences (1). For example, food, music, clothing and shared understanding (1).
- Brings people together and helps improve communication between them (1). Helps to reduce inequality and discrimination (1).

Accept any other valid response.

## 127 Racial discrimination

1 Award 1 mark for each belief. Award a second mark for development of the belief, up to a maximum of 4 marks.
- Muslims believe Allah created everyone to be equal and racial discrimination is wrong (1). The Qur'an promotes this idea in Surah 49:13 (1).
- Muslims believe the ummah demonstrates equality (1). If all humans are equal, racial discrimination is wrong as races all deserve to be treated the same as promoted by Muhammad (1).
- Muslims recognise that people are different, but this does not make them unequal (1). All humans should be treated the same, as this is what Muhammad did and Muslims want to follow his example (1).

Accept any other valid response.

2 Candidates must underpin their analysis and evaluation with knowledge and understanding. Candidates will be required to demonstrate thorough knowledge and understanding, as well as accuracy, of religion and belief when responding to the question and in meeting AO2 descriptors.

Arguments for the statement:
- Muslims believe they have a duty to stand up against injustice in the world. They believe all humans were created equal by Allah and the Qur'an states that they should treat them equally.
- Muslims demonstrate racial equality through many of their religious practices. They believe the ummah demonstrates racial equality, and they have practices such as Zakah, Sawm and wearing white robes on Hajj, which demonstrate this belief.
- Muslims believe that Muhammad demonstrated that racial inequality is wrong and treated everyone the same. As he did this, Muslims feel that they should follow his example and behave in the same way.

Arguments against the statement:
- Some people may feel it is not their individual responsibility to stand up to racial discrimination. They may feel that this is what the law and government are there to do and enforce.
- There are examples of people standing up for racial equality and losing their lives as a result, for example Martin Luther King Jr, who was assassinated. It may be too dangerous to stand up to racial discrimination.
- Some people may argue that one person cannot make a big difference and it needs to be a majority group that can bring about change. They may feel that this issue needs all people to be united.

Accept any other valid response.

## 128 Social justice

Award 1 mark for each reason. Award further marks for each development of the reason, up to a maximum of 4 marks. Award 1 further mark for any relevant source of wisdom or authority.
- Muslims believe that they have a duty to help care for others (1). This is stated in many teachings within the Qur'an (1): 'Those who follow the Messenger, the unlettered prophet, whom they find written in what they have of the Torah and the Gospel, who enjoins upon them what is right and forbids them what is wrong and makes lawful for them the good things and prohibits for them the evil and relieves them of their burden and the shackles which were upon them. So they who have believed in him, honored him, supported him and followed the light which was sent down with him – it is those who will be the successful. (Surah 7:157) (1).
- Muslims believe that all humans are equal as they are created by Allah (1). If they are all created the same, they deserve equality and a fair life through equality in social justice (1): 'O mankind, indeed We have created you from male and female and made you peoples and tribes that you may know one another. Indeed, the most noble of you in the sight of Allah is the most righteous of you. Indeed, Allah is Knowing and Acquainted.' (Surah 49:13) (1).
- Shari'ah law promotes social equality (1). This code of behaviour argues the basic requirements every Muslim should have (1).

Accept any other valid response.

## 129 Wealth and poverty

Award 1 mark for providing a reason. Award a second mark for development of the reason, up to a maximum of 4 marks.
- Muslims disapprove of greed and waste (1). They believe possessions ultimately belong to Allah and should be shared (1).
- Muslims are expected to act responsibly and help those in need (1). Allah created all humans to be equal, and this should mean in what they have as well (1).
- Muslims give Zakah as part of the Five Pillars and sadaqah voluntarily (1). These are used to help the poor and are key ways of putting Islamic beliefs into practice to help others (1).

Accept any other valid response.